Outdoor Life

GUNS AND SHOOTING YEARBOOK

1986

Published by
Outdoor Life Books, New York

Distributed to the trade by
Stackpole Books, Harrisburg, Pennsylvania

COVER: Photograph by Randy Lamson, Director of NRA Photography.

At top is the new Thompson/Center Hunter Model of the TCR '83 single-shot rifle. This model features an adjustable single-stage trigger, and interchangeable barrels are available in eight calibers. The scope is a prototype of a new Leupold 6X42mm model, designated the M-8, which should be on the market by the time you read this. The mounts are also by Leupold.

The shotgun is a Winchester Model 21 trap gun with factory-installed vent rib. The delicate engraving, gold duck inlays, and elegant California claro stock are by Pachmayr Gun Works of Los Angeles.

The pistol is the 9mm Parabellum Beretta Model 92SB-F, recently adopted by the U.S. armed forces. It carries the military designation M-9. This is a double-action auto with a 15-round magazine capacity. It utilizes an inertia firing pin and an extractor that acts as a chamber-loaded indicator.

Copyright © 1985 by Times Mirror Magazines, Inc.

Published by
Outdoor Life Books
Times Mirror Magazines, Inc.
380 Madison Avenue
New York, NY 10017

Distributed to the trade by
Stackpole Books
Cameron and Kelker Streets
P.O. Box 1831
Harrisburg, PA 17105

Produced by Bookworks, Inc.

ISBN 0-943822-58-0

Manufactured in the United States of America

Contents

Preface by Jim Carmichel

Part 1:   RIFLES

What Makes a Rifle Great? *by Jim Carmichel*   **2**

Holland's .375: The World's Greatest Big Bore *by Tony Sanchez-Arino*   **6**

Thompson/Center's One-Gun Battery *by Bob Milek*   **15**

Remington's Custom Shop *by Stanley W. Trzoniec*   **21**

The Return of the Varmint Shooter *by Jim Carmichel*   **24**

Kricotronic: Electronic Thunderbolt! *by Dave Hetzler*   **28**

Part 2:   HANDGUNS

Colt's Early Automatic Pistols *by Patrick F. Rogers*   **33**

A New Pistol for the U.S. Armed Forces *by Chuck Karwan*   **42**

The .357 Magnum: Ideal for Beginners? *by W.E. Sprague*   **46**

Handgun Stocks: The Exotic Alternative *by Al Pickles*   **51**

Part 3:   SHOTGUNS

Skeet Gun Trends *by Nick Sisley*   **53**

Trapguns: A Breed Apart *by Hugh Birnbaum*   **60**

The All-Around 20-Gauge Shotgun *by Jon R. Sundra*   **67**

The Big 10 *by Jim Carmichel*   **74**

The Winchester Model 97 *by Pete Dickey*   **77**

Part 4:   MUZZLELOADERS

Shooting & Hunting with the Small-Bore Muzzleloader *by Sam Fadala*   **82**

Blue Steel & Gray Smoke *by Toby Bridges*   **87**

Colonel LeMat's Grapeshot Revolver *by Phil Spangenberger*   **94**

Part 5:   AIR GUNS

The Air Gun of Lewis & Clark *by Ashley Halsey, Jr.*   **101**

Surveying the Air Gun Alternative *by Kerry Watkins*   **106**

**Part 6:   BALLISTICS, AMMUNITION,
AND HANDLOADING**

The World's Greatest Handgun Cartridge
by John Lachuk   **117**

The Grand Ballistic Illusion *by Jim Carmichel*   **127**

Analyzing Accuracy Data
by William C. Davis, Jr.   **130**

A Study in Stopping Power
by John F. Thilenius and William R. Meehan   **134**

Hunting Rifle Accuracy: Full-Length Versus
Neck-Sizing *by Dave Scovill*   **143**

Now You Can Get the Lead Out
by Jim Carmichel   **147**

**Part 7:   ALTERATIONS, IMPROVEMENTS,
AND GUNSMITHING**

Glass Bedding Remington Rifles
by R.L. Jamison   **150**

Gun Lubricants & Preservatives
by Roy Dunlap   **156**

The Sanded-In Finish *by David Simpson*   **161**

Accurizing the M-1 Rifle *by J.B. Roberts, Jr.*   **166**

Appendix: ANNUAL UPDATE

Gun Developments *by Jim Carmichel*   **170**

Scope Developments *by Bob Bell*   **175**

Index   181

Preface

The 1985 edition of the OUTDOOR LIFE GUNS AND SHOOTING YEARBOOK was a hard act to follow, but we've done it again. Our objective was simple: To select the most informative and best-illustrated articles from the world's leading firearms and shooting publications.

You'll find an outstanding selection of articles from the *American Rifleman* magazine. As the official journal of the National Rifle Association (with its sister publication, the *American Hunter*), the *American Rifleman* is a consistent leader and innovator in the field of firearms publishing. The *Rifleman's* knowledgeable and well-equipped staff, supported by excellent test facilities, is a continuing source of in-depth, well researched articles on all facets of firearms and shooting.

The best of *American Shotgunner, Guns & Ammo, American Handgunner,* and *Gun World,* all leaders in the field, are represented in this annual with articles by their top writers.

Another never-ending source of high-quality articles is the Dave Wolfe Publishing Company, whose bi-monthly magazines, the *Handloader* and the *Rifle,* offer hardcore but easy-to-read articles on the more technical aspects of handloading, gun design, and ballistics, plus do-it-yourself projects.

In addition to selecting the best articles by the best writers, our emphasis was on bringing you the latest trends in firearms design and performance. Articles such as Dave Hetzler's review of the revolutionary electronic firing system, Nick Sisley's "Skeet Gun Trends", Chuck Karwan's report on the new pistol adopted by the U.S. armed forces, and the article on home computer analysis of accuracy data by William C. Davis, Jr. — these and others tell you where shooting is today and where it's going tomorrow.

One of my own contributions from *Outdoor Life* deals with the resurgence of the varmint rifle in all its latest versions, and another gives you the lowdown on handloading with steel shot — which has at long last, become truly practical. Speaking of things practical, even some of the most venerable forms of do-it-yourself gun tinkering have taken on ultra-contemporary twists. Take stock finishing, a procedure that no longer requires the tedious old pore-filling methods recommended with boiled linseed oil. Whether you're working on a rifle or shotgun stock, the modern oil-modified finishes give you a better finish — and you'll find it here. You'll also find more exotic wood replacement stocks for handguns than you may have dreamed existed. Then there's a report on gun lubricants and preservatives — more of them than you may have known about, all better than ever.

If you're a black-powder shooter, you'll find plenty of good information on hunting with a small-bore muzzleloader. Or if you're interested in serious pellet shooting, you'll be intrigued by "Surveying the Air Gun Alternative" presented here — and by the world-class air guns appearing on the market. You'll find all this plus the "Annual Update" on gun and scope developments — both new models and variations. Indeed, the list of these newsworthy reports is a long one, and the Yearbook's coverage of the latest trends and what's best in shooting will put you way out in front in firearms knowhow.

Or if you want to sit back and enjoy a rich treasure of firearms history and nostalgia, our historical articles will be a rare treat. They are written by such well-known experts as Ashley Halsey and Pete Dickey.

Whatever your interests in guns and hunting, there's a lot here for you. It's the stuff shooters like to read over and over again. That's why we printed it on the best paper and put it between handsome, hardback covers — so it will last a lifetime.

Jim Carmichel

PART ONE

RIFLES

What Makes a Rifle Great?

Jim Carmichel

If I were able to poke around in your gun cabinet and you were to prowl in mine, we'd probably find a rifle or two that each of us would consider truly great. And we'd probably find some other rifles that we'd agree are not so great. The fascinating thing about this is that the rifles we'd consider not so great would in all probability be as accurate, as reliable, and as handsome as those we feel possess true greatness. What then is the dividing line between good and great? Through what prism in our perception of excellence is the spark of genius transformed into the lightning bolt of greatness?

Can a master gunmaker take his seat at the drawing board, pick up a pencil and say, "I will design a great rifle"? No. He cannot. He can pour every loving atom of his genius, experience, and inspiration into what he *hopes* will be a good rifle, but greatness is not his to give. Greatness comes later, bestowed in a million moments, one at a time. Moments on the mountain when exhaustion becomes exaltation. Moments in the African bush when the cutting edge between death and survival is a shot aimed true. Moments alone contemplating an immortal union of walnut and rifle steel.

Such greatness as a rifle may possess may in fact be a reflection of the times and the men who carry it to distant lands. The Hawken rifle, as made in St. Louis by brothers Sam and Jacob during the fur-trade era, is a ringing example of this form of greatness. Possessing neither the beauty and grace of past generations of American rifles, nor the exquisite workmanship of rifles being made a few hundred miles to the east, the Hawken was, by comparison, a club-like affair with no frills in its bonnet. But in doing the job for which it was intended — holding Indians at bay and blasting grizzlies to kingdom come under the worst possible conditions of climate and abuse — the Hawken was without peer. It became a legend because it was equal to the men and the needs of the time. When the grizzled mountain man nestled his rifle in the crook of his arm and went forth to the hills beyond the plains, he carried the Hawken to greatness.

And so it was with another legend — the great Sharps rifle. Only a comparative handful of these magnificent breechloaders were ever made, and the term of their manufacture was marked by financial strife, bankruptcy and, eventually, failure. But when

Photo by Stanley W. Trzoniec

At left is Mauser M-98 in one of its many current incarnations, a Parker Hale sporter in .30/06. At center is Winchester M-70 Featherweight chambered for .257 Roberts, and at right is Remington M-700 varminter in .250/3000. By Carmichel's logical standards of greatness, all three qualify as great rifles.

the wicked-looking Sharps thundered across the target ranges and plains of the buffalo its effect was awesome. Is there something in a name? Hawken and Sharps have a noble resonance. And how about Garand?

Sometimes a combination of circumstances, superb design, timing, and adventure, come together in a rifle in such a way that greatness is thrust upon it. Such a rifle is the M-1 Garand. Ask any infantry veteran of World War II what he disliked most about the war and he'll probably tell you it was stripping, cleaning, and lugging the heavy M-1 rifle. But it was a love/hate relationship because the Garand was one piece of government equipment that never gave up. Who can remember an M-1 that ever malfunctioned? It was the rifle that General Omar Bradley called the "finest instrument of battle ever devised."

Old-guard Army staff and a cadre of romantics left over from World War I had a hard time trading in their beloved 1903 Springfield bolt rifle for the porpoise-bellied M-1, but the German army had a wholly different view. As they saw it, the 1903 Springfield was a poor copy of their Mauser, which was exactly the case. Their view of the M-1, on the other hand, was one of awe. One defeated German field marshal summed it up very neatly: "We had everything — except the Garand rifle."

The old Garand M-1 evolved into the M-14, which was an even better rifle in just about every way. Yet the M-14, during its term as the standard U.S. musket, never had an opportunity to earn greatness.

If sheer omnipresence is a hallmark of greatness, then there is no denying the title to the Winchester Model 94 lever-action carbine. They have been made by the millions and, even back when this century was new, they had made lasting inroads into every form of North American hunting. In a very positive way, the Model 94 represents *all* lever-action rifles and, as such, stands for all that is great about this uniquely American rifle mechanism. It has been nearly a century since the Model 94 was introduced and, during the intervening years, hundreds of rifles have been designed, marketed, and forgotten. But the old 94 is still alive and active and, by any odds, it is the most widely and immediately recognizable rifle on earth. Is there any surer sign of greatness?

Another mark of greatness in a rifle is the effect it has on the mechanical design and styling of other rifles. When, for example, the Remington Model 721 and Model 722 bolt-action rifles (the 722 was only a short-action version of the 721) were introduced back in 1948 there seemed to be little to cheer about. The price was agreeable but the Models 721 and 722 lacked the touch of handcraftsmanship so apparent in pre-war Remingtons. And in no way did the new rifles seem to present competition to Winchester's Model 70. In short, both the 721 and 722 were as plain as a picked chicken and the bent-metal trigger guards looked to have been borrowed from a Japanese toy. Could such a rifle exist for long in the hothouse of post-World War II competition?

That was three dozen years ago and the design for the Models 721 and 722 rifles has not only survived but is one of the most influential of all time. The original model number has been changed — it's now called the Model 700 — but except for a new stock design, a different trigger guard, plus some minor cosmetic changes, the heart of the rifle is unchanged. This is the rifle that taught us most of what we know about accuracy and it's so imitated that it's hard to find a rifle of post-World War II design that doesn't incorporate some features first seen in the old Models 721 and 722.

Stylistically the Weatherby rifle has been so influential that the "California look" has become part of the shooting idiom. Whether or not you are a Weatherby fan is not the issue. We are discussing Weatherby's tremendous impact on rifle styling. When major rifle manufacturers, such as Remington and Winchester plus a host of foreign manufacturers, are compelled to adopt white-line spacers, Monte Carlo combs, and glossy finishes in order to copy the "Weatherby look," you can figure the original has achieved a position reserved only for the great. And that's without even considering the overwhelming effect Weatherby has had on ballistic thought and development. Weatherby did not invent the word "magnum," he invented the word's meaning.

Back in the mid-1930s when the engineers at Winchester poured themselves a fresh cup of coffee and sat themselves down to design the Winchester Model 70 bolt rifle, they already had a good thing going. Their Model 54 was a good looking and solid performer that had already proven itself in the game fields. So their task was simply to make a good thing better and this they did in dazzling fashion. The result was a combination of beauty, workmanship, style, accuracy, and reliability that has made the Model 70, not only the most cherished bolt-action rifle in America, but one of the greatest sporting rifles of all times. This was the rifle that weaned more than a few African professional hunters away from their traditional English rifles because it was more gun for less money. It also showed the world that Mauser and Mannlicher didn't have a lock on bolt-action rifle making. It has become the American standard by which other bolt rifles are judged and there is no surer standard of greatness.

There are many reasons the Model 70 has become a legend, but essentially they relate to the way it manages to do everything so well. For example, if an industrial designer were to try to design an action for the sake of appearance alone, he would be hard pressed to improve on the beauty of the Model 70. It has a relatively slender profile with clean lines and the look of rugged simplicity.

But its beauty is more than skin deep. Few rifles can equal its accuracy. For nearly a half century it has been the undisputed king of the long-distance rifle ranges. Whether in the lightning-fast, rapid-fire events or on the methodically precise 1,000-yard course, the Model 70 is still the rifle to beat. And in the game fields from Africa to the Arctic, be the quarry ground squirrels or elephants, the Model 70 gets the job done so reliably that praise is gross redundancy.

In truth, when we discuss Model 70 Winchesters we're talking about four different rifles. The first is the so-called pre-war model, which was the most beautifully finished of the Model 70 series. The second series continued until 1963 and, though marked by a succession of changes, few of which were for the better, the basic mechanism was the same as that made before World War II. In 1964 the Model 70 was offered in a redesigned form that was so stylistically ill-conceived that its good points were buried. The most recent series dates from the late 1970s and represents a sincere effort to recapture the essence of the earlier Model 70 while retaining worthwhile mechanical improvements introduced in 1964. If today's Model 70 (especially in the trim Featherweight version) had been the form introduced in 1964, the transition would have been much less troublesome and there would be no black stain on the rifle's manufacturing history. Today's Model 70 is indeed a great rifle; it has earned greatness on its own.

What is the greatest sporting rifle of all? Is it some royally priced double-barrel rifle of London make? I think not. Though the top doubles are truly magnificent rifles and their life-against-death performances in the world's most dangerous game fields are the stuff of which legends are woven, their total numbers are so few and ownership is so limited that their greatness will remain as remote as their price.

Hawken-style caplock lives on in several versions, this one made by Thompson/Center.

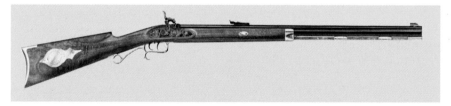

U.S. M-1 Garand; General Omar Bradley called it "finest instrument of battle ever devised."

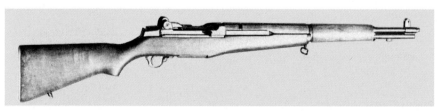

Winchester M-94 — longevity, popularity, and reliability give it high rank.

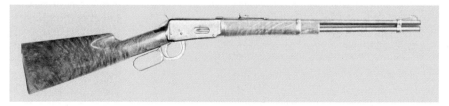

Thus, when we speak of the great double rifles of African lore we're not singling out any particular make or model but rather a class of rifles that have in concert achieved greatness. One of the best, the exquisite Holland & Holland Royal, represents great doubles.

When Ernest Hemingway placed a trim 6.5mm Mannlicher-Schoenauer in the hands of the fictitious Mrs. Francis McComber and bid her blow the craven brains from her buffalo-fearing husband, he pretty well summed up that rifle's place in history. Clearly it's the sort of rifle that shows up in the "right" places in the batteries of the "right" people. Never ostentatious, never out of place, always getting the job done, and always in style — like a Brooks Brothers suit. The Austrian-made Mannlichers ranked in the top 10 of the world's great rifles for well over a half century and will always be considered the most classic of bolt rifles from the standpoint of both styling and workmanship. These peerless rifles were made in the early 1970s and their passing was the end of an era. The Austrian firm of Steyr still makes a rifle called Mannlicher but it's something else entirely.

The greatest of the great has to be the Model 98 Mauser. In terms of numbers, the Model 98 has been made in more millions, by more manufacturers, and has been adopted by more countries as the official service weapon than any other arm in history. As a sporting rifle it has been chambered in so many calibers and offered in so many styles that a complete listing would fill a sizable catalog. Its effect on rifle design has been so pervasive that the Mauser influence is evident in all turnbolt rifles. It can be argued that the Model 70 Winchester, the 1903 Springfield, and a host of other bolt-action rifles are little more than modified Mausers.

As a mechanism the Model 98 is obsolete and has been since, as one astute observer put it, the Germans used it in losing World War I. Yet the momentum of its functional excellence will easily carry it to the end of this century and beyond.

And what other rifles are on the high road to greatness? Ruger's Model 77 is a contender along with their Number One Single-Shot. Marlin's little Model 60 rimfire autoloader is a shoo-in by popular demand, and Remington's inexpensive Model 788 will probably be around long enough to earn a halo.

Take a look in your gun cabinet, you might find the signs of greatness. Rifles aren't just born great, they have to be given greatness. By you and me and a million other riflemen, moment by moment.

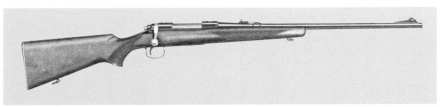

Remington M-721 — this rifle and the Remington M-722 were forerunners of the entire Remington 700 series.

Pre-1964 Winchester M-70 — often called "classic" and the "rifleman's rifle."

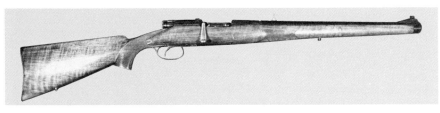

Typically full-stocked Mannlicher-Schoenauer carbine, combining elegance and shootability.

Custom sporter built on all-time greatest action — Mauser 98 — which has been produced in greater numbers by more manufacturers than any other firearm design in history.

Holland's .375: The World's Greatest Big Bore

Tony Sanchez-Ariño

For the last 32 years I have been a keen and happy user of rifles chambered for the .375 Holland & Holland Magnum cartridge in my work as a professional hunter in Africa. After such a long time I cannot remember exactly the quantity of game shot with it, but certainly it included several hundreds of elephant and buffalo, some dozens of lions and rhino, and about 2,000 other non-dangerous heads of game.

I mention these figures just to explain that my experience with this caliber is based on 98 percent practical use in the field and only two percent on theoretical facts. I shall try to write about the .375 in hunter's terms, avoiding designations that could be difficult to understand. Articles with many ballistic datums in the form of mathematic figures, with formulas, etc., look very impressive and lend credence to the author as a "real expert," but do not help much to clarify things to the people who want a simple and easy answer to their problem.

The .375 is a fantastic cartridge. The father of the Magnum clan; an old and glorious veteran of 72 years and it is still going strong — so much so that without any doubt it is the most popular and appreciated big-game bore all over the world today. Introduced at the turn of the century by Holland & Holland, the new .375 Magnum, as opposed to the .275 Express, was designed between 1910 and 1911, and placed on the market in 1912.

Lost with the passage of time is the name of the very brilliant cartridge designer who created this unrivaled caliber. Whoever he was, his cartridge was far ahead of its time.

Shortly after the introduction of the .375 Magnum, Holland & Holland also created a flanged version, without the belt, to be used only in single-shot or double-barrel rifles. After World War II, fewer and fewer .375 flanged Magnums were manufactured, and the ammunition became obsolete. Today, when somebody wants a double-barreled rifle chambered for the .375 Magnum, the rifle is manufactured to use the normal rimless cartridges employed in bolt-action rifles. However, the rifle is fitted with special extractors based on the original system introduced by Westley Richards many years ago, which still works perfectly and without any problem.

The .375 belted Magnum, mated with the Magnum Mauser, was the nearly ideal "all around rifle" that was used on all kinds of game, including the biggest animals of Africa, Malaya, and India. The unknown Holland & Holland engineer must have had a very clear view of the hunting future to develop a Magnum caliber totally different from the .400 or .500 caliber class of cartridges so much in vogue at the time. He chose a .37 caliber housed in a long case with a novel belt to reinforce the shell and avoid

This article first appeared in *GUNS & AMMO.*

Traditionally .375 H&H came in three different bullet weights; 235, 270, and 300 grains, each with a niche depending on the game being hunted. Today's handloader has a wide choice of projectiles to choose from.

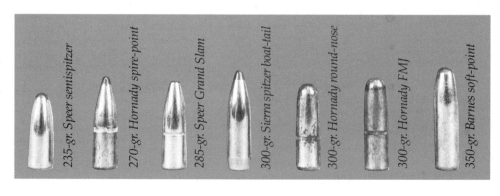

235-gr. Speer semispitzer · 270-gr. Hornady spire-point · 285-gr. Speer Grand Slam · 300-gr. Sierra spitzer boat-tail · 300-gr. Hornady round-nose · 300-gr. Hornady FMJ · 350-gr. Barnes soft-point

extraction problems. In rimless form it was used in bolt-action rifles which, by the way, were not as popular as massive double-barrel, big-game rifles in those days. Today, the .375 H&H Magnum is still a "modern" cartridge and has either outlasted or has remained a strong competitor to the theoretical rivals that were introduced by other firms to compete with it — the .350 Rigby Magnum, .338 Winchester Magnum, .358 Norma Magnum, and the 9.3X64 (.366) Brenneke, which have all claimed to be the ideal "all around rifle."

Originally, three different weights of bullets were designed to cover every species of game all over the world. The light 235-grain bullet was intended for the lighter varieties of soft skinned game generally shot at long range. The 270-grain bullet took on the heavier varieties of soft skinned game shot at medium ranges, including the big cats like lion and tiger, all the different bears, and plains game. The 300-grain bullet provided smashing power at close quarters and was, and is, used against such big and dangerous game animals as elephant, buffalo, and rhino.

Modern improvements in the ballistics of the 270-grain bullet are such that the 235-grain bullet has become less and less popular. Factory cartridges loaded with this bullet weight have not been manufactured since 1945. Today we can shoot with the 270-grain at ranges originally reserved for the 235-grain bullet, with the extra advantages of more bullet weight and killing power. The factory loaded 235-grain load had a muzzle velocity of 2,800 fps with a muzzle energy of 4,100 foot-pounds. The 200-yard drop was just 2.6 inches. Today, the modern factory loaded 270-grain .375 bullet has a muzzle velocity of 2,740 fps with a muzzle energy of 4,500 foot-pounds and a 200-yard drop just .3 inches more than the 235-grain load, 2.9 inches.

The killing power of the .375 Magnum can only be properly appreciated after one has shot a large variety of game and seen its terrific paralyzing effect. Its ballistics make it almost perfect for all types of game, with only a few minor limitations. There have been some problems among hunters who were overly enthusiastic and believed in the most blind way that the .375 Magnum could be used — for instance —against elephant under *any* conditions and in *any* terrain. In heavy forest with its attendant poor visibility, hunting elephant with a .375 just reaches the minimum safety standard required and the hunter must place his relatively light 300-grain solid bullet very carefully in order to get the maximum advantage of its superb penetration. The .375 Magnum just does not have the stopping power of heavier rifles in the .400 and .500 caliber class at close range. When used with common sense it can be employed with the greatest satisfaction and confidence, as there is no animal in Africa, Asia, or the Americas that cannot be killed cleanly with this

Among the many animals author has taken with .375 is this old buffalo in northern Tanzania. Utilized under the proper conditions (not in tight cover) he feels .375 is the single most versatile of all calibers, even for dangerous game.

caliber when shooting with the proper bullet. Whenever a hunter fails to kill his trophy successfully, it is quite common for the rifle to be blamed; that's human nature. But it should not be forgotten that the rifle can do nothing on its own, and at any given moment success or failure depends on the skill of the hunter.

After seven decades of extensive use in game fields throughout the world, the .375 has proven itself and is becoming more and more popular due to its great versatility and the fact that it can cover perfectly all the needs or requirements of modern hunters. Despite the fact that rhino hunting is virtually a thing of the past, and in the whole of Africa,

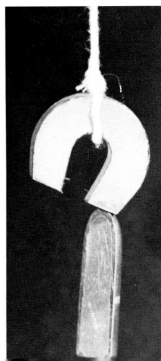

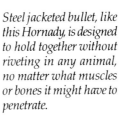

Steel jacketed bullet, like this Hornady, is designed to hold together without riveting in any animal, no matter what muscles or bones it might have to penetrate.

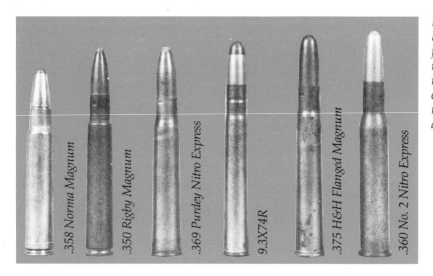

Down through the years .375 H&H has received a great deal of competition from other cartridges, but none have managed to push aside the Holland round as the most popular big-game cartridge worldwide. .375 has it all; moderate recoil, outstanding accuracy, and a reputation for quick kills.

the elephant are also in a difficult position due to indiscriminate poaching; at best, the hunter will be able to shoot one animal per season, something he will do perfectly with his .375 Magnum. So, it is not necessary to buy a more potent rifle just to fire two or three cartridges occasionally, if he is lucky. The only really big and dangerous game still found in abundance is the Cape buffalo, but the 300-grain solid bullet from the .375 Magnum will do the job as well as any bigger caliber, due to its great penetration. For soft skinned game, the .375 Magnum is still ideal as its 200-yard trajectory rivals that of the popular light calibers, but it uses a much heavier projectile. This is why, under present and future conditions in Africa or elsewhere, the .375 Magnum

is *the* right answer for the sporting hunter who is planning his dream safari.

As far as the professional hunter goes, the .375 Magnum is an extremely useful gun which can cover normally up to 85 percent of the situations arising in the hunting business. I have used the .375 as my regular working tool with the greatest satisfaction, backing it with my old .416 Rigby or the potent .505 Gibbs or .577 Nitro which I use for very particular occasions such as hunting elephant in very thick brush or rain forest where a heavier bullet with greater stopping power is required.

I am the happy owner of two fine .375 Magnum rifles, one with open sights and another fitted with a scope sight, and double set triggers. The first one,

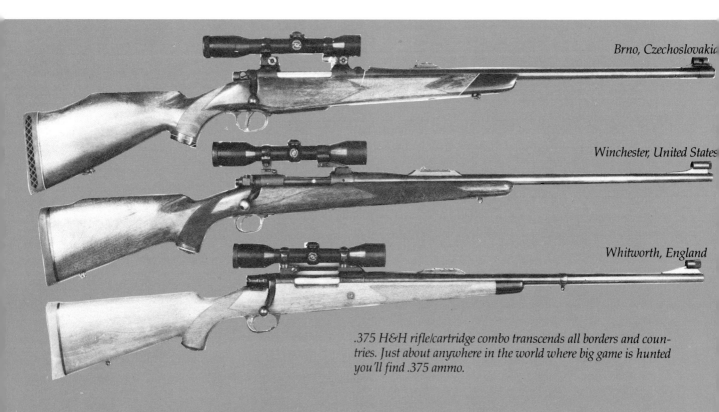

.375 H&H rifle/cartridge combo transcends all borders and countries. Just about anywhere in the world where big game is hunted you'll find .375 ammo.

with its open back sight, is made by Holland & Holland of London, with the long Magnum Mauser action, which is ⅛-inch longer than standard, with a square bridge and four-round magazine. This stock is my favorite as it is made of seasoned Spanish walnut. This gun fits me like a glove and I employ it for general work, where visibility is more or less limited. For open spaces and difficult shots I use the second .375 Magnum, made to order for me 25 years ago by the Belgian gunmaker Mahillon of Brussels. This rifle is very light and handy and is extremely accurate. It is topped with a Kahles 3-9X variable scope. This gun is also made from an original Mauser action — like all my bolt-action rifles —with a five-round magazine. In my opinion — based on 32 years of experience — the old and pure sporting Mauser actions are by far the best ever made to withstand the rigors of hard and constant use with high powered cartridges under the worst tropical conditions.

Why did I choose a .375 fitted with double set triggers (hair triggers) and a variable scope? Simply because I have concentrated on elephant hunting all my life and many times it was practically impossible to approach, to shooting range, a particular bull standing in the middle of the herd surrounded by females and younger animals. On these occasions, I took my .375 with the scope, a good tripod and went to the herd side, against the wind, to wait and wait until the moment the animals permitted me a sight of the bull's shoulder. Then I placed a bullet through his heart in the most careful way using the hair trigger and the proper scope power according to the range and the light. This system

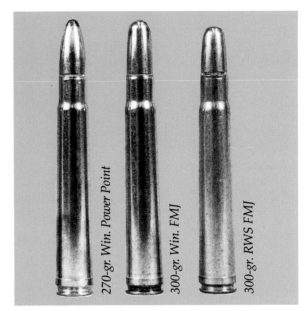

270-gr. Win. Power Point
300-gr. Win. FMJ
300-gr. RWS FMJ

All of the pictured cartridges have been used by author; he's especially fond of the soft-nose for thin-skinned game.

also works very well to pick up a fine buffalo head from a big herd.

For general use on soft skinned game I carry the scope set at 3X or 4X, but other hunters prefer to have their .375 Magnum rifles fitted with a 2.5X scope. As far as my experience goes, this caliber is so versatile that it can be used perfectly with variable power scopes, especially when mounted, like mine, with the German mount system which permits

This shows the moment of impact of a 300-gr. solid on a Cape buffalo. He staggered, took a few steps, and fell.

Contemporary of author, John "Pondoro" Taylor felt the .375 H&H was the perfect all-around cartridge for the Dark Continent's game animals.

The RWS solid (R) was used on a buffalo. It looks little different from the unfired Hornady FMJ solid.

Janet French took this buff using .375, proving the recoil isn't too much for a small-framed person.

removal of the scope in a second and use of the open iron sights when close-range shooting at dangerous game. I never will recommend that a gun to be employed against dangerous game be fitted with a fixed scope. I do not agree with the theory that when following a wounded animal a low-powered scope is as fast as any iron sight.

For a charging dangerous animal — or a running beast — it is just common sense to understand that an open, iron sight will be faster to bring the target to the hunter's eye, and he will be able to fire more rounds much quicker than with the scope. This is especially true in places where branches and leaves can confuse the vision through the scope. The detachable scope mount, with a claw or other system, is my choice for rifles that may be used against dangerous game.

Personally, one thing I have never done is to load my own ammunition because — apart from the

A solid's job is to penetrate through caked mud, thick hide, and bone to reach vitals without breaking up or riveting.

normal prohibitions against this in many African countries — I used to spend eight months per year in the bush without too much free time for this interesting activity. Thus, I always used standard factory ammunition. Over the years I have fired and experimented with all kinds of .375 Magnum ammunition found on the market. In the early days I used Kynoch ammunition, practically the only one available in Africa at the time. In general this ammunition was very good. The round gave great penetration and, with the 300-grain solid bullet, I shot many elephants and buffalo without any problem. The only possible criticism of this ammunition, which was made in England by Imperial Chemical Industries (I.C.I.), was the corrosive primers used which darkened the rifle bores if they were not properly cleaned every time it was used. However, I considered it a minor problem because of the excellent results obtained. To compete with Kynoch, other international firms have also manufactured .375 Magnum ammunition. Winchester, Remington, DWM (later replaced by RWS), and Norma all offer ammunition of excellent quality.

I found only two particular bullets I dislike. The first one was introduced years ago by Winchester. It had a little flat point, which pretended to be a solid but, on the practical side, was the most unreliable bullet I have seen in my life. It acted in the most unexpected or unwanted way, often deforming and not keeping a direct course, and sometimes even fragmenting. Fortunately, Winchester, a very responsible firm, stopped production of this aberration and now it is only a bad memory on which to comment as an anecdote.

I am not going to discuss all the existing bullets for the .375 Magnum because many of them are only available for handloading (i.e., Sierra's Spitzer Boat Tail, the Speer Grand Slam, and several Hornady bullets). I shall refer only to the standard factory ammunition, that which is available over the counter, all over the world.

After long experience in the field, my favorite solid bullet for big, heavy, and dangerous game is manufactured by Remington in the United States and RWS in Germany. Both feature magnificent reinforced full metal jacket bullets. These two particular bullets are extremely strong and on broad shots to elephant heads quite often go from one side of the skull to the other. When after Cape buffalo, the hunter must avoid shooting at an animal with another behind it to prevent wounding both of them, as the bullet will often go clean through one animal on broadside shots and wound a second.

Years ago, when RWS absorbed DWM and placed their new solid 300-grain bullet on the market, I was asked by a well-known gunsmith to try them both for accuracy and practical results. Luckily at the time I was shooting some marauding elephants so I had the ideal chance to test the bullets. Using my Holland & Holland rifle with open sights I started my double work — to eliminate the marauders from the local plantations and see how well the new RWS solid bullets worked. Backed by my .416 Rigby, "just in case," I shot elephants, taking them from different angles and positions, in the most careful way. After shooting a total of six, I found to my surprise and great satisfaction that all of them were killed with one bullet each. I recovered some of the bullets and all of them were in perfect shape, virtually looking like they were unfired. Later on I had a similar

Author and many other knowledgeable African hunters insist on having quick-detachable mounts that will return to absolute zero on a dangerous game rifle. Mount on this M-70 is the justly famous EAW unit made in Germany.

experience with Remington solid ammunition. Both manufacturers employ non-corrosive caps and the rifle bores do not suffer from their prolonged use. My two .375 Magnum rifles, after so many years in the African bush, have bores shining like mirrors — but I must confess that I am extremely fond of my guns and clean them with great enthusiasm every day.

For soft skinned game there are two weights of bullets, 270 and 300 grains, but according to my experience the best by far is the fantastic 270-grain Winchester Power Point. This is the one I prefer whether the game is dangerous or not. At close range, with a muzzle energy of 4,500 foot-pounds, it can be used perfectly for any emergency against the big cats and the largest bears. In the last two years I have shot four charging lions previously wounded by clients, and all of them fell in their tracks after receiving the 270-grain Power Point bullet. Personally I have shot 118 lions, some very easily and some

This impala taken at a paced 200 yds. shows the versatility of the .375 when bullet is matched to game being hunted.

Express sight is the professional's choice after the scope has been removed from a .375 H&H.

under quite difficult conditions, using all kinds of calibers from the .30/06 up to the giant .577 Nitro. I can assure you, without any passion, that the .375 Magnum loaded with the 270-grain Power Point is a fantastic lion gun. The killing power of this bullet is really amazing as it has great versatility and can be used safely at close range to shoot dangerous game, as well as to take soft skinned game at long range. It has extreme accuracy and a flat trajectory. Only some few months ago a client of mine wounded a large eland bull with his .300 Magnum rifle, employing the 180-grain bullet; the animal was hit a little to the middle of the body and started galloping like mad toward thick bush, maybe 400 yards away.

I waited for the second shot of the client, a clean miss, and then he called for me to shoot and give him a hand. Normally I try not to shoot when on safari, leaving the whole question in the hands of the sporting hunter so as to have him savor the last drop of his hunt. I take an active part only when a dangerous animal charges — for obvious reasons. On this occasion, I acquiesced to the hunter's request. My first shot broke the eland's rear right leg. The animal still continued his way, albeit more slowly, a little to the right which gave us a good sight of his body.

The client fired again without any apparent effect and told me to shoot again to prevent the animal from entering the bush. By now I had the rifle perfectly rested on a branch with the scope at 6X. Touching the hair trigger of my Mahillon .375 Magnum, I sent another 270-grain Power Point bullet against the eland's shoulder. At the same time I felt the recoil of the gun I saw the animal collapsing as if hit by lightning. We paced off the distance which measured about 144 yards up to the point of the client's first shot. My first shot was at 209 yards and the final, killing shot was taken at 267 yards,

Africa's greater kudu, slightly smaller than America's elk, demands a cartridge with the power of a .375 if he's any distance away.

more or less. Of course, this is not a record range, but it does show the versatility of the 270-grain Power Point bullet which worked as well as any one of the lighter .30 caliber Magnums, a clan famous for their flat trajectory. The .375 Magnum derives more power because of its extra bullet weight and diameter.

In Africa, with the exception of desert and mountain hunting, the normal shooting range is between 75 and 200 yards, very seldom up to 300 and exceptional beyond this. Those shots referred to by some authors, normally killing game at 400 and 500 yards are, I am afraid to say, just pure fantasy. They are trying to impress readers who believe anything they see in print. The super-long shots are the remarkable exceptions and not the rule as some pretend.

Many famous and experienced hunters have been extremely fond of the .375 Magnum. First on that list is that great elephant hunter from Uganda, Pete Pearson, who used nothing else for elephant in the open right from the day the .375 Magnum was placed on the market. He also used his big .577 Nitro double-barreled Express rifle when hunting in heavy forest. In more recent times we have the case of my good friend Harry Manners, who killed around 1,000 elephants in Mozambique with his .375 Magnum, a Winchester Model 70, which was his all around rifle. Another friend of mine, George Rushby, who was an ivory hunter in the old Belgian Congo and French Equatorial Africa up to 1929 and recently an Elephant Control officer in Tanganyika,

Author has a .375 with double set triggers for long-range shots; this .375 Czech Brno has a single set trigger for the same use.

Howard French poses with lion taken with a single shot. His choice of rifles? A .375.

was a great lover of the .375 Magnum for his particular job. He bagged over 800 elephants with the .375 H&H.

In Mozambique, meat hunters, shooting buffalo for big companies to feed their African workers, used the .375 Magnum with the greatest success. Many of these hunters shot, individually, between 4,000 and 5,000 buff with a few shooting well over these figures. The well known professional hunter, the late Syd Downey, one of the top "white hunters" from Kenya, always advised his clients to use the .375 Magnum for heavy and dangerous animals, together with something in the .300 class for the rest of the game. Just to put an end to these names I shall say that my old friend John "Pondoro" Taylor, author of many books about rifles and hunting, was extremely keen on the .375 Magnum and he told me that he fired more .375 cartridges than the rest of the calibers put together — well over 5,000 rounds — including all kinds of game in the bag.

The best recommendation we can give today for the .375 Magnum is the fact that since 1912, with generation after generation of hunters, it has been the most popular big game cartridge the hunting world has ever seen. There has been a continuous

demand for this particular round from the tyro to the most experienced nimrod.

If we always keep in mind its particular limitations when hunting elephant in very thick bush or rain forest with poor visibility, where a heavier bullet of great stopping power is required, then it can be stated that the .375 Magnum has the "green light" to be used in the most generous and general way with maximum safety and satisfaction. Do not forget that the happy days of Pete Pearson, John Taylor, Rushby, Manners or even myself are virtually over — unfortunately. The elephants, due to increasing poaching and tremendous pressure on them, are becoming extremely aggressive and in a permanent state of irritation.

Thus, elephant, in places with very dense vegetation where you can see only up to the muzzle of your rifle, can be a serious business difficult to handle. This is why I insist so much on not being over-confident when using the .375 Magnum in this unique situation.

However, with this one limitation the .375 Holland & Holland will continue to be the world's best all around cartridge, just as it has been for the last 72 years.

Thompson/Center's One-Gun Battery

Bob Milek

As my son, Bill, and I crept through the growth of chest-high sagebrush spotted with jack pine and gnarled juniper trees, the sun disappeared and ominous gray clouds settled over the area. Within minutes the wind picked up, moaning as it raced through the trees, and then we were in the midst of a howling blizzard. Wet snowflakes stung our faces and clung to our clothing like glue.

"The wind's right," Bill whispered, "but if this keeps up we won't be able to see those elk."

"Don't worry, we'll see 'em," I hissed in reply. "Just keep that scope clear of snow so you can shoot."

We were working along the crest of a high ridge that separated two forks of Ditch Creek. Opposite our position, both east and west, steep slopes and rocky outcroppings formed the rims of the canyon. The elk herd we were stalking was in the east fork — at least a mile above where our truck was parked.

I tapped Bill on the shoulder and whispered: "They should be almost directly below us now. When we get into them, shoot either the biggest bull or the smallest calf. I'd prefer the latter for packing, but if there's a decent bull, take him!"

Bill nodded, then stopped while we shed our backpacks to cut down on any noise we might make. This done, he pushed the top lever of the Thompson/Center TCR 83 single-shot rifle with his thumb and pivoted the action open to be certain the chamber contained a .30/06 round. Satisfied that everything was in order, we moved, a step at a time, toward the edge of the ridge.

The snowstorm was worsening and the cold wind whipped my face, numbing my ears. We were in a half-crouch, covering ground just a step at a time and pausing after each step to look and listen. Then, as if on cue, the wind stopped, the clouds parted, and sunlight flooded the canyonside.

We froze at the sight before us. We were damned near right in the middle of 50 head of elk! Yellowish-brown bodies milled around in the deep sage, the closest not over 25 yards away. Antlers — spikes, three-points, four-points — appeared and disappeared above the backs of cows. A calf raised its head, looked me right in the eye, then went back to feeding. Bill was just in front of me and I could see that he was searching for a good bull among the bunch. He still held the rifle at his side, but the safety was off and he was ready for action.

The herd seemed to separate a little and there, 60 yards away and all by himself, stood a dandy bull — six points on one side, five on the other. His head was nothing out of the ordinary, but in body size the bull dwarfed everything around him. Very slowly Bill raised the rifle, sighted through the Burris 3-9X scope, and there was an audible "click" as the rear trigger set. In that mountain stillness it sounded like a hammer hitting a horseshoe and I expected the bull to bolt in alarm. Instead, he just stuck his head and neck behind a juniper, forcing Bill to shift his aim from the bull's neck to the chest.

"Baroom!" The roar of the .30/06 was ear-splitting. I saw hair fly from high and behind the bull's shoulder and heard the 165-grain Nosler solid-base spitzer bullet hit with a resounding thump. My stomach did a flip-flop at the realization that Bill had scored a lung shot, a high lung shot at that. By all the rules that bull would boil off the mountainside and stack up only when he reached the boggy tangle along the creek far below. Our pack job would be four times more difficult if we had to follow the creek out.

But to my amazement the bull didn't head downhill. All around us elk were stomping, squealing,

This article first appeared in *GUNS & AMMO.*

Like T/C's Contender pistol, TCR 83 rifle has interchangeable barrels. This European-styled arm, available in .22/250, .223, .243, .30/06, and 7mm Rem. Mag., is capable of taking just about any game in North America, from varmints through elk and bear. T/C is adding additional calibers to increase the gun's versatility.

and running, lining out for the top of the ridge. Even though he was mortally wounded, Bill's bull followed the herd. By this time Bill was reloaded, but instead of shooting he just took a rest over a big sage and tracked the bull in the scope. When he was about 150 yards away and 50 yards below the top of the ridge, the elk stopped and turned, looking very much like he was now ready to head down country.

Bill didn't give him the chance. The .30/06 barked again, the muzzle blast creating a shower of snow from the sage, and the bull's legs went out from under him. His neck was broken!

"Sure wish he'd kept goin'," Bill mumbled as he plucked the fired case from the chamber. "I'd have

broken his neck right on top of the ridge and saved us that long uphill haul."

"Now that's confidence," I mused, "especially when you're shooting my rifle — one you haven't worked with much."

"I have no problem with this Thompson/Center," Bill replied. "I've shot it enough to know where it shoots and that's what counts."

I guess Bill's statement about the TCR 83 rifle just about sums up my feelings. After a year in the field with it, there is little to criticize.

The Thompson/Center TCR 83 rifle was introduced in 1983 as a companion to the popular Contender pistol. Like the Contender, the rifle has

Author found TCR 83 to be a strong, accurate, reliable sporter that handles well in the field. Its interchangeable barrel design provides the shooter with varmint-to-big-game versatility.

interchangeable barrels for a number of popular calibers. However, the TCR 83 is not simply an enlarged Contender. In fact, interchangeable barrels are the only similarity between the two Thompson/Center products. Even the method of interchanging barrels is vastly different.

The TCR 83 is a single-shot rifle built along the lines of the classic European single-shot sporter, but its design is quite advanced. Being a tip-up break-open action, it's much shorter than bolt-action sporters of similar barrel length. Barrels on the TCR 83 are 23 inches long, yet the overall length of the rifle is just 39¼ inches. Such a short rifle is easy and quick to handle, even at close quarters. But, it isn't a light rifle. My .30/06, topped with a Burris 3-9X Mini scope set in a Burris mount, tips the postal scale at seven pounds, 14 ounces.

As a complete TCR 83 rifle comes from the factory, it's equipped with open sights. Up front is a gold bead. The rear unit is adjustable for windage and elevation and the rear blade folds down. The monoblock has four holes drilled and tapped in it for attaching a scope mount. Because the scope attaches to the barrel, not the receiver, scoped barrels can be swapped back and forth without changing the zero.

Provisions for attaching the barrel to the receiver are contained on the monoblock into which the barrel is threaded. Flat on top and measuring 2.865 inches long, the monoblock contains the extractor, the barrel pivot, and the locking flange for the bolt. Forward of the monoblock about 3½ inches is a piece welded to the bottom of the barrel to which the fore-end fastens.

The 23-inch-long .30/06 barrel I tested has a muzzle diameter of .6 inch. At a point immediately in front of the monoblock the barrel measures 1.05 inches in diameter. These figures are essentially the same on my .223 Remington barrel.

The TCR 83 receiver is a solid piece of 4140 steel which contains the hammer mechanism, the sliding underlug bolt assembly, and the top lever which withdraws the bolt and allows the barrel to pivot open. The bolt is a massive piece of round steel, the front portion of which is cut flat on each side so that it engages the lug on the rear bottom of the mono-block. This lug is hardened so it can't spread open when subjected to high pressure.

The trigger setup on the TCR 83 is usually the first thing that catches the shooter's eye. It's a double set trigger like those popular on European sporters. Pulling the back trigger sets the front one so that only a few ounces of pressure are required to release the front trigger for firing. If you so desire, the rifle can be fired by simply pulling the front trigger. To set the trigger on my rifle, it takes a pull of 18½ to 19 pounds on the rear trigger. Once set, the front trigger pull is so light I have no means of measuring it accurately. To fire the rifle by pulling the front trigger in the "unset" mode, a force of seven to 7½ pounds is required.

As you might expect, the trigger on a rifle design like the TCR 83 isn't a simple thing. To begin with, the trigger mechanism itself is set in the bottom of the receiver while the hammer is located well above it. In order that the hammer can be held in cocked position by the sear, yet the sear be released by the trigger, the sear has to be quite long. It's a round, hardened steel rod that attaches to the froward portion of the trigger, then runs vertically up into the receiver. When the trigger is pulled, the sear is drawn down so that it releases the hammer to be propelled forward by the hammer spring. There's a

Removing TCR's barrel is as simple as unlatching the forearm and then opening the action and rotating the barrel downward out of receiver. Removing and replacing a barrel takes less than a minute.

As TCR 83 does not have sling swivels, author installed his own by drilling stock for rear (L) and using Michaels of Oregon barrel clamp for the front mounting.

lot going on in that mechanism, particularly when the set trigger is used.

The crossbolt safety on this rifle locks the sear when it's pushed to the right. Once on safe, the safety is locked in position by a spring-loaded button entering from the front of the trigger guard. This button must be depressed and held in while the safety is pushed left to the fire position. The safety lock complicates the system a bit, but it's an attempt by Thompson/Center to head off one of those crazy lawsuits so prevalent these days. Thompson/Center devotes most of the space in its TCR 83 instruction manual to the operation of the trigger and the safety, and the hunter is well advised to read this carefully.

The buttstock and fore-end on the TCR 83 are made of walnut. There's not much figure in the stock of my rifle, but it looks good and is nicely

With its sleek European styling and diminutive size, the TCR 83 is a joy to take into the field.

finished. The buttstock, which is anchored to the receiver via a bolt passing through the center of the stock, has a classic comb design, a dainty cheek-piece, and cut checkering on the pistol grip. A rubber butt pad is standard equipment. The length of pull on my rifle is 13½ inches to the rear trigger, 14¼ inches to the front trigger. The fore-end, which attaches to the barrel shotgun-fashion, also has functional cut checkering.

I learned a number of things during my load development and accuracy tests with the TCR 83 .30/06. First, this rifle is not more nor less accurate than any good .30/06 bolt-action sporter. This is really quite a compliment when you consider that all too often break-open and falling-block actions won't perform on a par with a rigid bolt gun. Second, my TCR 83 .30/06 digests heavy loads just as well as do my bolt guns. There's a lot of steel in the massive receiver and plenty in the locking bolt system of this rifle, so you needn't worry about it balking when you feed it any reasonable handload.

Once I got the .30/06 tuned in, I switched over to the .223 Remington barrel so I could use it on a variety of varmints. Here again I found the accuracy to be good, and it handled all of my handloads very well. Unfortunately, my .223 barrel doesn't shoot any factory load with pinpoint accuracy. Remington Power Lokt hollow-points and Federal spitzer boat-tail ammunition turn in the best performances. Three-shot groups with these two particular factory loads run around the 1¼ to 1½ inch mark.

Handloads, though, produce some excellent results, and a few give the really superb groups I was hoping for. For hunting I settled on two loads. One, 22.8 grains of H4198 behind the 50-grain Sierra Blitz bullet, produces a muzzle velocity of 3,208 fps, and three shots will consistently group in ½ inch at 100 yards. This is the load I prefer for prairie dog and chuck shooting. For large varmints — badgers, coyotes, etc. — I prefer the Hornady 55-grain SX bullet pushed by 24.5 grains of H335 powder. This one gets out of the muzzle at 3,140 fps and makes mighty quick work of a varmint. The accuracy isn't

The double set trigger is great for bench shooting, but author feels it's a poor choice for hunting.

quite as good as with my small varmint load, but groups hang in there at around .8 inch for three shots.

When you're shooting the TCR 83, bear in mind that it's a hunting rifle — a sporter — not a varmint or target rifle. The barrel is sporter weight. If you try to shoot multi-shot groups with it, or pour round after round at varmints, the barrel will heat up and the point of bullet impact will change.

The first time I headed into the field with my TCR 83 for some serious varmint hunting, I encountered a problem I'm certain will plague many a hunter. I was driving my 4X4 pickup down an old rutted trail when a flurry of dust a hundred yards ahead caused me to brake to a stop. A badger was busy digging right in the center of one of the tracks. When I opened the door and grabbed the rifle from the gun rack, the badger stopped digging and stood half in

and half out of the burrow, looking right at me. There was no time to get a steady position.

Standing offhand, I found the badger in the scope, pulled the back trigger to set mechanism and reached for the front trigger. "Wham!" The bullet hit a foot above the varmint. I wasn't anywhere near on target when I reached for the front trigger, and in the excitement of the moment I forgot that only a few ounces of pressure set that front trigger off. I bumped it with my finger and missed by a foot. At the bench the set trigger poses no problem, but during the excitement of the hunt — well, you have to be extra careful. With cold hands it becomes quite a problem. As far as simply firing with the front trigger is concerned, forget it. A seven-pound trigger pull is way too heavy for any hunting rifle.

As I see it, the double-set trigger on the TCR 83 is a mistake. Not one hunter in a hundred is expe-

TCR's massive bolt (shown in locking position) engages a locking lug on bottom of barrel monoblock.

TCR 83's trigger mechanism requires a long vertical sear to hold the hammer in the cocked position. Though all TCRs originally had set triggers, new models offer the option of a single trigger.

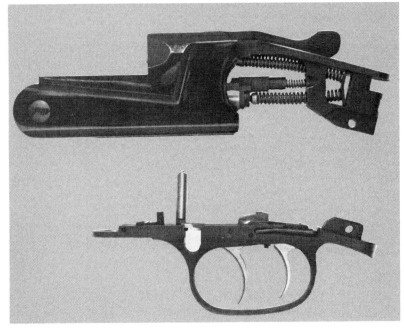

rienced enough to handle it safely in the field. If the front trigger were adjustable to 2½ pounds, that would be different. But under the circumstances I think a good single-stage trigger will be the salvation of the TCR rifle. I have it on good authority that such a trigger will be available by the time you read this.

Following my own field tests of the TCR 83, I let other experienced hunters use it to bag a variety of varmints, a couple of pronghorns, and the bull elk Bill collected. Following these hunts I asked for carefully considered comments. In every instance, the hunters felt that the TCR 83 needed a good single-stage trigger rather than the double-set design and all agreed that sling-swivel studs should be standard equipment. A couple of shooters said that they would prefer automatic ejection to the simple extraction system, but most of the hunters like the idea of plucking the case from the chamber rather than having it flipped out into the mud or snow.

Overall, the consensus agreed with my evaluation — the TCR 83 is a strong, accurate, well-constructed hunting rifle. Aside from these rather obvious attributes, the feature of the TCR 83 that appeals most to me, and drew high praise from the others who used it, is interchangeable barrels. The initial cost of a complete rifle is $425, but for just $140 per barrel you can add whatever you need to cover everything from small varmints to the biggest game in North America. Such versatility at low cost can't help but be impressive. I wouldn't be surprised to see a varmint-weight barrel for the TCR 83 in the

Topped with a Bausch & Lomb 3-9X scope, author's .223 TCR managed 1½", 100 yd. groups. With handloads, author feels he can trim spreads to ½".

not-too-distant future, and a shotgun barrel may be forthcoming. Consider the possibilities for just a moment and you'll understand why I predict that the Thompson/Center 83 rifle is destined to become one of America's most popular hunting rifles.

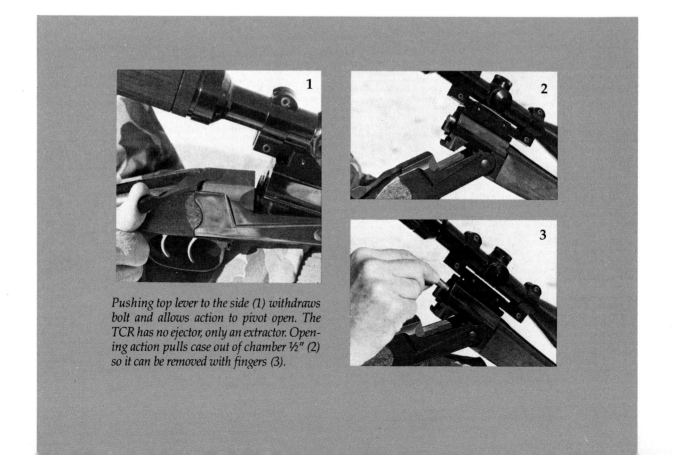

Pushing top lever to the side (1) withdraws bolt and allows action to pivot open. The TCR has no ejector, only an extractor. Opening action pulls case out of chamber ½" (2) so it can be removed with fingers (3).

Remington's Custom Shop

Stanley W. Trzoniec

Though gun manufacture in the United States and abroad today is largely given over to the most modern machinery and production techniques, one of the nation's most successful long-gun makers still shelters a custom shop where the customer and the craftsman reign. "We're here to serve the needs of the American shooter," said Tim McCormack, the head man at Remington's Custom Shop in Ilion, New York, which has catered to the special needs of Remington fanciers since its beginnings in the 1940s. Under the direction of Mike Walker — who worked 40 years for Remington — standards of the production-type shop evolved to rival even the best one-man operation.

In the early days, emphasis was aimed at the target shooter, the 40XB'er, if you please. The shop still turns out finely tuned arms for competition, as well as high grade shotguns, but today's bread-and--butter line is the Model 700 centerfire rifle. It is here, too, that Remington Safari Grade rifles are assembled.

Made in four ascending grades, the custom Model 700s begin where the company's ADL, BDL, and Classic lines leave off. In fact, what used to be the "C" grade (for Custom) years ago, is now Grade I. From there the scale goes up through Grades II, III, and IV. Each is distinct in form, finish and, of course, price.

During a tour of the shop, Tim McCormack plotted the sequence of steps from the moment of logging in the order for a custom rifle (or shotgun) to final packing and shipping. But before Remington begins work on a custom firearm, the customer must go through a basic checklist of just what's available.

This article first appeared in THE AMERICAN RIFLEMAN.

Remington's Custom Shop gunmaker Ross Tarbox hand sands a stock blank destined for a Safari Grade rifle. Shop is a bastion of craftsmen in an era where the machine is the king and high-volume production an economic must.

After selecting one of the four grades, caliber choice is the primary concern for the dedicated shooter. In all, 20 options are listed on the sheet, but McCormack acknowledges he will chamber 700s for calibers not on the list. But no wildcats.

Next to caliber choice, wood selection is a major consideration. American, Claro, and English walnuts are the current offerings, with the last type available as an option on the three higher grades at higher cost. When placing an order, the customer may request a certain type of figure or grain pattern. While the shop cannot absolutely promise to match such requests, the staff makes a real effort to pick

something along the customer's line of thought, McCormack said.

Stock configuration is another important consideration, and here the Remington craftsmen will help in any way possible. Maybe the customer would like a field grip, no fore-end tip, classic or Monte Carlo comb, a cheekpiece with or without the shadow line, no cheekpiece, reinforcing pins, wood grip caps in rosewood or ebony, white-line spacers, a specific length of pull, high comb, low comb, RKW high gloss or a genuine satin hand-rubbed oil finish. Whatever the whim, the Remington Custom Shop will attempt to accommodate within the chosen grade.

For additional accoutrements, the shop's gunmakers offer some interesting possibilities. Exterior polishing can be had in a satin or high finish (again depending on the grade), with a matte finish available at extra cost. Butt pads? No problem, the shop has rubber pads in two or three thicknesses, as well as the Model 700 rifle buttplate in solid or skeletonized steel, again at a slight increase in price.

On the upper three grades, the floorplate and grip caps (steel) are made to Remington's specs by Pete Grisel and Al Biesen, respectively. All triggers are hand fitted to ensure the proper sear engagement, resulting in a superior trigger pull.

Available barrel lengths run from 18½ to 24 inches. Polished and fitted at the shop, barrels normally come without metallic sights, but they can be installed as an option for the modest fee of $25. The receivers are available in either long or short action lengths, with the long action available in *all* calibers, in either right- or left-handed versions. Yes, southpaws too can own a custom-built Remington with a left-hand bolt in their choice of caliber.

Also, all stocks, no matter the grade, are hand checkered to a pattern befitting that grade and price range. Lines per inch start at 22, then become finer and show greater detail through the progres-

Stockmaker John Remington hand finishes a Remington 700 stock (above) and fits a skeletonized buttplate (left). Custom Shop provides its patrons many special options.

sive grades. In fact, the major distinctions between grades boils down to the elaboration of checkering patterns, engraving coverage, and final finishing of the metal.

McCormack pointed out that the shop is constantly upgrading the lines. To prove the point, he motioned to the checkering pattern in the Custom Shop brochure, then grabbed a corresponding rifle from the rack, showing a difference in the point pattern. The newer pattern had a few additional points, and overall, did look much better.

Other rifles available from the shop include the Models Four, Six, and Seven. The first two are offered in "D" and "F" grades, which parallel shotgun grades, while the Model Seven comes in the regular bolt-action rifle grades available in the Model 700.

The Model 870 pump and Model 1100 automatic shotguns can be had through the shop with many of the items listed for the turnbolt rifles. Like the Models Four and Six rifles, the scatterguns with their expansive receiver surfaces furnish a perfect field for engraving. The "D" grade is akin to a Tournament grade, and the "F" designation equals Premier and is available with gold inlays of hunting dogs, game birds, or other special designs.

The real story of the Remington Custom Shop lies in the craftsmen who perform the work, the metal workers, stockers, and engravers. They are the pulse of the operation whose individual talents combine to produce the final assembly that the customer will judge.

John Remington — the name's a coincidence — has been at his stock and trade for many years. Yes, he is a stockmaker. During the tour, he was busy working on a high-grade rifle. The barreled action had reached him, and he was in the process of mating it with a stock blank into one beautiful firearm.

All inletting is roughed in by machine, then hand

Barrel specialist Don Eckler turns and finishes a barrel destined for a Custom Shop rifle. Bolt-actions are the primary fare, but autoloading and pump shotguns and rifles are turned out there.

fitted to the exact dimensions, precisely blending metal to wood. The loading port is marked and raked to a pleasing angle, for the beauty here is in the fine detail. During the course of this work, the action is in and out of the stock many times to make absolutely sure the finished product is exactly what the customer expects.

The shop's final assembly inspectors fire all the guns they work on — from the shoulder — then rework them if the gun is not shooting to standard. After inspection, a certificate attests to the quality and workmanship of each gun.

A visitor can sense an air of relaxed assurance throughout the Remington Custom Shop. As the visitor moves from one group of craftsmen to the next, a confidence that breeds excellence is apparent. This excellence is found in the people and in the guns they produce.

Prices? Well, considering the time involved (the shop produces only about 10 rifles a week) and the necessary level of talent and worksmanship required, they are reasonable. Grade I rifles retail for $1,100, IIs list for $2,000, IIIs are $3,000, and Grade IVs — you guessed it — top the list at four grand. Waiting time as of this writing is six to eight months on most guns, up to one year on the higher grades.

If your interest in acquiring one of Remington's custom beauties has been whetted, by all means drop a note requesting a brochure to The Remington Custom Shop, Remington Arms, Ilion, N.Y. 13357.

Sally Cable checkers a rifle stock. A Grade II M-700 and an "F" Grade 1100 (pictured on page 21) are typical wares.

The Return of
the Varmint Shooter

Jim Carmichel

Have you ever wondered what happened to the love affairs that American shooters once carried on with their varmint rifles? From the late 1940s until the mid-1970s, varmint shooting was so popular that no gun rack was considered complete unless it held at least one high-velocity, flat-shooting, track-driving varmint rifle. From the manufacturers' viewpoint, varmint rifles and ammunition were bread-and-butter items, and the major gunmakers competed head on to turn out the most accurate rifles and the fastest ammunition. Some riflemakers staked their reputations on the performance of their varmint rifles, while some others made or sold nothing but varmint rifles. The honored Finnish firm of Sako, for instance, first cracked the American market with their sweet little varmint rifles and did not offer big-game rigs until years later. Similarly, the great reputation for accuracy enjoyed by Remington's post-war, bolt-action rifles was established in large measure by the performance of their Model 722 varmint rifle in .222 Remington chambering. Until that rifle was introduced, such fine accuracy from an off-the-shelf rifle was almost unknown.

But toward the end of the 1970s, varmint shooting got lost in the shuffle. The sport didn't exactly go out of style, but what with the high price of gasoline plus the escalating cost of rifles and ammunition, a day trip to the woodchuck meadows became a considerable investment. When the recession hit, varmint shooting really took a nose dive because the firearms industry, always the first and the longest to suffer during hard times, couldn't spend much money on the development of varmint-hunting equipment and spent even less money promoting the sport.

Times are brighter now, and a couple of gunmakers boasted that 1984 was their best year ever and geared up to offer newer and better varmint rifles. What we will see in the way of new varmint rifles and cartridges over the next few years will be the best ever, providing that there is no new recession and that the gunmakers keep the faith.

Another happy piece of news is that the varmint population — mostly woodchucks (we call them groundhogs in Tennessee), crows, prairie dogs, jackrabbits, Western marmots — has flourished over the past few years. The South Dakota Game

Some well-known varmint rounds (from left): .17 Rem., .22 Hornet, .222 Rem., .223 Rem., .222 Rem. Mag., .224 Weatherby Mag., .22/250 Rem., .225 Win.,. .220 Swift, .243 Win., 6mm Rem., .240 Weatherby Mag., .250/3000 Savage, .257 Roberts, .25/06 Rem., .257 Weatherby Mag.

Photo by Stanley W. Trzoniec

Department will even provide you with a map showing how to get to the state's big prairie dog towns.

Varmint hunting is just what the name implies — hunting pest species that most landowners would rather be without. A few anti-hunting agitators foam at the mouth about killing non-edible animals. Little do they realize that the varmint hunter is not only the friend, but also the protector of hundreds of thousands of prairie dogs. I know ranchers who refrain from poisoning their "dog towns" because the pup count is kept in check by varmint shooters. Even when a serious varmint shooter fires several hundred well aimed shots a day for days on end, he can kill only a small percentage of a town's population. Poisoning, by contrast, is total and permanent. I shoot groundhogs on several farms where the landowners would otherwise poke lethal exhaust hoses into their dens to wipe out the springtime litters.

Varmint shooting is the artful bridge between hunting and target shooting. It requires game-spotting and stalking skills, patience, and needle's-eye marksmanship. As varmint shooting equipment has improved over the past generation, the empha-sis has shifted away from the artful stalk and toward scientific marksmanship. The shot is the thing, and the longer the better. A good rig easily reaches out beyond 300 yards to center a sun-bathing marmot or chuck.

It takes wonderfully accurate rifles and ammuni-tion to hit small targets at such long distances, and that's why many hunters who balk at laying out $300 for a deer rifle will happily write a check for two or three times that much for a respectable varmint rifle and scope. That's also why riflemakers consider their varmint rifles the jewels in their crowns or, in some cases, their crown of thorns. Varmint shooters are a particular breed who may fire a hundred shots on a test range for every shot they fire at living varmints. If a rifle won't put five shots inside a one-inch circle at 100 yards, they scream bloody murder and try to have the rifle's maker drawn and quartered. But if the rifle turns out to be a half-incher, they wrap it in swaddling clothes and write love letters to the manufacturer. That explains why riflemakers' reputations for accuracy rest so heavily on their varmint rifles.

Of course, factory-loaded ammunition is widely used, but long-range varmint shooting is largely a handloading proposition. Questing for that Holy Grail of Rifledom, the one-hole group, dedicated varmint hunters fervently develop the best possible combination of bullet, powder, case, and primer for their rifles. In fact, much of what we know about ammunition and rifle accuracy was learned by varmint shooters. The ultratechnical game of benchrest shooting is itself an outgrowth of varmint hunting.

THE ROOTS

Today's varmint rifles and cartridges represent the most modern shooting technology, but the sport's roots are deeply planted in the last century. I once saw a Winslow Homer painting of a straw-hatted lad aiming a caplock rifle across a summertime meadow at what could only have been a woodchuck.

Then, as now, varmint hunters were an elite who enjoyed the challenge of long-range shooting at small, elusive targets. They were at the forefront of rifle and ammunition development and were the best marksmen of their era. The best varmint rifles of that time were high-performance target rifles chambered for .22 and .25 caliber centerfire cartridges that did dual service in the field and on the target range. With muzzle velocities in the 1,500-fps range, these blackpower cartridges wouldn't cause much excitement today, but they had enough punch for kills out to nearly 200 yards.

The more popular varmint or "pest" rounds, as they were called then, were the .22/15/60 Stevens (.22 caliber/15 grains of blackpowder/60-grain bullet), .25/20, .25/21, and .25/25 Stevens. The favored varmint rifles were the Stevens single-shot target rifles, which were among the most accurate rifles made at the time and were very popular with target shooters. In case you're wondering, yes, they did use scopes back then — some pretty good ones, usually 6X magnification or close to it.

MODERN TIMES

The modern era of varmint cartridges began in the 1920s with the introduction of the .22 Hornet. This classy little number, which churns up nearly 2,700 fps, was developed from the old .22 W.C.F. by Townsend Whelen, who was then the shooting editor of *OUTDOOR LIFE.*

The Hornet was a honey and still is. But with a maximum practical range of only about 200 yards it really whetted the varmint shooters' desire for more velocity, flatter trajectory and, of course, more range. This demand climaxed in the appearance, in 1935, of the awesome .220 Swift. In one quantum leap, the Swift staggered the shooting world with its muzzle velocity of 4,100 fps with a 48-grain, .22 caliber bullet. Fifty years after its introduction, the

Swift is still the fastest factory-loaded cartridge ever cataloged, which ought to give you some idea of the sensation it caused back in 1935.

Later in the decade, two more .22 caliber varmint rounds, the .218 Bee and the .219 Zipper, were introduced, but neither approached the Swift's performance and they were primarily designed to work in lever-action rifles or inexpensive bolt guns. However, the lever-action concept was never compatible with varmint shooting and the Bee and Zipper were never very popular. In fact, rifles in .219 caliber are now collector's items.

The next benchmark in varmint shooting was the introduction of the .222 Remington in 1950. Introduced with a 50-grain bullet at 3,200 fps, the .222 Remington was no match for the Swift in a footrace but, by the same token, it didn't spook cattle in the next county and was available in Remington's inexpensive but wonderfully accurate Model 722 bolt rifle. The Model 722 sold for $75 back then, and a Weaver K-10 scope cost $60. For less than $150, a shooter could buy a rig that could hit a chuck's head at 200 yards. The .222 ushered in the golden age of varmint hunting.

Varmint cartridges that followed were the .222 Remington Magnum, .223 Remington, .224 Weatherby, .225 Winchester, .22/250 Remington, .243 Winchester, and .244 Remington (which later became the 6mm Remington). The .243 was an overnight sensation because, in addition to being a superb long-range varmint round, it was also fine for deer and antelope hunting. The .225 Winchester and the .222 Remington Magnum got lost in the shuffle, but the .22/250 was a solid hit because it had gained considerable fame as a do-it-yourself, hand-loaded wildcat round before Remington gave it an honest factory name. Wildcatters made .22/250 cases by necking .250 Savage cases down to fire a .22 caliber, hence the name. Remington also showed great originality with the introduction of such radical cartridges as their 5mm rimfire and the .17 Remington centerfire. The 5mm is now dead and I understand that the .17 is in serious trouble. However, the .17 Remington was a noble cause and still is.

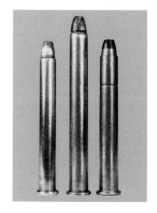

These antique varmint cartridges are (from left): .22/15/60 Stevens, .25/25 Stevens, and .25/21 Stevens. Ultra-long cases were necessary to accommodate large powder charges.

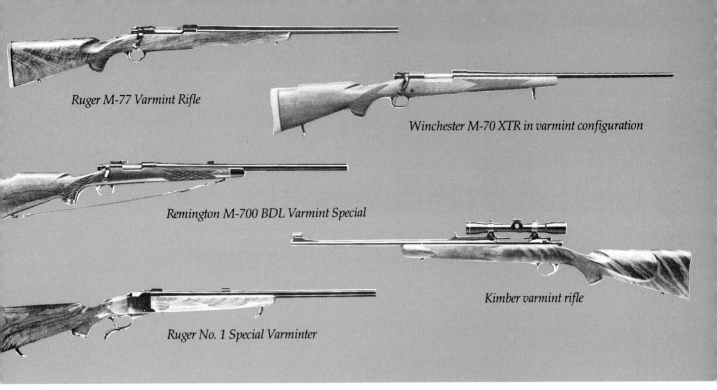

Ruger M-77 Varmint Rifle

Winchester M-70 XTR in varmint configuration

Remington M-700 BDL Varmint Special

Kimber varmint rifle

Ruger No. 1 Special Varminter

THE FUTURE

If I had to guess which varmint round holds the most promise for the future (other than *OUTDOOR LIFE'S* own sainted .224 CHeetah), it would have to be the .223 Remington. It has all the accuracy of the .222 Remington, has a respectable muzzle velocity of 3,240 fps with a 55-grain bullet, and has the overwhelming advantage of currently being the official U.S. small-arms cartridge. In other words, it may well become the .30/06 of the varmint kingdom.

About everyone who makes a good rifle these days turns out a good varmint rifle. Ruger offers their Model 77 bolt rifle in a medium-heavy varmint configuration, and also makes the stylish Number One Single-Shot in a heavy-barreled varmint version. Remington offers varmint calibers in their standard-weight Model 700 bolt guns as well as a special heavy-barreled profile. New for 1985, Winchester (USRAC) is making a Sporter Varmint Model 70 bolt rifle with the short action that they introduced in 1984. They also offer the varmint calibers in other short-action versions of the Model 70, including their high-style Featherweight.

Browning has a newly revamped bolt gun in a couple of fast-stepping varmint calibers and, if you want to spend a little extra money for something really pretty, take a look at Weatherby's short-action Varmintmaster rifle in .22/250 or .224 Weatherby Magnum. And, of course, if you want to get dead serious about long-range varmint shooting, the rifles to consider are the Remington 40-X, the Shilen DGA, or the Wichita varmint rigs. I have a Shilen DGA in .220 Swift that still groups about ⅜-inch after more than 5,000 rounds have been put through the barrel. Shilen and Wichita also offer

rifles in .224 CHeetah chambering, if you're a handloader and feel that you're ready for 4,300 fps. (It's a whole new world.)

Of course, many other varmint rifles are available. The foregoing list just gives you an idea of where to start looking. If you want to ease your way into the upcoming varmint season, why not try a .22 Rimfire Magnum or even some of the new .22 Long Rifle ultravelocity loads? The working range isn't much more than 100 yards, and some varmint shooters look down their noses at rimfires. But what the hell, any kind of varmint hunting is fun.

I have to say that the most logical and necessary varmint rifles aren't on the market. If I were designing rifles for Remington, Ruger, or Winchester, here's what I'd do. For Remington, I'd start with the Model 700 action and omit the big hole where the magazine box fits. This would make the action more rigid and, therefore, more accurate. Of course, the rifle would then be a single-shot, but that's fine. Varmints seldom call for fast follow-up shots. Then I'd redesign the stock so that the forearm would have a semi-beavertail shape with a flat bottom so that it would lie on a rest solidly. The barrel would be 26 inches long, with a straight taper, and it would be heavy enough to make the rifle weigh about 11 pounds.

I'd do the same with the Winchester Model 70 and the Ruger Model 77 short-action rifles. Leaving out the magazine cuts in both these rifles would be a great aid to accuracy. Both would also benefit from an updated stock design. The name of the game is accuracy, and these few improvements would significantly enhance performance without increasing manufacturing costs. Who could resist making and buying such wonderful varmint rifles?

Kricotronic: Electronic Thunderbolt!

Dave Hetzler

It has been said that the last 40 years have seen our entrance into the Atomic Age. However, I'm not so sure this is actually the fact. Certainly, a few nations have nuclear weapons, and some of the world's power comes from nuclear generating stations, but by and large, the average man on the street has no contact with fissionable materials, and the respective good, or evil, that comes from them.

On the other hand, practically everybody has some kind of contact with electronics. All civilized nations are powered by electricity, and even the most primitive third-world nations rely on that mysterious force we call electricity. Electricity is nothing new to firearms either. Some artillery is fired by an electrical charge, and electronic triggers are found on many target arms. But something that hasn't seen the light of day is electronic firing of sporting arms using *standard* ammunition — until now. The Krico Sporting Arms Co. (Krico GmbH) has developed a system wherein standard ammunition can have the primer ignited by an electrical charge.

At the moment, the Kricotronic System, as it's called, is meant basically for the target shooter for two reasons; first, a silhouette .22 rimfire rifle is the only arm the system has been adapted to, and second, the recycle time of the twin capacitors isn't fast enough for a quick follow-up shot. The recycle period is being improved all the time, however, and in future it is hard to say just how rapid it might become. I first heard about the Kricotronic system at the 1984 SHOT Show in Dallas, Texas. The Krico public relations people stated that recycle time was in the neighborhood of 6½ seconds. In June of 1984, when I first saw and fired the system at Krico's factory in Stuttgart, West Germany, the recycle time had been reduced to four to 4½ seconds. By the end

This article first appeared in *GUNS & AMMO*.

Prototype rifle, first seen in Germany, carries all electronics in the forearm. Newer version tested in U.S. uses essentially the same system except it is powered by only two 9-volt batteries instead of four used in the earlier version.

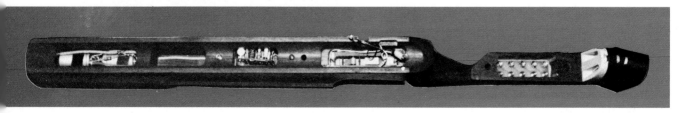

M-340 Silhouette is a shooter in and of itself. This group measured ½"; it was fired with Eley Match ammunition in a tunnel at 100 meters.

of last year (1984) when the prototype test rifle was unveiled, the recycle period was down to three to 3½ seconds. Interestingly enough, during this transition the battery pack also got smaller. At first the system was powered by six 9-volt transistor radio batteries. In June the pack was down to four batteries, and by the time the rifle got to America the battery pack contained only two 9-volt units.

Before we get deeply into the Kricotronic system let's talk about the rifle itself, because in this case it is almost secondary to the revolutionary new method of lighting the fire. The basic rifle is Krico's bolt-action Model 340 Silhouette five-shot .22 rimfire. Fitted with a 21½ inch heavy barrel, the Model 340 is meant for the rapidly growing game of .22 rimfire silhouette shooting. It boasts a target-styled walnut stock that is stippled on both the pistol grip and forearm. Stippling, while not as decorative a finish as checkering, provides a slightly better grip for the competitive shooter. The barrel is totally free-floating. The receiver is grooved for tip-off mounts, and on our particular test gun we fitted a Leupold 8X scope in Beeman rings.

Unfortunately, we weren't able to do serious accuracy testing. On two different trips to the Petersen ranch (where we tested the rifle), we were met by 35 to 40 mph winds, certainly not conducive to accuracy when testing any rifle, to say nothing of a .22 rimfire. At best, with Lapua Match ammunition we got slightly under ½-inch groups at 25 yards — nothing to write home about. However, I did get to fire another prototype (of the Kricotronic system, not the Model 340 Silhouette rifle) in Krico's 100-meter test tunnel. Using Eley Match ammunition, that gun was capable of under ½-inch groups at the full 100 meters. Using that as a basis, along with groups I've shot from other Krico rifles, I think it's safe to say that the Krico brand has proven to be highly accurate.

The rifle is fed from a five-round detachable magazine, the same as the standard Model 340 Silhouette. In fact that's a point I want to stress. Other than the installation of the Kricotronic system, the rifle *is* the standard Model 340 Silhouette with the exception that now there are *no* mechanical lockworks — none, zip, nil! Only extraction and ejection

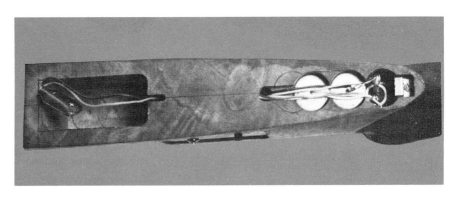

Unlike the earlier version, a second prototype seen in Germany had capacitors moved back to the buttstock from the forearm. Like so many prototypes, Kricotronic is in a constant state of flux.

Off/on switch activates Kricotronic system. Light blinks when system is charged.

sudden the rifle goes "bang" and you've sent a shot downrange. I guarantee you that first shot goes before you expect it — it has with every person I've seen shoot the rifle. It is almost uncanny how detached you feel from the trigger/switch movement. At first I didn't like it because I felt I had no control over when the shot was going to be fired. It was almost as though I had nothing to do with it. But when I got used to it I can honestly say I shot better groups than I ever had before. Once you understand the feeling, the Kricotronic system does wonders for your accuracy.

Basically the system works on the same principle as a spot welder — low voltage and high amperage. The two 9-volt batteries, in series, provide 18 volts. The voltage is stored in two capacitors until the shooter releases the trigger. When the trigger is pulled a thyristor (a one-way electrical switch) opens and allows 300 amps to flow through an electrode that resides in the bolt where a firing pin would normally be. This electrode, made from tungsten, is spring-loaded so that it can rest, under tension, on the rear of the cartridge case (on a .22 rimfire of course it rests against the rim). Because the electrode is so small in diameter (.040 inch) when compared with the surface it's resting on (the primer), opening the thyristor releases the stored charge against the primer. Because it happens so rapidly the charge is converted into heat in microseconds. At the point of contact the heat reaches 3,500 degrees C, and since primers only need 400 degrees C in an instantaneous situation to detonate, the primer is fired. In essence, all this means is that for all practical purposes there is *no* locktime. You pull the trigger and the shot is fired — right now!

are the same as a standard rifle. Dual extractors are used, and a solid projection that resides in the bottom of the bolt raceway provides ejection.

Firing the Kricotronic the first time is a bit unsettling. Subconsciously, you're aware of the sear breaking on a normal rifle — you *feel* it break, if you will. This system is something else altogether. First of all, the "trigger pull" (it's not a trigger in the normal sense of the word; it is a switch) is almost unmeasurable. Our standard pull gauge doesn't even come close to determining the lightness of the Kricotronic's pull. I can only guess it is in the one to three ounce range — and that's with a two-stage trigger! And even then the first stage, through a series of adjustment screws, can be adjusted out.

So there you sit, slowly trying to "take up the slack" on a trigger that you can *barely* feel. All of a

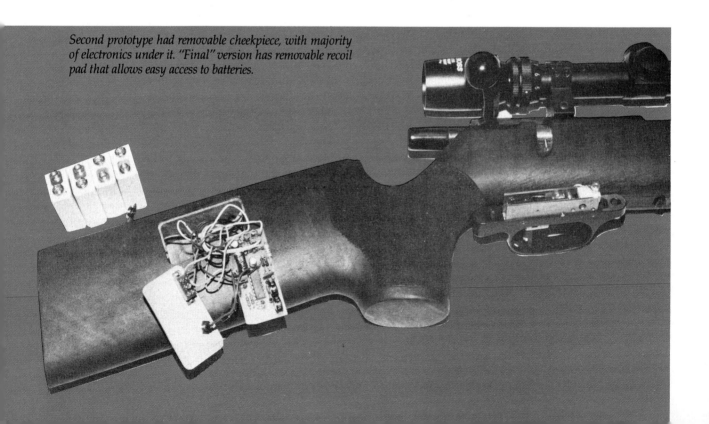

Second prototype had removable cheekpiece, with majority of electronics under it. "Final" version has removable recoil pad that allows easy access to batteries.

Small protrusion in bolt handle channel (right) is the only "safety" the Kricotronic has. Unless the bolt presses it down, rifle can't be fired. After removing electrode wire the bolt is removed by pressing in on bolt release (far right).

The switch to turn on the system is located on the right of the buttstock. Along with the switch is a warning light that goes on the instant the switch is activated. In about three to four seconds the light starts to blink, indicating the capacitors are charged and the rifle is ready to fire. In many ways it acts like, and works like, a modern strobe unit for a camera.

As you may have guessed by now, there is no safety provided with this system because none is needed. And since there are no mechanical parts in the lockworks it would be impossible to use a safety as we know it. Instead, when the switch is turned off, the rifle is as safe as a loaded gun can ever be. In a conventional firearm a sear can always break, or something can go mechanically wrong. The Kricotronic, on the other hand, is totally safe when the switch is turned off.

One problem did surface with the Kricotronic system during testing. However, it must be remembered that both guns we used — one in America and one in Germany — were prototypes and the problem will be cured. The difficulty was simply this: the rifle didn't fire every time the light said the capacitors were fully charged. This situation didn't occur often, perhaps one in 15 times — but it did happen enough to warrant mentioning it. Once or twice the fault was traced to the ammunition instead of the gun. On a rimfire .22 cartridge, the priming compound is spun by centrifugal force into the rim area of the case. Because the electrode is only .040 inch in diameter, the heat it produces is concentrated into a very small area, and if there isn't priming compound directly under the electrode, nothing will happen.

The few times the cartridge wasn't at fault, it was necessary to recycle the bolt handle, which then allowed the capacitors to recharge.

With the electrode transferring such high heat, it does burn itself away after about 500 rounds have been fired. Arndt Kriegeskorte, the designer of the

Kricotronic system, feels that Beeman Precision Firearms, who will be the distributor for this gun in North America, will be able to supply replacement electrodes for under $8. The batteries also have to be replaced about every thousand rounds, but any drugstore will be able to supply the shooter with them (or rechargeable batteries could be used). In fact, there is a plan to offer the system in the future with rechargeable batteries.

For accuracy testing we fitted Kricotronic with 8X Leupold scope. However, the California weather didn't cooperate; twice we were blown away by 30-plus mph winds. There's no reason it shouldn't shoot as well as it did in Germany, though.

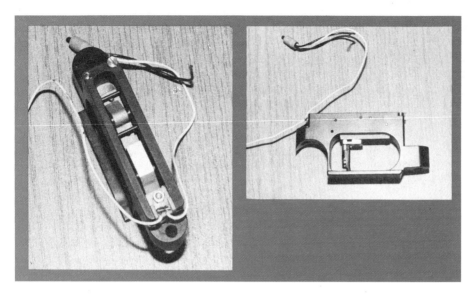

(Far left) Adjustments for various functions of the trigger are accomplished via two small screws at front of unit.

(Left) The trigger, actually an electronic switch, is fully adjustable for weight of pull, creep, and overtravel. Being a target-type trigger, let-off is measured in ounces.

So there you have it; not the Atomic Age, but the Electronic Age, so far as shooters are concerned. And what does this electronic marvel cost? Well, since we are talking about a prototype, it's hard to say. But here's a guide to go by. The basic Model 340 Silhouette costs $649.50. I was told in Germany the addition of the Kricotronic system would up the price about $110. I think most target shooters would be happy to ante up an extra hundred bucks if it would guarantee their scores going up. And so would target shotgunners. Presently two famous shotgun makers from Italy are talking to Krico about including the system on their target guns.

Also, plans are underway to make the system available on centerfire rifles.

So for the first time in many decades, we have an all-new method of igniting the primer of standard ammunition that seems better than the age-old style. It still has some minor glitches, but undoubtedly they will be resolved before the production system ever hits your dealer's shelves. What we have here is a small revolution in firearms. I'll bet that in a few years it will have grown into a full-scale insurrection!

For more information on the Kricotronic system, contact Beeman Precision Firearms, 47 Paul Drive, San Rafael, CA 94903.

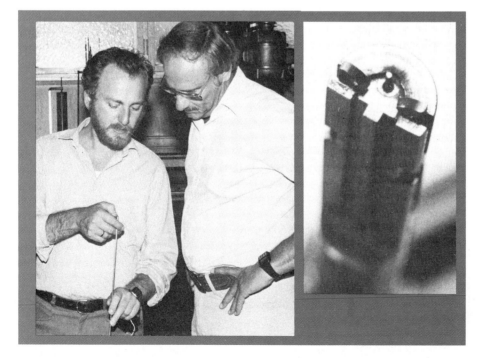

(Far left) Arndt Kriegeskorte, designer of Kricotronic system, explains part of the manufacturing process that goes into making Krico rifles so accurate.

(Left) Instead of a firing pin, Kricotronic uses spring-loaded electrode that rests on the primer. Periodically, melted brass must be removed from bolt face with a knife.

PART TWO

HANDGUNS

Colt's Early
Automatic Pistols

Patrick F. Rogers

Eighty-four years ago, John Browning revolu-
tionized the handgun world with a design so
basically correct in all respects that it has
never been equaled.

There were other automatic pistols on the market
in early 1900, when Colt began production of
Browning's .38 automatics. The Mauser, Mannlicher,
Luger, and Bergmann had all achieved production
status. Today, all are gone, remaining only as collector's items, while developments of the basic
Browning design have become the most widely
used automatic pistols in the world. No other
design since Samuel Colt developed the first practical revolver has had equal impact on the history of
handguns.

Browning's success came from two strengths. He
possessed an inherent genius in mechanical design,
and was an enthusiastic and experienced practical
shooter. This enabled him to visualize what an
entirely new type of gun should be like and then
design a weapon to realize the concept efficiently.

In addition to being a superior gun designer,
Browning was a master gunsmith and machinist.

Better than any other gun designer of the day, he
knew how guns were made. He would move along
a production line watching the work, occasionally
picking up a tool and demonstrating how an operation should be done.

He had the greatest respect for the men who
made his guns, and the feeling was mutual. Browning's production line workers nicknamed him "the
master."

Lacking a formal education, Browning had trouble with blueprints. While working with Colt on the
prototypes of his automatics, he would visualize a
part, cut out the outline from drafting paper, and
take it to the model shop. He would ask for a part to
be made to match the outline and specify the thickness. His visualizations were so accurate that, with
minor hand fitting, the parts could be assembled
directly into the prototype pistols.

Browning started work on military automatic
pistols in 1894. His work proceeded along two lines,
resulting in successful prototypes of gas-operated

This article first appeared in THE AMERICAN RIFLEMAN.

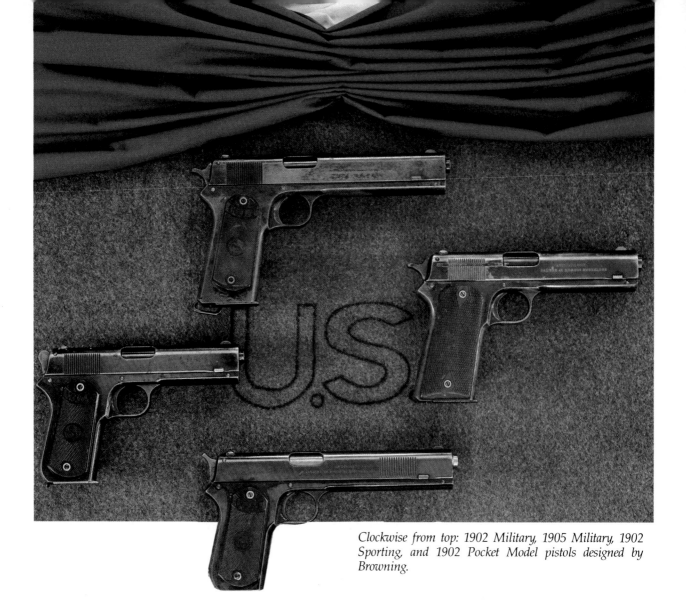

Clockwise from top: 1902 Military, 1905 Military, 1902 Sporting, and 1902 Pocket Model pistols designed by Browning.

and recoil-operated .38 automatics. The prototype pistols were demonstrated to Colt company officials and extensively tested from 1895 to 1898. Both designs were successful, and both were superior to existing military automatic designs.

In 1898, Colt selected the recoil-operated pistol for production. Development of the gas-operated model was dropped. It is not hard to see why. The gas-operated pistol used a toggle action actuated by a gas-driven lever. It was a fascinating design, but it was inherently more complex than the recoil-operated design. It would also have been less reliable with the ammunition available in the 1890s.

The recoil-operated pistol design incorporated all the features which characterize subsequent Browning designs. The pistol was the first to use the operating slide principle. The slide, a single strong piece, enclosed the full length of the barrel and contained all operating parts with the exception of the barrel, hammer, and trigger mechanism.

The slide moved backward and forward on grooves machined in the frame. The barrel was attached to the frame by links and pivoted down and back to unlock. The recoil spring was located under the barrel and was compressed when the slide moved to the rear. It then drove the slide forward, stripping a fresh cartridge from the magazine and pivoting the barrel forward and up to lock.

With the exception that post-1911 models replaced the forward link with a barrel bushing or a slide/barrel support surface, this system continues to be used in all locked-breech Browning designs to this day.

Nothing about the description sounds particularly remarkable. Most high powered automatic pistols built today, whether Browning designs or not, incorporate some or all of these features. Browning's remarkable accomplishment was to invent these concepts and introduce them all simultaneously in one pistol design.

If the new pistol's design was remarkable in 1900, its ammunition was sensational! The .38 Automatic Colt Pistol (ACP) was the first American pistol cartridge designed to use smokeless powder. It fired a 130-grain jacketed bullet at a velocity of 1,260 fps and a muzzle energy of 460 foot-pounds.

The standard .38 Government revolver cartridge in use in 1900 fired a 148-grain lead bullet at a velocity of 750 fps. The .38 ACP would penetrate 11⅞-inch pine boards. The .38 service revolver cartridge would penetrate only five.

Only two other smokeless powder automatic pistol cartridges were available in the United States in 1900. The .38 Colt ACP outperformed both, as the three cartridges were loaded at the time.

The .30 (or 7.63mm) Mauser, introduced in Europe in 1896, fired an 85-grain bullet at a velocity of 1,323 fps with a muzzle energy of 330 foot-pounds. It would penetrate 11⅞-inch pine boards.

The .30 (or 7.65mm) Luger cartridge was introduced in 1900. It was not as powerful as the .30 Mauser. The Luger cartridge fired a 93-grain bullet at a muzzle velocity of 1,160 fps with a muzzle energy of 278 foot-pounds. It would penetrate 10⅞-inch pine boards.

The .38 Colt ACP with its larger, heavier bullet was a much more effective cartridge than either of the two German rounds. Contemporary shooters agreed with his evaluation.

The .38 automatic pistols provided shooters in 1900 with entirely new capabilities. The .38 Colt automatics were the Magnums of their time. The 70 percent increase in muzzle velocity over the .38 revolver cartridge gave long-range accuracy and penetration never achieved before. The original load was reduced to 1,200 fps before World War I, primarily to improve accuracy. It also reduced nominal chamber pressure from 35,000 to 28,000 psi, which tended to prolong barrel life. In the late 1930s, muzzle velocity was reduced again to 1,100 fps. Penetration dropped to nine ⅞-inch pine boards.

The new .38 automatic was a radical step forward. The shooting public was interested but not wildly enthusiastic. Colt sold 3,500 of the new Model 1900 automatics in the first two years of production. While commercial sales were important, Colt's main goal was to sell to the Armed Forces, and the Army was definitely interested. The service pistol played a far more important part in the battle tactics of 1900 than it does today. It was particularly important to the cavalry and the artillery.

Cavalry units were expected to make mounted charges against enemy units. The cavalryman's carbine could not be used effectively when he was mounted. The sword and the pistol were the weapons used in the charge. American officers, with the combat experience of the Civil War and the Indian Wars behind them, knew that the pistol was the most important weapon. They considered it the principal offensive weapon of the U.S. Cavalry.

The artillerymen fired their cannons directly at enemy troops from positions in or very close to the front lines. Hostile cavalry charges to kill the gun crews and capture the cannon were considered to be a major threat.

Artillerymen were trained to fire their cannons at the enemy cavalry charge until the hostile horsemen were at point-blank range. Then, they took cover around the guns and fired at the cavalrymen with their revolvers, the last defensive weapons of the artillery.

A successful automatic pistol appeared to offer three significant advantages. First, it would hold more rounds, eight to 10 ready shots compared to the revolver's six. Second, if properly designed, it could be rapidly reloaded with spare magazines. This allowed sustained rapid fire without the long pauses required to reload revolvers. Third, it offered a far faster aimed rate of fire under combat conditions. This resulted from the self-cocking action of the automatic, allowing rapid aimed fire without breaking the shooter's grip to cock for each shot.

The first two points seem obvious. The third seems strange today. We are accustomed to the idea that a double-action revolver can be fired as rapidly and as accurately as an automatic. Modern practical pistol matches have demonstrated this many times.

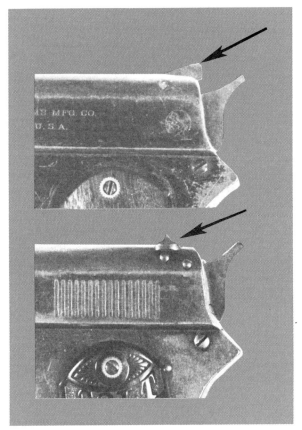

The first pistols combined the rear sight with a safety lever. The feature was discarded for separate safeties and sights.

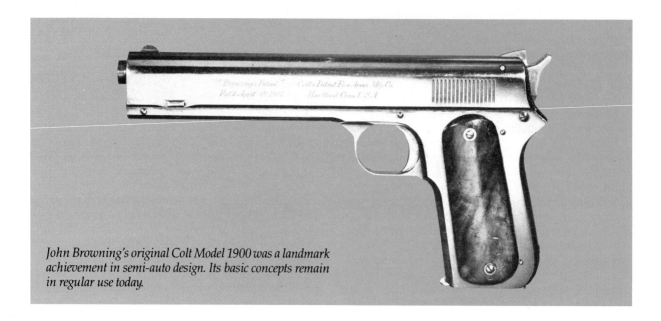

John Browning's original Colt Model 1900 was a landmark achievement in semi-auto design. Its basic concepts remain in regular use today.

This is true with modern revolvers and skilled double-action shooters. Neither were available in the 1890s. Double-action revolvers were relatively new then. The average soldier was far from being a skilled double-action shot.

Double-action shooting was regarded as useful only in emergency situations at point blank range. Ammunition for pistol practice was limited. Most practice firing with the revolver was done firing single-action.

Single-action firing required breaking the shooting grip to cock the hammer before each shot. The effective rate of aimed fire achieved with the revolver was low. A self-cocking automatic pistol offered the possibility of accurate, aimed rapid fire.

The military potential of the new pistol was obvious. A single specimen was tested by a U.S. Army Board of Officers between January and April 1900. The Board was favorably impressed. In its report it stated:

The test to which this pistol was subjected was in every way more severe than that to which revolvers have been heretofore subjected, and the endurance of this pistol appears to be greater than that of the service revolver. It possesses further advantage[s] as follows:

- Very simple construction.
- It is easy to operate.
- It is not liable to get out of order.
- It is capable of a very high rate of fire.
- It can be conveniently loaded with either hand.
- It gives a high initial velocity and flat trajectory.
- It is more accurate than a revolver.

The Board recommended that the .38 Colt automatic be considered for adoption as the service pistol and that a trial lot of pistols be purchased for field testing.

An initial Army order for a small lot of the pistols was placed in the spring of 1900. A second order was placed in early 1901. The number of pistols in each lot is unknown, but Army records indicate a total of 200 Model 1900 pistols was delivered to the Army at Springfield Armory. The U.S. Navy was also interested and placed an order for a small lot of pistols late in 1900. The exact number of pistols in the Navy order is not known, but is estimated to have been less than 50.

Unfortunately, no records of the Army and Navy trials of the 1900 Model Colt appear to have survived. However, we can deduce the probable military reaction by the modifications in design which Browning made for Colt in 1901.

Despite its many excellent design features, the 1900 Model had its faults as a military pistol. The principal problems were the combination rear sight-safety and the lack of any method of knowing when the pistol had been fired empty. Both problems required actual field service in order to become apparent. They had to be fixed if Browning's .38 automatic was to become an effective military pistol.

The pivoting rear sight-safety was effective as a mechanical device. It positively locked the firing pin when applied, but as a practical safety it was nearly useless. When the 1900 Model is held in the hand in a normal shooting grip, the safety cannot be touched by the shooting hand. It can only be activated by reaching over the slide with the free hand. This is awkward and slow.

It is possible to bring the pistol up to shoot, only to discover that the safety has been forgotten and the pistol will not fire. In 1900, when few U.S. firearms had safeties, this problem must have been common. The small size of the notch in the safety which served as the rear sight did not give a good sight picture. While usable for precise shooting under slow-fire conditions, the sight picture could not be picked up rapidly. This was a serious defect in a pistol intended for military or police use.

This was easily corrected. The pivoting rear sight safety was replaced with a fixed rear sight with a larger notch. This design was retained on all future Browning .38 automatic designs. Colt also applied the new sight design to the original 1900 Model with no other changes. The new variation was named the "Sporting Model." In 1903, a 4.5-inch barreled version was produced as the "Pocket Model."

The second problem was more severe and required more extensive redesign to correct. There was no hold open or indicator device to show that the last cartridge had been fired. It was possible to fire the 1900 Model empty without realizing it.

Under the mental and physical stresses of close combat, it is easy to lose count of the number of shots fired. If the pistol lacks a method of indicating that it has been fired empty, the first warning is likely to be the dismal click of the hammer falling on an empty chamber.

Allowing the slide to run forward on an empty chamber also delays reloading. If a 1900 Model has been fired empty, reloading requires removing the empty magazine, inserting a loaded magazine, and pulling the slide to the rear and releasing it to chamber a cartridge. What was needed was a device to indicate that the pistol was empty and to facilitate reloading.

Browning's solution was simple and elegant. A sliding lever was added to the left side of the pistol frame. When the pistol was empty, the magazine follower pushed the lever upward to a notch cut in the left side of the slide, locking it to the rear. The shooter thus had an immediate visual clue that the pistol was empty.

When a loaded magazine was inserted, downward pressure on the sliding lever released the slide. The slide was immediately driven forward by the recoil spring. The slide stripped the first cartridge from the new magazine and loaded it into the chamber. The pistol was instantly reloaded, cocked, and ready to fire.

By the simple addition of one new part, minor additional machining on the slide and receiver, and a slight change in the magazine design, a major defect in the original design was corrected.

Colt incorporated this improvement in a new version of the Browning design. The new pistol was designated the Military Model and placed in production in 1902. In addition to the slide locking and release lever, the Military Model also incorporated a lengthened grip which allowed an increase in magazine capacity from seven to eight rounds. A lanyard ring was added to the lower left side of the grip. This looks strange to modern shooters. It was considered essential in 1902, however, when the majority of military pistol users fought mounted and a pistol dropped from a horse was lost if not secured with a lanyard.

Government interest in the Military Model was immediate. Two hundred pistols were delivered to Springfield Armory in 1902. The military future of the new pistol appeared bright. It combined a powerful and accurate cartridge with a simple and reliable mechanical design. It was superior to the .38 Colt service revolver in almost all respects.

If events had taken their normal course, it is probable that an improved version of the .38 Military Model would be our service pistol today. But outside events intervened. Browning had designed a .38 caliber automatic because that was what the Government wanted. Suddenly, this was no longer true.

In 1899, the U.S. Army became involved in heavy fighting in the Philippines. In the close-quarter infantry combat which followed, the .38 Colt service

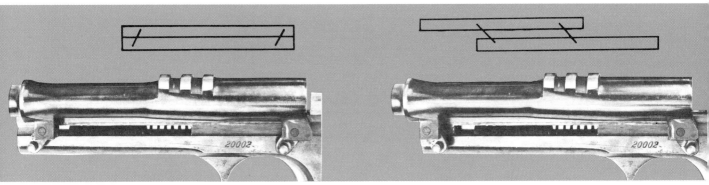

Browning may have gotten the idea for his recoil operating principle from the action of a parallel rule. The double links of the pistol act in the same way as the connecting links of the rule. As the barrel recoils, it drops out of engagement with the moving slide.

revolver repeatedly failed to stop determined attackers. In 1904, the Army established an investigating board headed by Colonels John T. Thompson and Louis A. LaGarde to investigate the failures of the service revolver and recommend changes if required.

The Thompson-LaGarde board conducted extensive tests with a wide variety of pistols and ammunition. Their final recommendation eliminated the Colt .38 Military Model as a potential service pistol. It called for the replacement of the .38 revolver with an automatic pistol or revolver of "nothing less than .45 caliber."

It was obvious that the Government would no longer consider a .38 automatic, no matter how advanced its features. It was equally clear that Browning's basic design was superior to all other contemporary pistols. Browning immediately set to work to design a .45 caliber model.

The first test guns were completed in 1904. Military reaction was immediately favorable. Browning continued to work to improve the basic .45 design. In 1905, Colt produced the .45 automatic for the civilian market as the .45 Military Model.

The Army tested the 1905 .45 Military Model in early 1907. Its impressions were basically favorable. It praised the Colt for "its certainty of action…, flatness, compactness, neatness, and ease of carrying." However, the Board criticized the Colt as "defective in having side ejection, no automatic indication that the chamber is loaded, and no automatic safety." The Board recommended the procurement of more .45 Colt automatics for testing, but only if their three deficiencies were corrected. This recommendation resulted in the last pistol whose design derives directly from Browning's original .38.

Colt modified the 1905 .45 design by incorporating a loaded chamber indicator, extending the ejection port upward and partially over the top of the slide, relocating the ejector to obtain vertical ejec-

Disassembled Pocket Model shows the somewhat complicated double-link mechanism used in early Browning .38s.

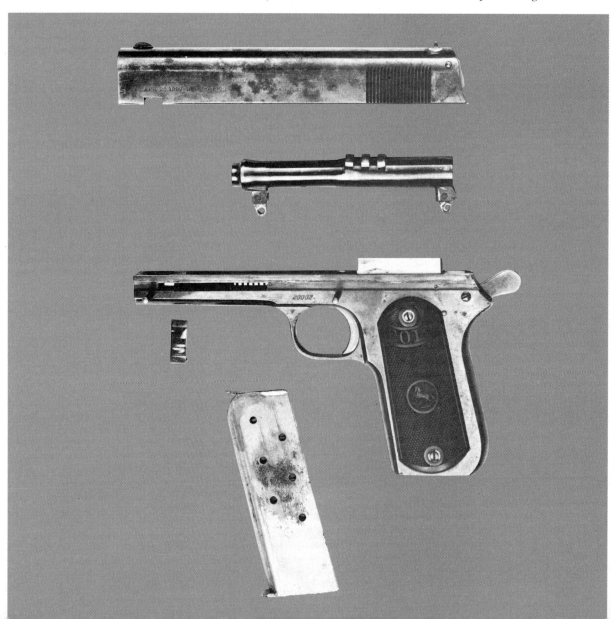

tion, and adding a grip safety to the frame. These modifications created a new version known to collectors as the .45 1907 Contract Type. Two hundred were manufactured and delivered to the Army for testing. Colt considered the 1907 Type to be sufficiently different from the Model 1905 to require its own serial number series running from one to 200.

The Model 1907 was the last of the models derived from Browning's original .38 automatic. In 1911, the U.S. Army adopted a modified version as the Model 1911. Seventy-three years later, the same basic design has remained in service with the U.S. Armed Forces. (For the latest developments see, *A New Pistol for the U.S. Armed Forces*, by Chuck Karwan, in this volume.)

The Government's decision to adopt the .45 automatic reduced the .38 automatic's sales. Nevertheless, Colt continued to produce them until 1929. The evidence indicates that they still had a devoted following. Colt replaced the .38 automatics with the

Colt .38 Super, a Model 1911 chambered for a more powerful loading of the .38 automatic cartridge.

It is always interesting to see what shooters thought of an obsolete gun before it became obsolete. The .38 Colt automatics received good reviews. In the early 1930s, General Hatcher compared the .38 automatic cartridge to the .45 ACP and the 9mm Luger, and wrote: "It is generally agreed that the Colt .38 automatic cartridge is the best highpowered pistol cartridge made...[When] the Army put its stamp of approval on the .45 caliber it was only natural that the Colt Company should give all their attention to the new model, for it was assumed that any and all buyers of military automatics would want what the Army wanted and so the .38 automatic was left to die.

"But it would not die. The ballistics of the cartridge were too good. People found that the new Army .45 fell short at long ranges at which the old .38 still held up, and that no pistol cartridge in the

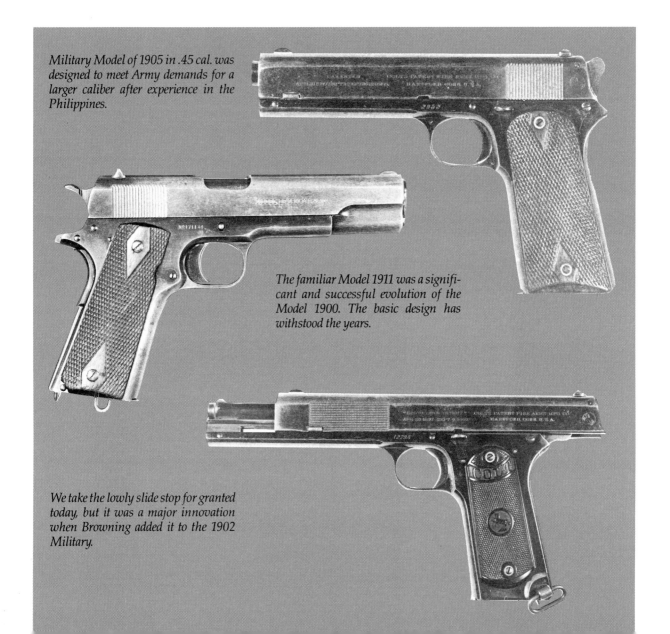

Military Model of 1905 in .45 cal. was designed to meet Army demands for a larger caliber after experience in the Philippines.

The familiar Model 1911 was a significant and successful evolution of the Model 1900. The basic design has withstood the years.

We take the lowly slide stop for granted today, but it was a major innovation when Browning added it to the 1902 Military.

world equalled the .38 automatic in penetration. So it happened that there has always been a call for that excellent shooting gun from long range pistol shooters and from people to whom deep penetration seems to be an essential feature. Thus the old .38 [automatic] continued to have a good sale in spite of the fact that its mechanical features were 25 years old. It was clumsy and awkward (compared to the 1911 Army automatic), its grip was at the wrong angle but how it did shoot!"

And it still will! A major part of the interest of gun collecting to me is the opportunity to test-fire the guns of previous generations and compare their performance with the guns and ammunition of today. I have test fired all the variations of the early Colt automatics and have always found them to be accurate. The .38 Sporting and Military automatics are particularly accurate. All you need is a pistol in good mechanical condition and proper ammunition. *Never use .38 Super cartridges.* They will chamber but are unsafe in the early .38 automatics.

I recently tested two .38 Military Models firing commercial .38 automatic ammunition. The test firings were done at 25 yards, using a two-handed hold with forearms supported. Both pistols delivered two to three inch groups consistently. The best group obtained was 2⅛ inches and the worst 3½ inches.

What made these results particularly interesting to me is that they were done at the end of a series of tests of 9mm automatics with modern ammunition. The old Colts equaled the best performance achievable with the 9mms and were superior to many combinations of modern 9mm pistols and ammunition. Not bad for an 80-year-old design and pistols manufactured in 1904 and 1906!

What made the early .38 Colt automatics accurate? First, they were expensive, top-of-the-line pistols when they were manufactured. Second, they were made in times when skilled labor for hand fitting and assembly was available.

But I think there is another significant factor. By today's standards, they were "long slides." Modern shooters trying to wring the last drop of accuracy from the current .45 automatic design often pay large amounts of money for pistols modified to include a six or seven inch barrel and lengthened slide.

The early .38 Colts came with six inch barrels with the exception of the Pocket Model. Their slides are tightly fitted, and the distance the slide is guided by the frame during its rearward and forward motion is more than double that of the modern 1911 design. In effect, the .38s came from the factory as "long slides" with accuracy jobs.

These early Colts offer an interesting field for the collector. A basic collection could consist of a 1900 Model, a Sporting Model, a 1902 Military Model, a Pocket Model, and a .45 caliber Military Model.

These five pistols would be a complete set of the early locked-breech Colts.

If a five-pistol gun collection seems small, don't worry. There is no need to stop there! The early Colt automatics display a fascinating variety of minor mechanical and marking variations. Changes in hammer styles, markings, and slide serrations have no effect on the basic design or shooting characteristics of the pistols. They do, however, create a splendid array of subtypes to fascinate collectors.

The pre-1911 pistols are easily identified. All .38 models are marked "AUTOMATIC COLT CALIBRE .38 RIMLESS SMOKELESS" on the right side of the slide. The .45 Military Model was similarly marked, with the caliber designation changed to ".45 RIMLESS SMOKELESS." Original 1900 Model .38s have smooth walnut grips. The .45 Military Model has checkered walnut grips.

All other models have identical black hard rubber grips marked "COLT" in large letters and the Colt trademark in the center of the grip. Occasionally, factory pearl or ivory grips will appear. These have small Colt medallions inset if they were made at the factory.

Some shooters preferred the smooth walnut grips of the 1900 Model to the later black hard rubber grips. This explains the occasional Sporting Model, Military Model, or Pocket Model which turns up with "incorrect" walnut grips. Since shooters, then as now, have always been individuals, it also accounts for Model 1900 pistols with the later black rubber grips installed in place of the original walnut.

Another interesting feature which creates fascinating variations for collectors is the location and pattern of the slide serrations. The purpose of the serrations is clear. They provide a rough surface on

the otherwise smooth slide. This allows the shooter to get a good grip when he is retracting the slide. So far, so good. However, the first three .38s, the 1900 Model, the Sporting Model, and the 1902 Military Model display an interesting series of changes in slide serration positions during their production runs.

Early Model 1900 pistols have rear serrations consisting of 16 vertical grooves. The first lot of Model 1900s delivered to the Army had the same serration pattern. The second lot of Army pistols, delivered in late 1900, showed a distinct change. The vertical serrations were moved to the front of the slide, approximately 1.3 inches to the rear of the muzzle. Commercial Model 1900s also changed to frontal slide serrations at about the same time and retained them to the end of the production run.

When the improved Sporting Model was introduced in late 1901, it retained the frontal vertical serrations. In 1906, the serrations were moved to the rear and remained there to the end of Sporting Model production in 1908.

When the .38 Military Model was introduced in 1902, it had frontal slide serrations of a new and distinct pattern. The vertical grooves used in earlier models were replaced with a sharply checkered rectangular area. This serration pattern was used only on the 1902 Military Models. In 1906, vertical groove serrations were introduced, and the serrations were moved to the rear. The vertical rear serrations were retained until production ceased in 1929.

The .38 Pocket Model and the .45 Military Models were not involved in these changes. They were introduced with vertical groove rear serrations and retained them throughout production.

Why this occurred is not clear. Apparently, the Army thought that a soldier could retract his pistol's slide more easily if he could grip the slide at the front rather than the rear. This seems reasonable, particularly for a cavalryman who must keep his reins in his left hand to control his horse. In theory, frontal slide serrations allow him to grip the slide with the fingers of his left hand while still holding the reins. In practice, the frontal slide serrations did not prove to be an advantage.

Colt appears to have switched from rear slide serrations to frontal ones because the Army requested it. When the Army lost interest, Colt returned to the previous rear-or-the-slide serration.

While this information will allow you to immediately identify any of the early Colt automatics, my best advice to anyone who is seriously interested is to buy books first! The best reference is *COLT AUTOMATIC PISTOLS*, by Donald B. Bady. This is a specialized book, devoted entirely to Colt automatics, and contains invaluable information for the collector. The general Colt reference books also have sections on the early automatic pistols which contain valuable information.

Forming a collection may be challenging because production of all models was limited. Only 3,500 of the 1900 Models were produced. Next in scarcity is the .45 Military Model with a total production of 6,100, followed closely by the .38 Sporting Model with approximately 7,500 produced. The .38 Military Model and the .38 Pocket Model are more common.

No matter how you look at them — as outstanding examples of John Browning's genius, an interesting phase in American firearms history, or superb material for a gun collection — the .38 Browning automatics were remarkable pistols. They are no longer in use, but the technology they introduced is marching on: a remarkable tribute to a gun designed in the 1890s by a man who died in 1927.

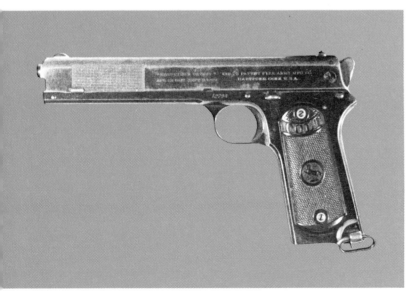

(Far left) Model 1902 Sporting pistol had vertical serrations at the front of the slide, carried over from the military version.

(Left) 1902 Military had the slide lock, lanyard loop, and eight-round magazine. Checkering provided grip at the front.

A New Pistol for the U.S. Armed Forces

Chuck Karwan

The reign of the venerable Colt M1911A1 .45 automatic as the primary U.S. military side arm came to a close on January 14, 1985, with the announcement by the Army of the Colt's successor, the Beretta 92SB-F 9mm pistol. The announcement was the culmination of a long and rigorous selection process that pitted most of the world's best 9mm service automatics against each other.

Included in the trials were entries from Beretta, Colt, FN Belgium, Heckler & Koch, SIG, Smith & Wesson, and Walther. The Beretta and SIG entries emerged from the testing as the finalists most suit-

Field-stripped, Beretta 92SB-F reveals contours of unusual open slide design. Magazine holds 15 rounds, with optional round in the chamber, carried with safety.

able for adoption. After evaluating the cost proposals and the best and final offers submitted by the two final competitors, the Army selected the Beretta to be the future service handgun for all U.S. armed forces.

The new Beretta 9mm has the commercial designation of Model 92SB-F, but it will reportedly receive the military designation of Pistol M9. As the Army is the procurement agency for small arms for all the U.S. services, the new M9 pistol will not only have to fill the holsters vacated by the M1911A1 .45, but will also replace the myriad other handguns in service in the Air Force, Navy, Marines, and Coast Guard. The latter are primarily .38 Special Revolvers of various makes and configurations. The service most desperate for new handguns is the Coast Guard and various sources in the Defense Department have stated that the Coast Guard will get the first Beretta 9mms issued.

The 9mm pistol contract awarded to the Beretta U.S.A. Corp. covers a five-year period and amounts to 315,930 pistols to be delivered at the cost of $56.4 million. This averages out to less than $180 per handgun. Some 52,930 pistols of Italian manufacture will be produced and delivered the first year. The second year Beretta will assemble and test 65,750 guns at its American plant in Accokeek, Maryland. Assembly in the second year will include using parts made in Italy with a gradual transition in the third year to a gun manufactured entirely in the United States.

In excess of $15 million of capital investment will be made for the contract as well as creating three hundred jobs in America. Beretta models already in production at its plant in Accokeek will be unaffected by the new contract. New equipment will be used to manufacture the pistol.

The Army's search for a replacement for the M1911A1 .45 was the result of a number of factors. The military service's inventory of M1911A1's is

This article first appeared in *GUN WORLD*.

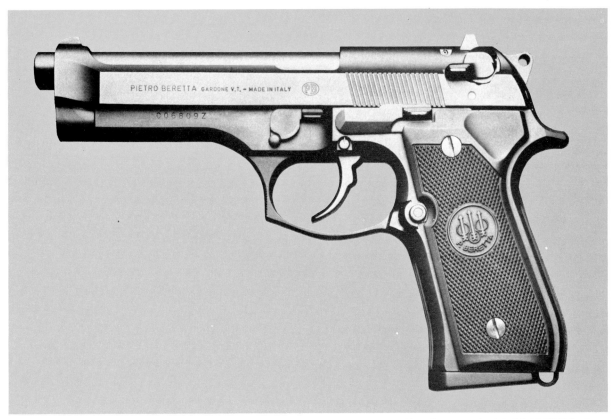

Beretta's entry into trials for a new U.S. military pistol, chosen to replace the old Colt M1911A1. Model 92SB-F in 9mm features new combat frame, non-glare finish, open slide design, ambidextrous safety.

elderly, since new specimens have not been procured since the end of World War II. As a result, a substantial portion of the inventory is in questionable condition. Agreements signed by the U.S. and its NATO allies clearly state that new small arms procurements will use NATO standard ammunition which is the 9mm Parabellum cartridge for handguns and submachine guns. On a service-wide basis there is a shortage of serviceable handguns and even those available are a long way from being satisfactory, particularly the .38 Special revolvers. Finally, the safety record of the M1911A1 in military service left a lot to be desired as a result of its design and handling characteristics.

The new Beretta M92SB-F offers a number of advantages and improvements over its predecessor. It can be carried with a round in the chamber and the hammer down with total safety. The .45 is subject to accidental firing anytime it is dropped on the muzzle and the chamber has a round in it. The Beretta's hammer can be safely lowered without touching the trigger, negating the possibility of an accidental discharge as can happen with the .45 if the hammer slips out of control in lowering. From its carrying mode, the Beretta requires only a pull on the trigger to fire, while the .45 requires chambering a round or cocking its hammer or release of its

safety before the trigger may be pulled, depending on how it is carried. Under the stress of combat, this kind of simplicity is a huge advantage. The Beretta has a 15-round magazine capacity verses seven rounds for the .45, offering more than twice the shots without reloading. Unlike the .45, the Beretta can be safely cleared without touching the trigger and with the safety engaged. In addition, the Beretta is ambidextrous while the M1911A1 is not. Though these are the major advantages of the Beretta, there are a number of other features, including a loaded chamber indicator, a large trigger guard for gloved operation, and a chrome-lined barrel.

Variations of the Beretta 9mm are already in global service. The weapon is the standard handgun of the armed forces of Italy, Brazil, Nigeria, and other countries. It is also used extensively by police forces throughout the world. For example, in 1983 Connecticut adopted the Beretta M925B 9mm as the official gun to be used by state police. There is little doubt that the Beretta M92SB-F is one of the finest 9mm service handguns extant and the most suitable to replace the 74 year reign of the M1911 .45 ACP as the standard U.S. service handgun.

On the day following the Army's announcement of the Beretta's adoption, a press conference was called at the Shooting, Hunting, Outdoor, Trade

(SHOT) Show at the World Congress Center in Atlanta, Georgia. Robert Bonaventure, general manager and vice president of Beretta U.S.A. and Ugo Gussalli Beretta, managing director of Pietro Beretta SpA in Brescia, Italy, answered questions about the Army's announcement. Both men were obviously pleased and proud that the Beretta 92SB-F had been chosen by the U.S. Army.

Beretta said the 92 and variations of the handgun have won every service trial in which they have been tested. Bonaventure, asked when Beretta 92SB-Fs would be available for commercial sales, said the 92SB-Fs were being shipped to the U.S. as he spoke and would be available for the trade shortly.

Another person present at the press conference was also pleased by the Army's choice. John Bianchi realized that if the U.S. armed services were adopting a new handgun, a new holster would be needed. Bianchi had a ready solution. The U.S. armed services now have thousands of holsters that no longer fit the standard pistol. Besides, the standard G.I. leather flap holster is an archaic design even more obsolete than the handgun it held.

Bianchi recognized this dilemma and put the considerable forces of his Bianchi International Company into designing a better holster for the new U.S. service pistol long before the government had even decided on what the pistol would be!

More than a quarter million dollars and a huge number of man hours went into the design of the military holster, offered by Bianchi to the commercial trade as the Model UM84. Richard Nichols, national marketing manager for Bianchi International, headed the development program of the nylon UM84. Under his guidance the UM84 developed into the world's first truly modern military service holster. The UM84 has many excellent features and is far superior to the current leather flap holster.

When Bianchi submitted the ballistic cloth holster design to the Army for test and evaluation, the reception was enthusiastic. The result of the Army's tests was the recommendation for adoption as soon as it was known what handgun had won the pistol trials. The UM84 was type classified and given the military designation of Holster M12. The primary version will be olive drab in color for the Army, with some services or units receiving a black version. A camouflage pattern will also be available.

It is not hard to see why the Army is enthusiastic about the new UM84 Bianchi holster. First, it is made from modern ballistic cloth construction that is stronger, more wear resistant, and, unlike leather, totally mildew and fungus resistant. One of the specifications for the new 9mm handgun was that it had to be ambidextrous; in fact, the new Beretta 92SB-F is just that. It would seem ludicrous to have

Beretta 92SB-F is a 9mm Parabellum semiautomatic pistol specifically designed for use by military. A remarkable, proven design in a combat weapon, 15 round firepower combines with flawless reliability and safety to make ideal combat weapon. Extraordinary firing mechanism will handle thousands of rounds without a malfunction. Ambidextrous triple-safety mechanism features a passive firing pin blocking bar, a slide safety that acts as a decocking lever, plus a unique rotating firing pin to positively insure that a falling hammer can never break safety and discharge accidentally. Key specifications are:

	U.S. Govt. Specifications	92SB-F Specifications
Weight	Max. 1,300 grams (with fully loaded magazine)	1,145 grams (40.89 oz.)
Length	Max. 221 mm	217 mm (8.54″)
Height	Max, 147 mm (with magazine inserted)	140 mm (5.51″)
Caliber	9mm Parabellum	9mm Parabellum
Barrel	Min. Length 102 mm	125 mm (4.92″)
Magazine	Min. 10 rounds Removable floorplate	15 rounds Removable floorplate
Rear Sight	Fixed, driftable for windage	Fixed, driftable for windage
Slide Stop	Holds slide open after last round, manually operable	Holds slide open after last round, manually operable

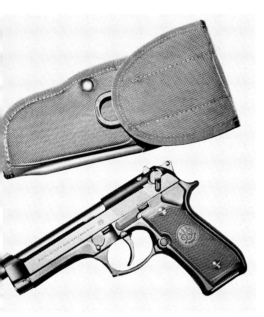

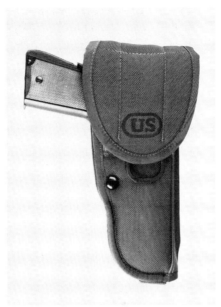

A new military pistol means a new holster. Bianchi's new design gets the nod from Department of Defense.

Bianchi's holster design is configured to fit almost any large automatic pistol, including the Colt M1911A1. Colors are black, olive drab, camo.

Top flap is easily removed, opens either side for left or right side wear, on belt or with shoulder harness. Features are patented.

an ambidextrous handgun and not have a versatile holster.

The Bianchi UM84 is ambidextrous. It can be switched from the right to left hand easily and quickly. It features what is known as a Quick-Lock belt fastener for easy installation and removal from the wearer's belt. It even has an integral cleaning rod pocket in the front part of the holster. In addition, the UM84 features modular construction that allows use with an optional shoulder harness or a special operations hip extender. Most importantly for a military holster, the UM84 has a silent yet effective flap closure that insures the handgun is going to stay in its holster no matter how rigorous the activity of its bearer. Admittedly, this is no quick-draw holster, but neither is it slow. Under test at this time by the Army is an extremely clever and effective chest harness that appears to be ideal for tankers, vehicle drivers, and aviators. The chest harness is lightweight and comfortable and can be rigged for either right- or left-hand carry.

Now that the winner of the 9mm pistol trials has been decided it is expected that the Army will soon be placing orders for the UM84 (as the M12). The UM84 is made in two sizes, fitting almost all the world's service automatics. One of its selling points is that the size suitable for the Beretta, the UM84I is also suitable for the old M1911A1 .45. Thus, units receiving the new holster before they receive the new Beretta pistol can still put the new holster to immediate use.

The UM84 is one of the best examples of how the free enterprise system can design and offer superior products before government agencies even realize that they have a requirement for them. Bianchi has every right to be extremely proud of its latest effort.

For more information on the UM84 or its military counterpart, the M12, contact Bianchi International, 100 Calle Cortez, Temecula, CA 92390. For more information about the Beretta 92SB-F or a copy of a brochure on the handgun, contact a Beretta dealer or Beretta U.S.A. Corporation, 17601 Indian Head Highway, Accokeek, MD 20607.

Right side view of new military pistol shows ambidextrous safety lever just below rear fixed sight.

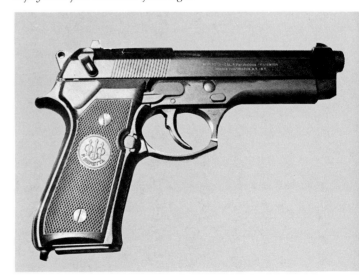

The .357 Magnum:
Ideal for Beginners?

W.E. Sprague

Since 1973, when the U.S. Treasury Department began keeping records on such things, the annual number of handguns made and sold in America has grown to the point where they now account for roughly half of all guns made and sold each year.

Yet surveys show that 18 percent to 20 percent of present long-gun owners do not own modern sidearms. That this percentage is shrinking, though, and will continue to shrink, is evidenced by both the continuing rise in handgun sales in general, and by a notable increase in the frequency of questions put to the various shooting magazines requesting advice on the choice of a "first" gun.

More often than not, that advice boils down to a .22 of moderate cost — preferably a revolver, since automatic pistols require additional training in order to be handled safely. The reasons a .22 is recommended are that it is generally cheaper to buy, and certainly cheaper to shoot, than larger caliber guns. Moreover, .22s are superbly accurate and offer minimum recoil. All of which are important considerations, since excessive cost, inaccuracy, and heavy recoil discourage the practice needed to gain proficiency and skill. Yet, oddly enough, in the view of many experienced shooters the ideal "beginner's gun" is the .357 Magnum.

Admittedly a minority, advocates of the .357 Magnum reason that if your purpose in owning a handgun is little more than the fun of informal target shooting, be it tin cans out in the countryside or paper targets at the range, then a .22 revolver is more than satisfactory. Also, if you want to have something to put in your tackle box or backpack, a .22 will serve. But if you want something for home defense or hunting, then why not start with a gun designed for such heavy-duty use, and one that will also serve your lesser needs as well?

Still, to say the least, the notion is heretical. In the popular mind, the .357 Magnum, with its loud report and normally heavy recoil, is hardly a gun for learning. Moreover, it's expensive, both to buy and to shoot — over 25 cents a round for its centerfire cartridges, compared to less than five cents a round for .22 rimfire cartridges. Yet, given certain conditions, it is no more costly to own and shoot than a good .22 revolver, and no more difficult to master.

Consider the .357 Magnum in light of the arguments put forth in support of the .22, beginning with the element of price. While a good .22 can be had for about $100 or so, it can also run as high as $300 and more. Presumably, then, a .22 of "moderate cost" is somewhere around the $200 mark. A really good quality .357 Magnum can be had for about the same money.

It goes without saying, of course, that prices in either caliber will vary from place to place, and even from dealer to dealer within the same community. But, unless one insists on paying the lowest possible price, the dollar-spread between the two will not be very great and, depending upon the individual's comparative-shopping skills, may even be nonexistent.

A more persuasive argument supporting the .22 is that of minimum recoil and superb inherent accuracy, both of which are technically unarguable. Yet, while it may be true that the .22 is probably unsurpassed in terms of inherent accuracy, it is equally true that virtually *any* modern handgun offers more in the way of that particular virtue than anyone short of an Olympic competitor can use to any real advantage. And insofar as recoil is concerned, while it certainly could be a problem in learning to shoot the .357 Magnum, thanks to the versatility of the gun, there are ways to get around it.

Originally developed as an improvement on the .38 Special, the .357 Magnum will readily accept the .38 Special cartridge, and is in fact designed to do so. Dimensionally, the .357 and .38 Special cartridges differ only in terms of case length.

To prevent its being fired in guns suited only for the .38 Special cartridge, the case for the .357

This article first appeared in *THE AMERICAN RIFLEMAN*.

Dan Wesson .357 offers the flexibility of interchangeable barrels in lengths from 2" to 8", in both blued and stainless steel.

Magnum is made about .1 inch longer. Ballistically, however, there is a world of difference between the two. Working at considerably higher pressures, the .357 Magnum is capable of delivering as much as three times the energy of the .38 Special cartridge.

For purposes of learning, then, the recoil of the .357 Magnum can be reduced dramatically by the simple expedient of using .38 Special ammunition, graduating to Magnum rounds once mastery of the gun has been achieved. Reduction of recoil can be further enhanced by using .38 Special "target loads" which, with their smaller powder charges and usually lighter bullets, produce even softer recoil.

Granted that even target loads may not reduce the recoil of a .357 Magnum to that of a .22, they can, however, narrow the gap to the point where any remaining difference is easily handled by the vast majority of beginners. For those who might still find it a problem, there is, as we will shortly see, yet another way to tame the .357 even more.

Perhaps the most persuasive argument supporting the .22 is that of inexpensive ammunition. Gaining pistol proficiency requires frequent practice. The expenditure of 100 rounds a week or more is not uncommon, and the number of weeks involved depends entirely upon the individual and the level of proficiency he or she pursues.

Maintaining that proficiency requires practice, too. The difference, then, between five cents a round or so for .22s and more than 25 cents a round

for .38 Specials can be considerable, amounting to $20 a week, if 100 rounds per week is used as a basis of measure.

However, it is this very fact — the cost and volume of ammunition required for practice and proficiency — that justifies the notion of the .357 Magnum as a "beginner's gun." Once fired, the .22 rimfire cartridge is forever gone; not so, the .357 Magnum case. The latter can be "rebuilt" several times over. Depending upon the components used,

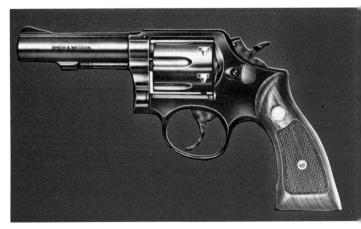

S&W M-13 is a .357 version of the heavy barreled M-10 with ramp front and square notch rear sights.

it can be done for just about the cost of a .22 rimfire cartridge.

The answer to low-cost ammunition for the .357 Magnum then — as well as to further reduction of recoil — is a minimum investment in reloading. And the key word here is *minimum*. For the long-gun shooter who already reloads for a rifle, that investment will consist of a modest stock of components and a set of .357 Magnum dies — which can also be used for reloading .38 Specials.

For those who don't reload at all, the cash outlay could be even less, since perfectly satisfactory ammunition can be produced with simple tools that cost no more than a box or two of factory .357 cartridges. Moreover, if one has never reloaded before, there is perhaps no better way to learn than by using one of these inexpensive tools.

The least expensive of these, and by far the most popular, is the Lee Loader. Produced by Lee Precision of Hartford, Wisconsin, it consists of a specially designed metal base into which various dies and accessories fit, with the power needed to perform the various reloading steps supplied by punches and a mallet.

A similar kit, the Unitized Loader, is made by MRC (Mequon Reloading Corp.) of Mequon, Wisconsin. Each of these kits contains a charge-cup, along with a chart for various powders to be used in a large variety of charge- and bullet-weight combinations.

And, for a few dollars more, the new reloader can get the Lee Improved Powder Measure Kit, a complete set of graduated-capacity charge-cups, together with a chart listing the capacity of each cup as used with virtually every powder on the market. With it, even the experienced reloader using a bench-mounted press and dies will find himself prepared for almost any powder/bullet/caliber combination.

If, in view of its price, either kit can be said to have any real disadvantage, it would have to be its speed of operation. Both are decidedly slow. But if increased speed is important, then either of two other tools, each available for very little money, might be an appropriate choice.

One is the Lyman 310 Tool by Lyman Products of Middlefield, Connecticut; the other, the Pak-Tool produced by W.H. English of Seattle, Washington. With either tool, the new reloader can just about duplicate the speed of reloading with a bench-mounted, single-station press and dies, since each, in effect, is a hand-held single-station press complete with dies or their equivalents.

The 310 Tool looks and even functions somewhat like an old-fashioned, pliers-type nutcracker, and is in fact often called a "nutcracker" tool. Its singular departure in appearance is a boss on one handle that is threaded to accept its various dies and chambers. Less apparent is a spring-loaded hook on the other handle, designed to catch the rims of the fired cases being put through the various operations.

The Pak-Tool, on the other hand, looks more like a steel tube with a full-length section of its wall cut away, to which an old-fashioned bottle-capper has been attached at one end. While the operation of each tool differs in particulars, both do indeed work much like a single-station press.

A different die, chamber, or accessory is put in place for a given operation such as priming or depriming and, one by one, all the fired cases are put through it — with the process being repeated until a finished lot of ammunition is ready for immediate use.

The ultimate in reloading is, of course, a bench-mounted press and dies. But, even here, cost can be kept to a minimum. A tool called the "Compac Press" has been recently introduced by Huntington of Oroville, California. Unorthodox in design, it is

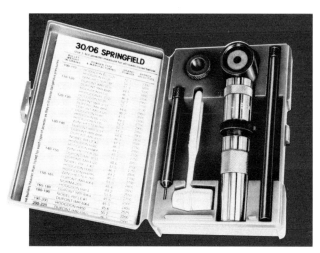

Lee Loader offers the ultimate in economy reloading; it costs less than two boxes of factory-made centerfire ammo.

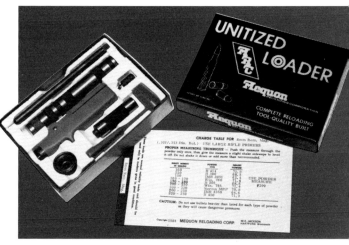

MRC Improved and Unitized Loaders include everything to reload at a price beginners can easily afford.

basically a single-station press that operates by simultaneously pushing its twin handles toward the "body" of the press.

Another recent introduction, and one with a much greater speed of operation, is an inexpensive turret press from Lee Precision. Once its dies are set in place and properly adjusted, a completely loaded round of ammunition is produced with just three turns of its turret and three strokes of its handle.

Although designed for permanent mounting, either press can be set up anywhere, even the kitchen table, with the use of C-clamps. Lee, in fact, also offers a carrying box that can double as a portable mount. And with a set of .357 Magnum dies, either press will permit the new reloader to go all the way for just about the cost of a half-dozen boxes of factory .38 Specials.

With the use of any one of these inexpensive tools, not only can one reduce the cost of shooting the .357 Magnum, but recoil can be completely tamed, since reloading allows the shooter to produce "target loads" that are not commercially available.

The *Lyman Reloading Handbook*, for example, lists loads for the .38 Special with bullets as light as 75 grains and velocities of less than 600 fps. Other published sources list so-called gallery loadings using 000 buckshot balls for bullets, with velocities as low as 400 fps.

There will always be those, of course, who, for various reasons, shy away from reloading, and for them the .22 revolver is undoubtedly the better choice. But even for non-reloaders, the .357 still has much to offer. Short-range practice loads, with virtually no recoil and suitable for indoor use, can be made with nothing more than a box of primers and a box of reusable plastic bullet/case assemblies obtainable at almost any gun store. These are especially useful for mastering basic technique.

Charter Arms "Tracker" .357 is among the least expensive guns on the market. It comes in 2½", 4", and 6" barrel lengths.

And, for economy with regular ammunition, Omark Industries of Lewiston, Idaho, offers its new line of CCI Blazer ammunition. Made with non-reloadable aluminum cases, Blazers in either .38 Special or .357 Magnum can cut the usual cost of shooting the .357 Magnum by as much as a third or more.

Still, the underlying premise here is that the amount of practice required to gain and maintain proficiency with *any* handgun, even a .22, is such that it easily warrants a small investment in reloading. This, plus the fact that perhaps no other handgun spans the ballistic range of the .357 Magnum, makes the investment quite worthwhile. For, once proficiency is achieved, the erstwhile beginner will have a gun that offers all the fun of a .22, and a great deal more besides.

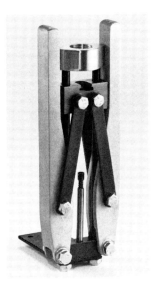

Compac Press can be used virtually anywhere, even on the kitchen table, with C-clamps.

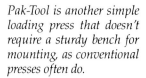

Pak-Tool is another simple loading press that doesn't require a sturdy bench for mounting, as conventional presses often do.

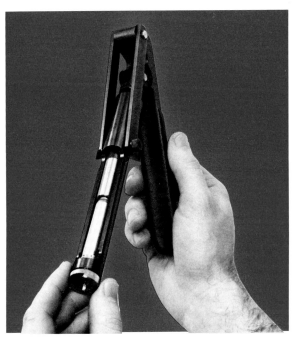

Beretta M-25 South American Ironwood

Exhibition-Grade Rosewood Colt Government Mode

Exhibition-Grade Bocote S&W K frame

Standard-Grade Bocote Detonics Mk V

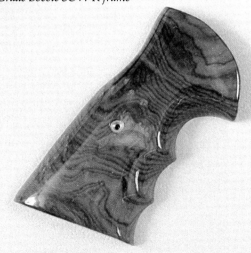

Exhibition-Grade Cocobolo S&W N frame

Standard Bocote Ruger Mk II

Walnut S&W M-59

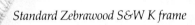

Exhibition Ebony Colt Government Model

Standard Zebrawood S&W K frame

Standard Cocobolo Colt Government Model

Handgun Stocks: The Exotic Alternative

Al Pickles

I recall, many years back, interrogating a stick-up man who had assaulted several policemen. He was armed when arrested by a lone patrolman, but had not offered resistance. Since he was in a talkative mood, I asked him why he had submitted so meekly. He stated he always looks at the grips of a cop's revolver before going for his own gun. He figured that any policeman with the same factory issue grips that came on the gun when new, was unpracticed and unskilled as a gunfighter. He did make an exception for "oversized" factory stocks.

The arresting officer was carrying a holstered Smith & Wesson Model 19 Combat Magnum with custom grips. He was also the department pistol champion at the time, a fact unknown to this hood. The incident is true.

Of course, custom grips will not make you an instant shootist, but they indicate you are "working at it." Factory grips are supposedly made for the average hand, yet seldom fit any hand properly. Happily there are a dozen custom grip manufacturers ready and willing to make you a handgun grip "just the way you like it."

A handgun grip, unlike a rifle, is not as limited in the materials from which it can be made. Since handgun grips do not have to take the stresses of recoil, they can be crafted from many attractive materials. If you are filthy rich, you can have your custom grips made of ivory with Frazetta's Moonmaid in scrimshaw. Stag is also attractive and relatively inexpensive. Mother-of-pearl, jade, and buffalo horn are flashy and are not intended for service guns. Engraved silver and pewter are also for show pieces and presentations. Obviously, many other materials can be used; such as hard rubber, neoprene, and plastics.

I have always had a personal preference for wood grips. Custom wood grips, be they plain-grained or

This article first appeared in *AMERICAN HANDGUNNER.*

fancy, compliment blue steel and give a warm beauty to an otherwise cold instrument. Wood looks equally good on nickel, stainless steel, or today's miracle finishes like Armaloy, Nitex, and Teflon. Space age plastics and aluminum may indeed have valid applications, but they can never replace the traditional beauty and service of blue steel, wood grips, and fine gunleather. One of the few factories still adhering to this tradition is Smith & Wesson whose classier guns, like the Models 19 and 66, come with beautiful oversize grips made of Goncalo Alves. This exotic hardwood is grown in the tropics and is characterized by a light and warm brown contrasted with a dark, high-figured grain.

At this point, I would like to insert a short course on woods. We have some domestic woods that are quite attractive. There is nothing wrong with American Walnut and, by using the crotch and burl, you can produce stocks with striking figure. The lighter colored Birds-eye and Curly Maple are equally eye-catching. Cherry, Apple, Beech, and Birch are good looking woods in their own quiet way. Mesquite, which Roy Weatherby used to use in his rifle stocks, is outstanding. Most of us would be quite happy with a nice looking set of grips made of any of these domestic woods. However, human nature being what it is, the thought of owning a stock made of rare and seldom seen wood from, say, Java, is intriguing. Some very colorful wood comes from rather remote corners of the world.

Cocobolo: Cocobolo is a Central American species of Brazilian Rosewood, but considerably denser. Color varies from purple to yellow, including browns and orange.

Bocote: This wood is from Southern Mexico and is usually gold and dark brown to black in color. Figure varies form straight, to wide stripes, to highly ornate patterns.

Rosewood: Although there are many Rosewoods, Bullshooter's gets theirs from East India. East India Rosewood is dark purple-brown to near black. Occasionally it is bleached to better show figure.

Kingwood*: A member of the Rosewood family, Kingwood comes from Brazil. It is usually straight-grained with fine to large brown stripes. Stripe color can sometimes vary to black or deep violet and occasionally show figure.

Satinwood*: This relatively common, strong, and durable wood grows in East India and Ceylon. It is blond, straight-grained, with subtle figure.

South American Ironwood: A very rich appearing, dark, tight-grained wood. Its figure can vary from straight to marbled. It has that "quiet class."

Macassar Ebony: One of the more expensive woods, this wood comes from the coastal forests of Celebes. This dark, hard, and brittle wood shows alternating light and dark stripes.

Bullshooter .45 stocks have unique finger grooves.

Zebrawood: This wood comes from Cameroon and Gaboon. It is very difficult to work. It is almost always straight-grained with highly contrasting stripes, like a zebra. This light and dark brown wood is an attention getter.

Bubinga*: If from the Cameroon it is called Bubinga, if from Gaboon it is Kevazingo. Color is generally medium reddish brown or purplish brown, with darker veining. Grain may be straight or interlocked.

The woods listed above, with the exception of those marked with an asterisk, are available from Bullshooter's Supply, which provided the samples in the photography. They also offer select American and exotic walnut, Birds-eye Maple, and Curly Maple.

Many of the Bullshooter grips offer a bonus; they wrap around the lower front of the frame and provide a set of finger grooves. While there is more bulk to grips like this, they make a natural pointer out of a gun.

Now for the super good news! Bullshooter's Supply sells their stocks for a ridiculously low price considering the quality. Walnut is $24.95; Standard Grade Exotics are $39.95; and Exhibition Grade or Macassar Ebony go for $85.00. Additional good news is that the grips will fit most of the Colt automatic copies. Also available is a line of grips for the Detonics .45, Berettas, S&W Automatics, and Browning HP. In revolver grips, Bullshooters offers models for S&W N and K frames and the Colt Python. Grips can be mail ordered from Bullshooter's Supply, P.O. Box 13446, Tucson, Arizona 85732.

Finally, since I obviously had to do some research into common and exotic woods so I could write with passing intelligence, I learned of another beautiful wood which I have never seen in a pistol grip. Maybe, some day, Bullshooter's will offer their grips in Lacewood Plane.

PART THREE

SHOTGUNS

Skeet Gun Trends

Nick Sisley

Thousands of shooters all over the country participate in skeet competition — both the international variety sanctioned by the NRA and the American skeet game sanctioned by the National Skeet Shooting Association. Thousands more use the clay-bird game to brush up on shotgun pointing for the hunting season, to put a new gun through its paces, or simply for recreation.

What kind of guns do the superstars of skeet use? Are some of these shootin' irons approaching the space-age complexity of trap guns? Not quite. In fact, guns that become popular on skeet fields tend to also become popular with hunters, as long as steep price doesn't become a factor. Some examples have been the Model 12 Winchester pump and the Remington 1100 autoloader.

Many skeet shooters are willing to spend a great deal more for some of their guns than hunters, even when those skeet shooters often can't afford it.

If there's one thing about skeet guns and skeet shooters that stands out these days, it's the philosophy to shoot only "one gun" in all four American skeet events — the 12-, 20-, 28-gauge, and .410.

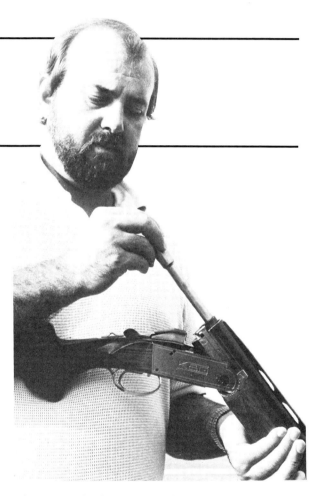

Ulm K-80 with tube set is a popular choice among competitive American skeet shooters.

This article first appeared in THE AMERICAN RIFLEMAN.

Though this trend might seem like a totally new one, it isn't.

Why one gun, anyway? The answer centers around total familiarity with one shotgun — one gun that's stocked the same, with the same length of pull, drop at comb and heel, same pitch, same trigger, same fore-end, same balance, same swinging qualities.

The "one gun" philosophy was in vogue almost right from the start. Skeet was a game invented by a small group of New England upland bird hunters in the 1920s. Evidently, these gents were trying to improve their gunning prowess, probably for grouse, woodcock, and quail, maybe even ducks.

The first shotguns to be choked for the new target game, and have "skeet" stamped on their barrels, didn't arrive on the American shooting scene until around 1935, many years after the first game of skeet was shot. That was when the Remington Model 31 pump was offered with an open-bored barrel (in 12-gauge that meant about .005 inch of constriction).

A very short time later, Winchester began offering its Model 12 pump gun — in 12-, 20-, and 28-gauge, and their .410 Model 42, with skeet barrels. There was a certain "one gunness" about this Winchester quartet. They were stocked similarly, swung similarly, had similar trigger pulls (or could have if they were worked on by an experienced gunsmith). In those early years, Model 12s (and the .410 version Model 42) dominated the winner's circle, but the search for the "one gun" concept was then only in its infancy.

World War II was a setback for the development of skeet guns. Other priorities necessarily came to the forefront in America. Though Remington came

out with its Model 870 pump in 1949, it wasn't offered in the four American skeet gauges until 1969. Even the great Model 1100 Remington autoloader, since proven one of the top skeet guns in history, wasn't offered in all gauges until 1969. That was the year both the 870 and 1100 were offered as a matched set in 28-gauge and .410 skeet versions — with matching serial numbers. However, it can be said that the set of four 870s or 1100s was another step in skeet toward the "one gun" ideal.

Simmons Gun Specialties, still located in Olathe, Kansas, developed the technology which permitted skeet shooters to come a giant step closer to the one-gun ideal. Simmons began taking 12-gauge over-unders, mainly Remington Model 32s and Browning Superposed guns, and making new 20-, 28-gauge and .410 barrel sets which would all fit the 12-gauge receivers.

This was a major advance in skeet gun technology, for now the shooter could compete in all four gauge events using the same stock, fore-end, and trigger. The gun in the smaller gauges handled much like it did with the 12-bore barrels affixed. Nationwide, overall skeet averages climbed upward.

The four-barrel set concept is still very much in evidence today. Simmons continues to make up barrel sets for many of the over-unders currently being marketed. And a number of manufacturers are offering four-barrel set skeet guns.

The most famous manufacturer of four-barrel sets is undoubtedly Krieghoff, whose over-under design is based largely on the Remington 32, with a number of internal improvements. Krieghoff four-barrel sets are available in many different grades. Today it'll cost you almost $4,000 to get your hands

Sub-caliber tube's integral extractor mates with shotgun's ejector to extract the spent cartridge case. Early tube sets required different ejectors for each gauge, but more modern tube sets can be installed without alterations to the shotgun's barrels.

on a used peasant's model, maybe more than $20,000 for one that's trimmed with gold dogs on point and silver flushing birds galore, plus ornate engraving. So it's not everybody's stomp-through-the-brush and scratch-the-stock huntin' gun, or everybody's skeet gun either.

For a short time Remington marketed its 3200 over-under in four-barrel configuration. Today you might still be able to find a new 3200 four-barrel set. Expect to plunk down more than $4,000 for it. Perazzi, a fine manufacturer from Italy, offered the four-barrel set in the Mirage Model, but it has been discontinued in favor of the current MX-3. I saw a recent ad for this one in four-barrel style — $5,300.

Beretta announced a four-barrel set in the Model 683 some time ago, but these have been as rare as the proverbial hen's teeth, ostensibly because the factory is so busy turning out other Beretta shotguns.

At the 1984 NSSA World Skeet Shooting Championships in San Antonio, July 1984, Winchester introduced a four-barrel set version of the long-popular over-under Model 101. A very sweet-swinging four-barrel set is being offered by Double M Shooting Sports, dubbed the Black Diamond.

The Krieghoff is on its way out from a manufacturing standpoint. It has been replaced by a model called the K-80, still the basic Model 32 Remington design, but with new, better-designed, and longer-lasting innards. Those who want a four-barrel set K-80 can have it. I just found one in an ad for $7,150. Finally, there's the least expensive four-barrel set of all, and maybe the best buy of the lot — the Browning Citori. A recent ad showed this one at $2,500 new.

The trouble with four-barrel sets is that many avid skeeters feel they're on their way out — well, sort of — replaced in most every instance by the skeet tube set. Of the 14 skeeters who made the 1984 All-American Skeet Team, 13 used tube sets. Just one used a four-barrel set. What is this skeet tube

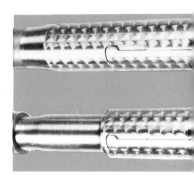

Extractor must be carefully machined into the tube to allow close fitting and to ease installation and removal during a tournament.

set deal anyway, and why is it making such a profound mark on the game of American skeet?

A guy named Claude Purbaugh in Monrovia, California came up with the idea. A skeet shooter himself by avocation, Purbaugh was a machinist by vocation. Before Remington 1100s were available in 28-gauge and .410, Purbaugh would sleeve 12- or 20-gauge 1100s to 28-gauge and .410, and rework the actions so these guns would function reliably. However, Remington soon came out with the 1100 in all four skeet gauges, effectively taking Purbaugh out of the 1100 conversion business.

Not to worry, however, for Purbaugh came up with an even better idea. He began putting his "barrel sleeve" brainstorm into over-under skeet guns. Ultimately, he was able to take a 12-gauge over-under and fit it with tubes in 20-, 28-gauge, and .410.

The tubes are machined from high-tensile-strength aluminum (except for the chamber section), then anodized for extra hardness. The chamber sections are made of stainless steel for strength. Some of the current manufacturers of skeet tubes offer titanium chambers in the .410 (some in the 28 as well), so gun weight can be almost identical, no matter which tube set might be installed. Today,

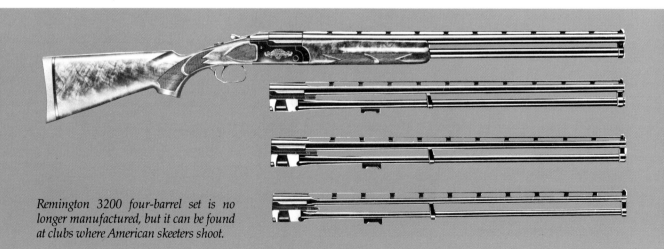

Remington 3200 four-barrel set is no longer manufactured, but it can be found at clubs where American skeeters shoot.

Screw-in choke tubes like these from Briley can be installed without altering outward appearance of a scattergun's barrels.

this is the ultimate skeet gun, a 12-gauge over-under fitted with tubes in the smaller gauges.

Why are these guns now considered the state of the art in skeet? In the first place, because 13 of the 14 1984 All-Americans used tubed over-unders. In the second place, because skeet averages in general have increased notably since their use came into vogue a few years ago.

Of course, the overall averages increased appreciably when four-barrel sets became popular, too. However, the improvement has been even more dramatic with so many skeeters using tube sets in competition these days.

Skeet tubes add approximately 14 ounces of weight to the barrels. This out-front weight results in a number of advantages. First, swings are necessarily smoother. Anyone who has ever shot one round or several rounds of skeet with a light shotgun adorned with a light, short, whippy barrel will easily understand how out-front weight results in a smoother swing.

A second advantage of the tubed skeet gun with the out-front weight is that it's more difficult for the shooter to slow or stop the swing. Doing either results in a missed target. A third advantage of those 14 ounces of out-front weight is recoil reduction, never a problem in the .410, seldom a problem in the 28-gauge, but sometimes it can be in the 20 if the skeet gun is light.

Remember, after breaking 100 straight skeet targets, competitive shooters then might fire scores or even hundreds more shells in the shootoff!

Most tubed over-unders weigh around 8½ pounds, some slightly more. A gun that heavy makes shooting hundreds of 20-gauge ⅞-ounce shells a piece of cake. Of course, hunters are seldom bothered by recoil because they fire so few shotshells in a day.

Purbaugh solved the problem of small-gauge shell extraction by machining separate extractors of the right size for the top and bottom barrels, a different size extractor with each gauge tube. Thus, when one of the tubes is changed, the extractor must be changed, too. Briley and Kolar, two other skeet tube makers, have integral extractors built into the tubes themselves. These integral extractors match the ejectors or extractors of the parent 12-gauge gun.

Today's dilemma in skeet centers around the 12-gauge. Thousands love the dampened recoil of the gas-operated autoloaders, like the Remington 1100, Winchester Super X Model I, and the Smith & Wesson Super Skeet. However, skeet experts have conscious and subconscious reservations about switching from their tubed over-unders, used in the small-gauge events, to a totally different gun. At the very least, they're going to want their 12-gauge autoloaders stocked exactly like their over-unders.

I had Jesse Briley of Houston, Texas fit .410 and 28-gauge tubes to my 20-gauge Ruger Red Label. Though I consider this one too light for skeet (mainly because I've shot heavier tubed guns for so long), I do love the feel of this gun for hunting. I've used it often to bag a limit of 12 doves — with the .410 tubes installed.

While some claim the .410, especially the 2½-inch version used in competitive skeet, to be useless as a hunting gun, I disagree. It all depends on the circumstances. If plenty of doves are flying close, which isn't unusual when the shooter is well positioned at a water hole or has them decoying, the man shouldering a little .410 need only have more patience, firing solely at doves within 25 yards.

Don't forget, we have dove limits. For me, it can be both exciting and challenging to limit out with the .410 in three or four hours, picking my shots, compared to not having to be so selective and limiting out with a 12-gauge in 50 minutes. Also, mainly because of experimental work done by the skeet tube makers, as well as the use of extra-hard shot, the little ½-ounce, 2½-inch .410 is now capable of even and lethal close-range patterns.

For people of small stature and youngsters, tubing a fairly light 20-gauge, in .410 and 28, could be the ideal set-up. The 28-gauge tubes could be inserted for firing both the 28 and 20-gauge events. That still leaves the dilemma of what gun to select for the 12-gauge, but there are now a smattering of skeeters, especially youngsters and those of smaller stature, who fire 12-gauge over-unders with 28-gauge tubes in 12-gauge competition.

With the popularity of tubes has come considerable experimentation with chokes. These days we're seeing tighter and tighter chokes in skeet guns, especially among the greatest shots. Their reasoning is based on psychology. They like the way totally puffed targets help their confidence.

Maybe they think this also demoralizes the opposition. If they're using wide-open chokes it's not always possible for even the top shots to determine where they were when they chipped a bird — in front, back, over, or under. If the shooter wonders too much about this, his high confidence level soon wanes.

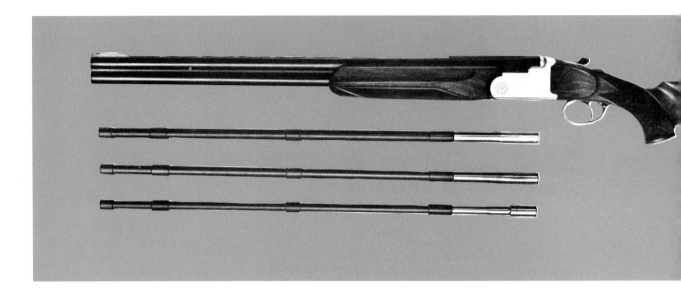

A close friend, Rich Drury, had Jesse Briley make him two sets of .410 tubes for his Browning Superposed, one set with .005-inch choke in both tubes, the other with .009-inch. Rich opts for the more open set when firing factory loads, his second set of tubes, with the tighter chokes, if shooting reloads.

Briley has rigged Rich's aluminum tubes and the stainless chamber sections with male and female threads. To add a different set of tubes, Rich merely unscrews the aluminum section from the stainless steel chamber section and threads on another.

A second alternative for changing chokes on these skeet tubes is threading the muzzle end of the tube sets to receive screw-in chokes. I had Briley rig my Beretta 682 with tubes, but he also rigged the 12-gauge with screw chokes, then put his screw chokes on my .410, 28-, and 20-gauge skeet tubes.

Today's skeet guns are fitted with higher combs than those of yesteryear. This same philosophy has been transferred to shotguns used for hunting. Guns with higher stocks permit shooters to stand more erect, which has proven more effective in competition, as well as in the hunting field.

While the 6¼-pound 12-gauge side-by-side was the classic game gun in Britain for decades, such a gun isn't seen on competitive skeet fields. The wider sight plane of the side-by-side doesn't permit precise leads, the lighter barrels don't permit the fluid swings which are essential to success in competition, and the light weight will quickly make for flinching when 400 and more targets are shot during a weekend.

One answer has been to add weights to the 12-gauge over-under when shooting it without tubes in the 12-gauge event. Several such weights are available in the shotgun marketplace, and can be positioned so that the 12-bore feels and swings very much like the same gun with skeet tubes inserted.

However, a 12-gauge fitted with such weights, firing 1⅛-ounce loads, can still produce too much recoil for many competitors.

So a second answer has been firing reduced loads in the 12-gauge. Most skeet targets are only about 21 yards from the gun, so 1⅛-ounce loads can be "overkill." The one-ounce factory target loads, now offered by Winchester, Remington, Federal, and a few newcomers on the shotgun shell scene, are available because clay target busters demanded them. Of course, many skeeters reload. Some of them have successfully tried ⅞-ounce and 15/16-ounce 12-gauge loads in their over-unders fitted with weights.

Such loads must be painstakingly patterned to determine if the effective pattern width and evenness is comparable to the 1⅛-ounce 12-gauge load. If they aren't, the skeet buff might as well stick with his 20-gauge tubed over-under for the 12-gauge events — and that's exactly what some are doing.

Bob Uknalis of Philadelphia, Pennsylvania, won the High Over-All at the 1984 NSSA World Skeet Shooting Championships. He used his Browning high-post Citori with Briley 20-gauge tubes to break 250 straight in the 12-gauge event. Incidentally, Uknalis, only 21, broke 550 straight clays to capture the HOA Crown.

At ranges of 20 to 22 yards, it's doubtful that the 12-gauge 1⅛-ounce load offers much of an advantage over the ⅞-ounce 20-bore shell. Averages posted by the top shooters in the nation at the end of each skeet year reflect this. Still, the dilemma among skeet shooters remains: what gun to use in the 12-gauge event? That dilemma has been caused, in the main, by the current switch to tubed over-unders in the three smaller gauges.

Beretta's 682 shows straight stock profile becoming popular among both four-gun and international skeet competitors.

Which shotgun brands and models are most favored today for tubing? Though it was introduced only two years ago (1983), the K-80 has great appeal among today's serious shooters. This is the tubed double such notables as Wayne Mayes, Phil Murray, Dave Starrett, Ed Scherer, and others chose. Ed is already in the Skeet Hall of Fame. The other three are eventual shoe-ins.

The Browning Citori with its high-post rib, shot by Bob Uknalis and many others, has proven ideal for tubing. This model, made in Japan, offers one of the most attractive over-under price tags. The Citori does have inertia triggers. They'll seldom set for the second barrel in the little .410 without careful

gunsmith work. Those who make tube sets are experienced in doing this. The Browning Superposed, formerly made in Belgium, is another excellent over-under for a tube set.

The Krieghoff Model 32 has been tubed by numerous serious skeet shooters. Ditto for Remington's recently discontinued 3200. This one, possessing plenty of weight, can be too heavy in the tubed versions for some, particularly those of small stature. The Rottweil can be seen on many skeet fields. Beretta's Model 680 has been discontinued in favor of the current Model 682 (with vent openings between the barrels), but there are a good smattering of both models around.

The 28-inch barrel length is the hands-down favorite among skeet experts, so few Ruger Red Label 12-gauge skeet guns, so far only available in the 26-inch skeet version, have been fitted with skeet tubes. The Valmet 412S could be the least expensive, yet reliable, over-under on the market today for tubing.

The trend on the skeet field is being matched in the hunting field. While pumps and autoloaders still outsell doubles, stackbarrels are now outselling side-by-sides, I'm told, by a significant margin. The only reason over-unders aren't outselling pumps and autoloaders today is price. Most pump and semi owners would love to have an over-under, if they could only afford one.

Skeet guns have changed dramatically over the years. The top shooters, in their continual quest for "...just one more target," keep coming up with new ideas, new concepts, new experiments. From this, everyone who swings a shotgun, even if only a few times a year, derives benefit.

Kolar makes this barrel weight, designed to equalize 12-ga. barrel's heft with that of the tube-equipped skeet gun.

Just as fleas have smaller fleas, tubes can be tubed with screw-in choke tubes like these from Briley. Some American skeet competitors like to shoot a tighter pattern for those confidence-building puffballs, and with choke tubes, they can.

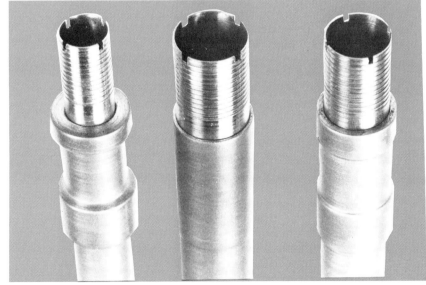

Trapguns: A Breed Apart

Hugh Birnbaum

Normal, right-thinking field shooters visiting a trap club for the first time often experience severe culture shock after a tour of the trap line and a glance at the gun racks. Many of the shotguns and much of the shooting paraphernalia seem barely related to conventional hunting equipment, and even ordinary-looking guns sometimes incorporate distinctly unusual features.

Most disorienting to the visiting hunter is that some highly regarded trapshooting exotica would be disadvantageous or even potentially dangerous if taken afield. Bizarre appearance and/or functioning notwithstanding, what may seem at first to represent a design aberration often proves to provide an elegant solution to a particular trapshooting problem. In a game in which a perfect score may merely be the entry ticket to an extended shoot-off, every advantage is welcome, even if it looks weird and won't play in a duck blind.

For example, consider the Ljutic Space Gun, so named because it looks like a prop from a sci-fi epic. Perhaps the most unusual-looking shotgun you can buy over the counter (not every counter, to be sure), the unconventional configuration and features of this single-purpose claybird cruncher are direct replies to trapshooting challenges.

It is straight as a water pipe to keep recoil in line with the shoulder, reducing the tendency toward muzzle jump. The abbreviated rib is extra high so the shooter can hold his head and neck comfortably erect. The heads-up stance is becoming increasingly popular among trapshooters because it is less fatiguing, provides a better view of the target area and, because the head is positioned high to begin with, reduces the likelihood of the shooter lifting it out of alignment with the rib and target, one of the most common trapshooting faults.

The Space Gun's full pistol grip provides good directional control and allows the shooter's right hand to soak up more recoil than a conventionally shaped stock wrist. The guardless trigger is a button nestled in the front portion of the grip. Pressing it

fires the gun, unless the shooter has specified a release trigger, in which case pressure sets the trigger and releasing the button fires the piece.

The Ljutic Space Gun is a single-shot bolt-action with the loading/ejection port at the bottom of the receiver. The upside-down configuration is convenient for trapshooters who save empties to reload (most do) as the hull simply drops into a waiting hand. The design also spares the shooter on the next post the distraction of seeing or sensing an

This article first appeared in THE AMERICAN RIFLEMAN.

empty sailing toward him while preparing to fire. Other Space Gun features include a speed lock to minimize firing delay and interchangeable screw-in choke tubes for fine-tuning pattern performance.

As one might expect of a firearm incorporating so many goodies, the Ljutic Space Gun has a hefty list price of $3,495. On the other hand, customizing a plain vanilla trap gun to a comparable state of the art with the aid of expert gunsmiths would end up costing at least that much, if not more. And then, you've got to consider the Space Gun's indisputable value in psyching out the competition when

you bring it to the line. There is a concept of winning through intimidation, and the Space Gun is certainly one intimidating piece of ordnance.

At first glance, Remington's 870 Competition Trap model appears to be, in its handsome way, as utterly conventional as any gun could be. However, beneath its Clark Kent exterior lies a unique design conjured up to neutralize the trapshooter's bane: recoil.

Field shooters accustomed to mastering monster Magnums often deride trapshooters for moaning about the recoil of comparatively pussycat-class loads. But the cumulative battering of touching off 100 12-gauge shells in fairly rapid succession and sometimes 200 or 300 in the course of a day is more than many people can take in the name of pleasure. Even if you don't perceive the recoil sensation as painful, it promotes fatigue, which in turn leads to lost targets.

A popular solution to the problem is to shoot a gas-operated autoloader, which spreads the recoil impulse over a longer time than does a fixed-breech gun, thus making the recoil feel less sharp. Some shooters, though, are reluctant to use autoloaders in competition because of qualms about possible malfunctions. For these skeptical souls, the Remington 870 Competition Trap offers the functional reliability of a classic pump gun combined with the recoil-damping of a gas system.

The 870 Competition Trap differs from the traditional 870 in having a gas-assisted recoil-absorbing mechanism that bleeds gas from the barrel against a spring-buffered inertia piston housed in the magazine tube. The result is, in Remington's words, a "...softer, longer recoil curve previously found only in guns such as Remington's Model 1100 gas-operated auto-loader."

Because of its unique gas system, the 870 Competition Trap cannot be used with standard Model 870 barrels, and it is limited to single-shot operation. Other functional features include a barrel-to-choke relationship specifically designed for competitive trapshooting, a stronger receiver with no shell-latch cuts, and a crisp target-type trigger.

Although the notion of a single-shot pump gun with a gas system may seem strange, the gun works as claimed. My subjective impression is that recoil sensation with the 870 Competition Trap is quite similar to what I feel shooting the same loads in a Model 1100, and noticeably less than what I experience with a standard Model 870. If I weren't a hardcore devotee of the Model 1100, I'd be sorely tempted. Remington has ceased quoting "list prices," however, they suggest that the 870 Competition Trap has a "fair retail market value" of $675.

Despite trapshooters' almost universal obsession with avoiding recoil punishment, many are unwilling to abandon a favorite shotgun that fits well and hits well in the search for softer recoil sensation.

Thus a thriving after-market has developed offering accessory recoil-reduction devices you can install in a gun you already own and would love if only it didn't beat you up. Two of the best known anti-wallop treatments in trapshooting circles currently are the Edwards Recoil Reducer and the Griggs Recoil Redirector.

The Edwards Recoil Reducer, on the market since 1966, is a metal cylinder containing a floating piston trapped between opposed springs. One end of the cylinder is fitted with an air-bleed valve. The unit is installed in the shotgun (or rifle) buttstock, parallel to the stock bolt or principal axis of the stock. Depending on how much recoil damping you feel you need and the size of the stock, you may fit one or two Reducers.

Installation usually requires drilling the stock to accept the Reducer. If you're skilled and have the proper tools and the guts, you can do it yourself. Otherwise have the unit(s) installed by a local gunsmith who knows what he's doing, or send your gun to the Edwards establishment for fitting. They promise one-day turnaround.

Each Reducer adds about 5½ ounces installed, so expect the gun's balance to change somewhat. Both the weight and the patented internal piston action damp recoil perceptibly for most shooters I know who use the system. Edwards Recoil Reducers are list priced from $45 to $49, depending on the specific model. Single and double installations by Edwards are priced at $65 and $125, respectively, including Reducer(s), shipping and insurance.

The Griggs Recoil Redirector, the new kid on the block in recoil-control circles, is exactly what the name implies: a cleverly contrived super recoil pad that uses recoil energy to move the buttstock down and away from the shooter's cheek. The main magic is achieved by two complementary aluminum wedges separated by a Teflon slip pad.

The assembly, which is complex in a beautifully logical way, replaces the conventional recoil pad on your shotgun or heavy-caliber rifle. It is about the weight and thickness of a deluxe trap or Magnum-style recoil pad, so does not change gun fit or balance appreciably. You can add spacers or remove wood to adjust pull length if there is a noticeable difference.

In operation, rearward recoil thrust forces the slope of the forward wedge against the mating reverse slope of the rear wedge. The slick Teflon layer separating the wedges allows them to slip freely with respect to each other, and the slant of the interface forces the forward wedge, and the stock to which it is attached, progressively downward as recoil drives the wedges together. The downward motion is retarded by an internal spring, adjustable to fine-tune tension.

As recoil thrust dissipates, the spring pulls the two wedges back into alignment. The net result is that some rearward motion is converted to downward motion, both softening the blow against the shoulder and moving the comb of the stock down and away from the cheek.

A trapshooter I know who installed a Griggs

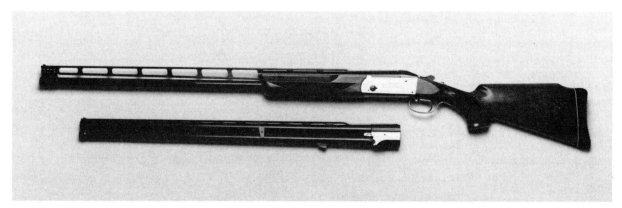

Shotguns of Ulm K-80 Unsingle, shown with interchange-able over/under barrel set, has an adjustment device at the muzzle for raising or lowering the center of impact by changing the relationship between the rib and the barrel.

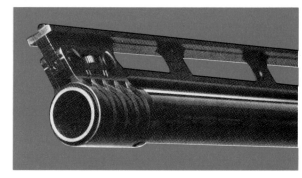

Shotguns of Ulm rib is adjustable to raise or lower point of impact. Knurled wheel over the muzzle is turned to adjust sighting rib upward or downward.

Recoil Redirector on an over-under that had been beating his right cheek into strawberry jam is an ardent proponent of the unit. His cheek is back to normal. He notes, however, that he initially found the downward and subsequent return motions of the stock a little unsettling, although he adapted to the action quickly after a few rounds of practice. He says he has no difficulty shooting doubles with the Redirector, as it returns to neutral quickly enough not to interfere with the second shot.

Griggs Recoil Redirectors are available in several models, differing in style of recoil pad, and in several color options. List prices range from $59.95 to $69.95. Installation is easy enough not to require a gunsmith's services if you're reasonably skilled with tools. Clear, detailed instructions for installation and adjustment accompany the unit.

Another approach to taking the ouch out of recoil is Meadow Industries' Recoil-Slip Pad, a familiar sight among trap and skeet shooters. Some shotgunners develop painful abrasions where the comb of the stock rubs facial skin raw during recoil because the skin is oily or moist and thus adheres to the stock instead of sliding freely.

The Recoil-Slip Pad is a smooth, thin patch of expanded vinyl that drapes over the comb and is held in place by two small Velcro fasteners, one on each side of the stock. The fasteners are low enough and small enough to let the pad slip fore and aft along the stock. Your cheek may stick to the surface of the Recoil-Slip Pad, but the pad will slide freely along the comb during recoil. Result: Your cheek doesn't get torn up.

List price of the Recoil-Slip Pad is $6.49. Meadow Industries points out that the pad can be used on high-powered rifles, too, but cautions against installing it on a scoped rifle. Under some circumstances, the slippage under recoil might exceed available eye relief, allowing the shooter's face to strike the scope.

It's a truism in trapshooting that you usually cannot hit targets well if you cannot see them well. As noted earlier, many trapshooters now believe that holding the head high rather than scrunching down yields a better view of the target area. Not many trapshooters, however, are in the happy position of being able to plunk down megabucks for the relatively few and costly trap guns that leave the factory with ribs high enough to facilitate heads-up shooting.

For shooters with champagne tastes and a beer budget, O.F. Mossberg & Sons, Inc. produces the Mossberg Model 500 Hi-Rib Trap pump gun. The Model 500 Hi-Rib is available with 28-inch or 30-inch barrels, both lengths boasting a so-called "Olympic style" high rib. In keeping with the lofty rib, the stock features a compatibly high Monte Carlo comb.

Both barrel lengths are available with interchange-

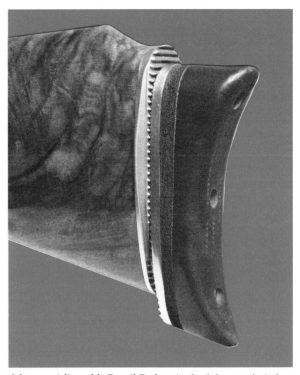

Morgan Adjustable Recoil Pad varies heel drop and pitch.

able Accu-Choke tubes that provide a choice of modified, improved modified, and full constrictions to suit the occasion. The 30-inch barrel also comes in a fixed full-choke version. List prices are $340 for the fixed-choke model and $350 for a gun equipped with an Accu-Choke barrel.

Trapshooters' fascination with ribs isn't limited to matters of height. Loiter long enough among trapshooters and eventually the conversation will turn to the intensely personal subject of just where a gun should shoot relative to where the shooter is looking. Most trapsters concede the virtue of barrels that launch shot charges neither to right nor left of center, but optimum vertical placement of the shot cloud isn't so clearcut.

Some shooters prefer guns that shoot dead on. Many trappersons prefer guns that shoot somewhat high, the better to crunch rising targets. And some want a gun to shoot flat when targets are flat or dropping, somewhat high when flight paths are normal, and quite high when the disks are climbing steeply. Still others prefer to have different impact points depending on whether they are bashing 16-yard clays or assaulting handicap birds.

The time-honored way of changing the impact point is to change the position of the master eye relative to the rib. But, some shooters object that changes the "picture," and anyway it isn't really precise, and it certainly isn't elegant. So how about changing the relationship between the rib and the barrel? The K-80 Unsingle trap gun by Shotguns of

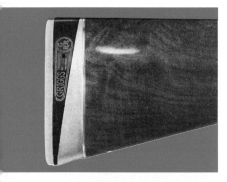

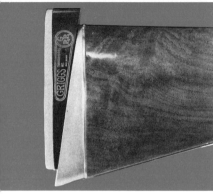

Griggs Recoil Redirector reduces felt recoil by making buttstock slip down and away from the shooter's face on firing.

Ulm, distributed in the U.S. by Dieter Krieghoff, allows you to do just that.

The K-80 Unsingle has a handsome, 12mm-wide rib secured at the muzzle by a complex locking collar that incorporates an adjustment wheel for altering the relationship between rib and barrel. Turning the wheel lets you change the impact point continuously from a claimed seven-inch low to 35-inch high at 38 yards.

Shooters I know who use the K-80 Unsingle tend to fiddle with the adjustment endlessly for a few weeks until they find a setting they like, then they bravely try to resist the urge to fiddle further. It can be terribly tempting to turn that little wheel, though, as an instant cure after a disappointing round. Best results are usually obtained by those who heed the maxim, "Don't fix what ain't broke."

The K-80 Unsingle is beautifully made and boasts nearly every competition-proven refinement a serious trapshooter could want. It is available with 32-inch or 34-inch full-choke barrels at a standard-grade base list price of $3,990, including case. Extra-cost factory options include interchangeable screw-in choke tubes and a release trigger instead of a standard pull trigger.

Note that over-under fans aren't out in the cold where impact adjustment is concerned. Shotguns of Ulm and Browning both offer trap stackbarrels that provide means of raising or lowering pattern placement of the bottom barrel.

More than any other shotgunners, trapshooters have fits about gun fit. Some of us really believe that

$1/16$ inch more or less will make the difference between winning the Grand American and finishing well back in the pack. And those of us who shoot year-round through four seasons really go bananas about gun fit, because it changes with each layer of clothing added or removed.

Reinhart Fajen, Inc., a firm that lists more stocks than a brokerage house, introduced the Fajen Adjustable Trap Stock a few years ago to deal with that problem. Available in models for most popular trap guns, from the ubiquitous Remington 870s and 1100s to the more aristocratic high-roller thundersticks, the basic stock looks for all the world like a trystock that's been through finishing school.

You can raise or lower the comb, lengthen or shorten the pull, and move the recoil pad horizontally and vertically. Playing with the adjustments is nearly as much fun as shooting, so you've got to develop self-control. An acquaintance who fitted one to his trap gun spent so much time trying to improve on perfection that he started muttering one day, "If I had any brains I'd throw the wrenches away and epoxy everything in place."

Prices for the Fajen Adjustable Trap Stock range from $475 through $775, depending on the grade of wood and gun to be fitted. On a less adjustable and less costly note, local gunsmiths have begun converting existing factory stocks to adjustable-comb types that are sometimes quite derivative of the Fajen version.

Some trapshooters, myself among them, find that conventionally configured trap stocks don't provide the desired view over the rib unless the recoil pad is seated awkwardly high or low against the shoulder area. There are two basic ways of dealing with this frustration. The elegant and expensive way is to spring for a custom stock.

The economical and, in my experience, gratifyingly functional alternative is to replace the standard recoil pad with a Morgan Adjustable Recoil Pad. The Morgan assembly consists of a metal mounting plate that attaches to the stock in place of the original recoil pad, and a recoil pad on a second metal plate that bolts to the mounting plate.

The attaching bolt is trapped in a vertical slot in the mounting plate that provides considerable scope for raising or lowering the pad. The two metal plates have deep horizontal grooves in matching ridged patterns that prevent vertical slippage when the bolt is tightened with an ordinary screwdriver inserted through an access hole in the rubber pad. Some pitch adjustment is also possible via two control screws.

The Morgan Adjustable Recoil Pad is available with either a curved or flat pad at a list price of $20. Installation is simple enough not to require a gunsmith unless you want a particularly neat job, foresee a problem you'd rather avoid or suffer from terminal tool trauma. Overall thickness of the assembly is similar enough to that of most standard trap pads to have little effect on pull length. I cannot honestly say that the Morgan Pad enhances the appearance of a gun, but it definitely does what it's supposed to do very well and the price is right.

The shotgunner who wants to alter the comb height of a conventional stock has no problem if the comb is too high. A bit of creative rasp work can do the trick, plus some refinishing. But if the stock is too low or the rasping has gone too far, building up a higher comb can involve painstaking and costly stock work. An alternative much in evidence at trap clubs comes from Meadow Industries in the form of their Variable Convert-A-Stock Pad sets.

Each set consists of two adhesive-backed Velcro fastener strips (one for each side of the stock), several Velcro spacers of different thicknesses that can be used individually or in various combinations, and a stretchable Naugahyde overpad. You select the right combination of spacers to raise the comb to the desired height, then stretch the pad over them to hold them in place. The ends of the overpad have Velcro fastener strips on each side of the stock.

The system is flexible, easy to use and effective, and the materials are light enough not to change the balance of the gun. If you make a mistake, no problem. Zip off the overpad, adjust the spacer stack, and try again. If you wish, you can remove the Velcro fastener strips from the stock easily by softening the adhesive with heat.

Variable Convert-A-Stock Pad sets come in two types. The VCS-6 kit permits raising the comb from $1/16$ inch through $3/8$ inch in six steps. The VCS-11 kit raises the comb from $1/16$ inch through $5/8$ inch in

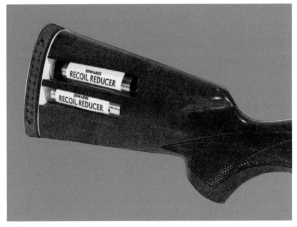

Edwards recoil reducers are cylinders with floating pistons trapped between opposed springs. They can be fitted singly or in pairs.

eleven steps. List prices are $11.95 and $14.75, respectively. A set of variable tapered spacers is available separately at a list price of $5.49.

Although Morgan Adjustable Recoil Pads and Variable Convert-A-Stock Pads are most often associated with shotgunning, both accessories are potentially useful for riflemen looking for custom fit without paying custom prices.

Since shotgunners in general and trapshooters in particular are a bit weird, anyway, it should come as no surprise that increasing numbers of competitive shooters are using release triggers. These infernal devices, which go click when you press them but don't go bang until you release them, were as recently as seven or eight years ago considered "old men's triggers" because they were usually encountered in guns belonging to veteran shooters who had developed severe flinching problems from decades of being battered by recoil.

The theory held, and still does, that relaxing the trigger finger to fire the shot is less likely to unleash the flinch mechanism than the more convulsive action of rapidly squeezing the trigger. That is a gross oversimplification of an imperfectly understood process, but it doesn't detract from the basic fact that flinchers who switch to release triggers often stop flinching.

Younger shooters began to wise up, and release triggers are becoming fairly common at trap clubs. Several major purveyors of competition guns offer release triggers as optional features and quite a few gunsmiths will convert conventional triggers to release functioning. One of the best known gunsmiths offering release triggers is Allen Timney, of Cerritos, California. His current catalog lists more than two pages of release triggers.

Of particular interest to owners of Remington Model 1100 and 870 trap guns, Timney makes all-steel replacement trigger units in both pull and

A trapshooter at North Jersey Gun Club, in Fairfield, N.J., mounts a Shotguns of Ulm K-80 Unsingle during a round of 16-yd. trap.

The gap between the comb and main buttstock is a clue that this trapshooter has equipped his Shotguns of Ulm K-80 Unsingle with a Fajen Adjustable Trap Stock. The combination of adjustable stock and adjustable rib provides maximum opportunity for fine-tuning gun fit and pattern placement.

release versions that come as close to being inde-structible as trigger units can be. Timney release triggers for the Model 1100 begin at $60 for a new Remington factory trigger converted to release action, and mount to $155 for the Timney all-steel unit (some options can raise the price still higher). If you think you may be interested in getting a release trigger, try before you buy. Shooting with a release trigger is very different from shooting with a pull trigger, and not everyone can make the personal adjustment required to enjoy the benefits of a release action. As one who cannot at all adapt to a release trigger, I speak from experience on this point.

If you decide to buy a release trigger, deal with a gunsmith with lots of experience and lots of satis-fied customers. A release trigger is one of those products, like an airplane engine or a parachute, that should not represent a low or midpoint on someone's learning curve. For the sake of those around you, learn to control the release trigger during practice sessions, not registered events.

Pay particular attention to mastering the appro-priate technique for unsetting the trigger when you wish not to fire after having set the mechanism. The procedure is sometimes tricky or awkward, but you absolutely must learn it cold to use the trigger safely. Friends who use and like release triggers suggest that the acclimation process requires shoot-ing about 500 targets to achieve reasonable ease and proficiency.

Because of the potential for accidental discharge, many users prominently display warning decals on guns with release triggers. Under no circumstances should a gun equipped with a release trigger be taken afield for hunting.

As trap guns tend to be heavy and the game involves considerable standing around, gun in hand, trapshooters often attempt to conserve energy by resting the weight of the gun on any nonhostile surface. Some clubs provide patches of rubber mat or carpeting at shooting posts on which to rest the muzzle. Some shooters, whose sanity I seriously question, habitually rest the muzzle on the tip of a shoe. Several shooters I know trail soft muzzle pads with them on a length of string as they move from post to post, looking for all the world as though they were walking squashed chihuahuas.

A clever solution to the problem of how to rest the muzzle safely without damage comes from Meadow Industries in the form of a lightweight muzzle rest you can attach to nearly any 12-gauge barrel. The muzzle rest is formed from sheet steel that is nicely blackened and contoured to conform to the outer curve of most trap barrels. The inner curve of the rest is lined with a layer of neoprene tape that will stick it securely to the barrel when you follow the clear instructions that accompany the device.

The business end of the muzzle rest, when prop-erly positioned, projects about ½ inch past the muzzle and roughly ⅓ inch away from the barrel. The rest ends in a black nylon bumper. Correctly installed, the muzzle rest is invisible to the shooter with the gun mounted. It lets you rest the gun weight (not your weight!) on any hard surface without marring the muzzle. If you ever decide you would rather live without it, you can remove it easily. The Muzzle Rest is list priced at $6.49. It sure beats terrorizing your toes and making black rings on your Nikes.

Lest you get the impression that trapshooting is impossible without a plethora of exotic equipment, I hasten to point out that in years of lurking at gun clubs I have yet to see anyone stagger to the line with a gun incorporating all of the innovations and/or oddities described above. Some, certainly. Not all. At least not yet. But it's only a matter of time. Particularly since I just spoke with my gunsmith about it. Just you wait gentlemen, just you wait!

The All-Around 20-Gauge Shotgun

Jon R. Sundra

I'm not exactly sure when I decided the 20 gauge was "my shotgun." Perhaps it was the morning I cleanly dropped a big Canada goose up in Manitoba at 65 yards. Maybe it was the time I dropped more doves than any of my five companions, all of whom were shooting 12s (I'm not really sure what I'd consider a crack wingshot, but then obviously neither were they). Or perhaps it was on the eastern shore of the Chesapeake one frigid morning when I got two doubles in a row on mallards and filled out in ten minutes.

It is understandable that we embrace a specific gun based on a few successful experiences in the field (which, in the long run, may prove not to have been representative at all), so surely those afore-mentioned incidents have something to do with my long love affair with the 20 gauge. But the kind of experiences cited above are few and far between, and my affair with the 20 is much more substantive than that; it's based on nearly 20 years of extensive use on virtually every type of winged game from dove and quail to geese and turkey. In all that time I can count on both hands how many times I felt I was handicapped by having a 20 gauge in my hands.

My first shotgun was a Mossberg bolt-action .410.

This article first appeared in *GUNS & AMMO*.

With modern high-performance hunting loads, 20-ga. handles pheasants nicely. Southpaw shown here is about to bag rooster crossing to right.

(Photo by Bob Elman)

Once considered a lady's and youth's gun, the 20 ga. has finally earned respect due to its performance.

I didn't have much of an opportunity as a youngster back in northern Ohio to shoot much game with it, but I sure did-in a pile of corn-marauding blackbirds for a farmer friend who rewarded me by paying me in shells. Next was a 16-gauge Ithaca double which I used long enough to decide I didn't particularly like looking over pipes oriented side by side (I know, I know; the Harris tweed and Ascot types are clutching their throats at that statement, but that's their problem).

Then I got my first 20, an Ithaca 37 pump, which I never fully appreciated until I decided to buy a stable mate — another Ithaca 37, but in 12 gauge. I had both guns fitted with a vent rib and Poly-Choke with the barrels both cut to 26 inches, reasoning I now had a battery for any and all wingshooting; two guns as close in fit and feel as 12- and 20-gauge guns could be.

But it wasn't close at all; one felt heavy and cumbersome, and I was always conscious of having to "move it around." The other felt so light and responsive it seemed to anticipate where I wanted it — and it was there. Sure a lot of it was in my head, but what the hell, most of our preferences for one thing over another boil down to arbitrary decisions, and I'll admit to being predisposed to light, fast-handling shotguns. I've always been a sports car buff, too, so I suppose there's some correlation there.

But enough of the subjective aspects. Sure I like the looks and feel of a 20, but I'm no fool; if my faith in it wasn't borne out by ballistic fact and satisfactory experiences, I wouldn't be so enamored with it. Now I'm not about to cite a bunch of carefully selected facts and figures, then through some convoluted reasoning process attempt to "prove" that the 20 gauge is somehow superior to the 12. Ballistically the 20 gauge never has and never will be as effective as the 12 gauge. Anything that can be done to improve the performance of the 20 gauge shell, either by the ammunition makers or handloaders, can be done with the 12 so it always maintains its edge.

How much of an edge is it? Well, a standard 2¼-inch 20-gauge one-ounce load contains about 350 pellets of 7½ size, 225 No.6s, 135 No.4s. A 1¼-ounce 12-gauge load tosses 25 percent more shot across the board. In the three-inch Magnum persuasions, the 20 gauge's 1¼-ounce payload is more than matched percentage-wise by the 12's 1⅞-ounce loading. No contest when it comes to pellet-pushing potential!

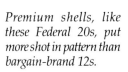

Premium shells, like these Federal 20s, put more shot in pattern than bargain-brand 12s.

In trying to evaluate relative efficiency of a given shotshell, the bottom line is not a question of payload per se but rather how much of that payload reaches the target. With a rifle cartridge, for example, there's nothing to debate; we know a 180-grain bullet exiting the muzzle is still going to be a 180-grain projectile when it hits the target, whether that target be 100 or 300 yards away.

With a shotshell, on the other hand, only a percentage of the original charge of shot hits or, in some cases, even reaches the target. As for the percentage of pellets that do make it into that 30-inch circle at 40 yards, a great deal depends on how the shotshell is put together and with what kind of components. Take the typical shotshell of 30 years ago. In my Dad's day, no one armed with a 12 gauge and "high brass" loads considered themself handicapped for any kind of wingshooting — ducks and geese included — yet today it's possible to buy over-the-counter 20-gauge one-ounce loads that will deliver as many or more pellets to the target than did the 1¼-ounce 12 gauge of the '50s.

In Dad's day, less progressive burning powders, less efficient over-powder and over-shot wads, rolled crimps, and the lack of shot wrapping all made for a markedly inferior shell than is available today. Add to that technology the widespread availability of extra-hard shot in factory loads and — well, it's just a whole 'nother ball game for modern shooters.

Without going too deeply into the internal ballistics of it, the improvements enumerated above allow a substantially greater percentage of pellets to emerge from the muzzle with sufficient sphericity to fly true. Whether a No. 2 or a 7½, any pellet with a flat spot or in any way out-of-round becomes an imperfect airfoil. The net result is that the distorted pellets not only lose velocity faster — and thus "string out" — but their imperfect shape causes

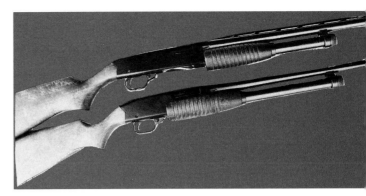

Though most 20-ga. guns are built on reduced-scale receivers, these Winchester 1300s in 12 and 20 are both same size and weight.

them to sail off and out of the pattern like so many little frisbees gone berserk. The better cushioning wads and more progressive burning powders in today's shotshells exert less violent forces to the pellets in the bottom third of the shot column, hence the "mashing effect" which flattens and otherwise distorts sphericity during initial upset is minimized. No sooner does the shot column get moving than it enters the forcing cone and gets mashed some more. Approaching the muzzle our pellets are further deformed by "scrubbing," (i.e., flat spots actually rubbed into the peripheral pellets in direct contact with the bore). With the development of shot sleeves, then integral shot cups, peripheral shot is protected during its bore travel. Sleeving also helps minimize pellet deformation as the shot column is again constricted passing through the choke. On today's premium-type hunting loads the addition of granulated polythylene buffering material further protects each pellet from being deformed

(Right) With crimp removed, premium-load 20 shows off those neat little copper-coated spheres that make it so effective. Filler acts as a buffer and helps protect shot by helping it "flow" through the restricting choke.

(Far right) Compared to 10 ga. Mag., even the mighty 12 (center) seems a bit skimpy. The 20 ga. at right is only 25% shy of the 12's average payload.

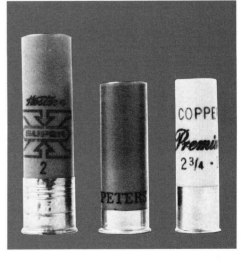

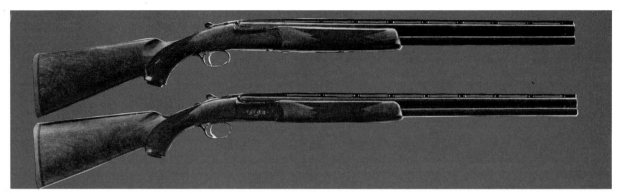

One of the nicest features of most 20-ga. guns is their reduced size and weight, as evidenced by the comparison above: the Ruger Red Label 12 (top) and its little brother the 20 ga. Red Label, below.

by its neighbor and also helps them "flow" through the choke more easily.

All the above advances in shotshell technology make for much more efficient shotguns in all gauges, but the collective degrees of their effectiveness ultimately depends on the hardness of the shot used. It costs money to add antimony to harden shot, so the inexpensive foreign promotional lines

Some skeet gunners prefer 20 ga. even for events in which they could shoot 12 ga. Versatility, comfort, and efficiency are hallmarks of the 20.

(Photo by Bob Elman)

of shotgun shells we see in discount stores commonly labeled "duck and pheasant" or "dove and quail" loads may use unhardened shot. With soft shot it is estimated that between 40 and 50 percent of the pellets in a given shell will deform a significant amount by the time they exit the muzzle. Bargain-price shotshells rarely come close to providing the nominal pattern percentages we're supposed to get from the various chokings, especially out beyond the 40-yard mark.

Next on the hardness scale is "chilled" shot, which contains some 1½ to two percent antimony, making it more resistant to deformation. All other things equal, chilled-shot pattern percentages may go up as much as 10 percent over an identical load using soft shot.

High-performance hunting loads advertising "high antimony," "Magnum" or "extra-hard" lead shot represent the next quality step above chilled. Here we're talking antimony content between 4½ and six percent depending on pellet size (larger shot sizes require less antimony), which further increases patterning efficiency another eight or 10 percent over chilled-shot performance levels.

Even more resistant to deformation than "Magnum" shot is the copper-plated stuff which, when used in conjunction with buffering materials, may actually provide almost 100 percent patterns with shot sizes of No. 4s or larger through a full choke at 40 yards! Copper-plated shot is nothing new, but its general availability in factory hunting loads is. Whether it's Federal's Premium, Remington's Premier, or Winchester's Super X Double XXs, copper-plated buffered shotshells are unquestionably the biggest improvements ever handed to the American shotgunner.

So good are they in fact, that the traditional choke percentages used in the past no longer apply and should be changed, especially for the coarser shot sizes used in duck and goose shooting — 2s, 4s, and 5s. In the "old days," nominal percentages for shot placement within that 30-inch circle at 40 yards were 40 percent for improved cylinder, 50 percent for modified, 60 percent for improved modified, and 70 percent for full, give or take five percent in all cases. With today's "super shotshell" you can add, say, another 10 percent to those figures using No. 6 or 7½ shot, and as much as 15 to 20 percent in a No. 2 or 4 load for a premium-type shell using buffered, copper-plated shot.

The point I'm trying to make here by dwelling on shotshell technology is simply this: By merely spending a few extra cents per shot for premium shells, today's 20 gauge surpasses the performance of even Express-type 12-gauge lead loads of the not-so-distant past. And the chap with the three-inch-chambered gun with its capability of digesting 1¼-ounce payloads has even more performance available to him.

I would again remind you that these advances have benefitted all gauges and therefore today's 12 gauge is as much superior to yesterday's 12 as in the case of the 20. The 12 gauge's edge is as wide as it's always been but at this point I think we have to ask ourselves just how much gun do we really need, and at what cost in terms of size, weight, handling, and pointing qualities.

It's really impossible to "measure" in a quantitative way the pointing and handling characteristics of a shotgun; those are things you feel. You know when a gun feels good yet, like trying to describe in absolute terms how a certain food tastes, find it impossible to do so other than by comparison with other tastes.

Two things we can measure and compare, however, which have a great deal to do with those attributes we can't describe, are size and weight.

Lower profile of 20-ga. is really appreciated when the gun is held in one hand. Fingers easily wrap around gun at its balance point and make all-day carrying far less tiring than with heavier and bulkier 12 ga.

Generally speaking, a 20-gauge gun will weigh around 12 ounces less than a comparable 12-gauge model. This, of course, assumes each is built on a scaled receiver, something not every maker does. Winchester's (USRAC) Model 1300 pump and Ranger semi-auto 20 gauges are built on 12-gauge receivers and therefore have the same bulk and weight of the larger gun. Most makers, however, do scale their 12- and 20-gauge guns accordingly — like Remington's 1100 and 870, Ithaca's 37, and Browning's B-80 and BPS to name a few. As such, 20-gauge receivers average about ⅜-inch less in depth than the comparable 12-gauge model. Since the shells themselves are of the same length in either gauge, length of receiver and overall gun measurements are the same though with the 20-gauge barrel being some

Even decoyed ducks and geese are fair game for hunter armed with Mag. versions of this versatile gauge.

Big rooster ringnecks were no match for the 20's Mag. load of #6 shot.

Pass shooting at high-flying ducks and geese may be stretching the 20's ability, though 20-ga. devotees claim their gun can do it.

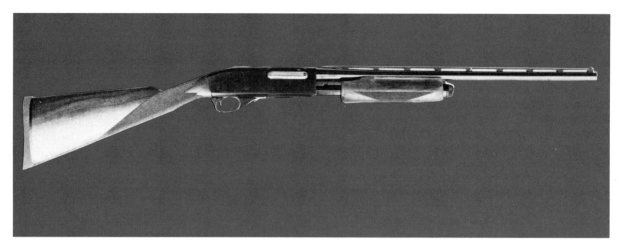

This is probably as close as anyone comes to the upland hunter's "dream gun," according to author. At 5 lbs. 14 oz., this Remington Special Field with its 21" barrel and straight-grip stock is a pleasure afield.

rel lengths and type (vent rib or plain), pull length, and stock style. As for dimensional differences, Ruger's 20-gauge receiver is nearly ¼-inch less in depth than the 12.

The feel, balance, and handling qualities of a single-barrel repeater and a twin-barreled gun are vastly different, of course. Personally, I prefer the over-under above all others, but I'll admit to having done some of my best shooting over the years with pumps and semi-autos, so I'm not too fanatical about that preference. No one has yet proven that one type of gun is in any way superior to the others with regard to one's ability to hit with it. If I had to hazard a guess, I'd say that given an unlimited number of shooters and targets, both live and clay, those using softer-shooting semiautos would post the best averages. Game shooting in the real world, however, does not provide the frequency of shots or consistency of target flight for us to make any kind of valid comparisons — like we can measure the grouping ability of two or more rifles fired from a bench — our choice of shotgun is based primarily on whether or not we're accustomed to it and how it strikes our sensibilities.

Fully realizing that the question of "how much gun?" is the subject of half the gun articles ever written, it is one that must be addressed. But how? Determining how much gun we "need" is futile enough when dealing with rifles, but nigh on impossible with shotguns. It doesn't take a great deal of gray matter to realize that, with individual pellet velocity being the same in either gauge, the one throwing the greatest number will have the edge. It may take a box of shells for that edge to manifest itself in the form of an extra bird or two, but sooner or later it will. But when a bird flies on without so much as a ruffled feather, how do we separate the flat-out miss from "not enough gun?" I

.115 inch thinner, there's less bulk and weight to be swung around.

With double guns, both over-unders and side-by-sides, the same physical differences between the 12 and 20 apply; all are scaled down accordingly and thus offer the same kind of bulk and weight savings as enumerated for the single-barrel repeaters. Ruger, for example, shows a difference of ½ pound between the nominal weights of his 12-gauge and 20-gauge Red Label over-unders, but the two guns I have, both with 26-inch IC/Modified barrels, show a ¾-pound difference on my scale. Indeed, I've found that the ¾-pound figure pretty much applies to all 12/20-gauge comparisons assuming comparable bar-

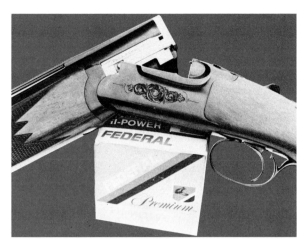

Most modern shotguns offer the 20 ga. with 3" chambers, making its combination with 1¼-oz. Mag. loads, offered by Federal and others, a good all-around gun that will handle most hunting situations admirably.

wish it were always that cut and dried but it's not; sometimes we hit and wound, and it's in those situations that we tend to wish for more gun. If we didn't we'd be rather callous jerks. But there's some point at which more pellets won't compensate for their being in the wrong place, so what's "enough gun" is a question each of us must answer for himself based on our assessed skill and the frequency we get afield.

The situations alluded to earlier, in which I felt undergunned with a 20, involved waterfowl in every case. I've killed my share of ducks and geese with 20s using both the 1⅛-ounce 2¾-inch load and 1¼-ounce three-inch Magnum loads, but unless the birds were decoying, I sometimes found myself wishing for the edge the 12 gauge would have given me. In these days of fierce competition often forcing hunters into pass shooting at birds 60 and 70 yards high, the 12 gauge should get the nod. Then too, steel shot regulations have now taken that decision out of our hands. Even where lead is legal I find myself these days opting for a 12 for all my waterfowling. I am convinced, however, a good, well practiced duck and goose shooter doesn't need any more than a Magnum 20; I'm just not in that league — and few of us are.

For everything else though — quail, doves, pigeons, grouse, chukar, even wild-flushing late-season pheasants — the 20 has always done the job for me. I'm just vain enough that if my companions using 12 gauges consistently brought down more game than I, I would have long given up on the 20. I mean, what else can we go by other than our own performance? The rest of it is all senses and perception. I like the petite size of 20-gauge guns. I like how they feel, how they mount, point, and swing. Sure it's subjective stuff; after all, the dynamics of balance and movement are not quantitative things,

and less weight and bulk are not inherently desirable attributes. So it must be a subjective decision that prompts one to opt for a 20 over a 12 because the former will always be ballistically inferior.

The 20 gauge guy is really no different from the gent who uses a 6mm for deer hunting or a .270 for elk. He knows there are more potent rounds he could use that will give him more of an edge under the worst of circumstances, but he's comfortable in the knowledge that his 20 will do its job if he does his. He knows that if on a given day he's missing with his 20, he'd in all likelihood be missing with a 12. Though over the course of the season he's aware the larger gun would probably add an extra couple of birds to his bag, that's okay with him because he doesn't measure the quality of the outdoor experience strictly in terms of success ratio. To him, the satisfaction of doing the job with a smaller, lighter, better-handling, easier-carrying gun more than makes up for whatever ballistic edge a bigger gun would give him. If that weren't the case, there'd be no such thing as a 20 gauge.

Author's son, Ian, is shown here with 20-ga. pump gun after highly successful dove hunt in Sonora. This bore size can handle everything from doves and quail to ringnecks and sage grouse.

Photo by Pete McLain

The Big 10

Jim Carmichel

Floyd is a veteran of many seasons in the goose pits and exhibits all the paranoia of a guide who has shivered through too many cold, wet days with clients who miss at every opportunity and greet sundown with unfilled limits. His motto is "Wait until they're closer!" which he chants like an Indian medicine man each time a flight of honkers makes a reconnaissance pass over his spread of stuffed decoys.

On this particular bluebird day, the geese wanted no part of Floyd's stuffed decoys and his blue-ribbon calling. Time after time, we breathlessly peered through the crosshatch of brown grass that concealed our whereabouts as flight after flight of geese dipped to within 80, 60, and 50 yards, and then turned with the wind and were gone.

Finally, about midmorning, with no birds in hand and no shots having been fired, a quintet of honkers cautiously coasted in 60 some yards overhead. Floyd could stand it no longer and said:"Let's take them, Jim."

I heard Floyd's load of No. 2s connect with the characteristic *whooshump* of a well-centered pattern. No need to look; I knew that the goose was falling. Just then, my finger tightened on the trigger. *Whooshump* and the honker was dead in the air. *Whooshump, whooshump* and two more geese fell. Floyd and I each still had a shot left in our Ithaca Mag 10 autoloaders.

Another hunter in our party had fired at the remaining goose with his 12-gauge Magnum. The bird, though hit, was pumping hard to get out of range. Floyd's last shot, a backup charge of BB-size pellets, caught up with the goose about 75 yards out, and that bird, too, joined our bag.

Floyd didn't have much to say, but I detected a trace of a grin breaking through his Chesapeake reserve. More geese came over during the morning and, when any of them dipped to 60 yards, he'd say: "That looks about right, boys. Take them!" Our own three-bird limits filled, Floyd and I passed our big guns to other members of the hunt who, for the first time, experienced the awesome reach of the modern, 10-gauge, 3½-inch Magnum shotgun.

The term Magnum is aptly applied to the 10-gauge 3½-inch shell but, for the record, it must be noted that the Big 10's magnificence is a phenomenon of very recent vintage. A short decade ago, the legendary 10-gauge Magnum was wheezing on its deathbed, already considered a relic of the bygone era of great waterfowl gunning. Then two things happened to miraculously improve the big gun's future. The first of these was Ithaca's introduction of their Mag 10 shotgun, the first and only commercially made 10-gauge autoloader. The second was an unprecedented population explosion of geese, especially wild and beautiful Canada honkers.

THE MAG 10

Ithaca introduced the Mag 10 in 1974 and I suspect that, if they had taken an opinion poll among hunters beforehand, the project would have been dropped. Ten-gauge shotguns had not been made in the United States for decades and, except for ordering a high-priced specimen from a few custom shops in England or on the Continent, the only new guns available in the United States were Spanish-made doubles.

I owned one of those doubles back in the 1950s. I bought it, along with a case of shells, at what seemed to be a bargain price. But after firing a box or two of the exotic shells at crows, I sold the gun and the remaining shells at an even lower price. Every time I pulled the trigger, the stock's thin, sharp-edged comb hacked me in the mouth like a dull chainsaw. Besides, I wasn't killing crows any higher than I did with my 12 bore, so I allowed that I could spend the rest of my days without the painful company of a 10-gauge shotgun. I imagine that is what just about everyone who tried one of the big doubles decided.

Despite the widespread negative view of the 10 bore, Ithaca had some compelling reasons to proceed with the development of their 10-gauge autoloader. One of these was the company's historic association with the big shell. Until 1948 or thereabouts, they had manufactured a double that was often said to be the best 10 gauge ever made in America. It was much favored by gun writers of the pre-war era.

Ithaca also had an ace in the hole in the person of Jim Tollinger, a firearms wizard who wanted to add a 10-gauge autoloader to his long list of design achievements. Tollinger realized that a gas-operated autoloader in 10 gauge would punish a hunter's shoulder much less than the 10-gauge guns of the past, thus eliminating the principal objection to hunting with the giant Magnum. Remington's Model 1100 gas-operated autoloader was a best seller by then and had effectively demonstrated the recoil-reducing advantages of the gas system. This system, in effect, spreads the recoil over a longer time period, thus reducing *felt* recoil. So, putting

their faith in Jim Tollinger, Ithaca labored and brought forth the Mag 10, one of the most daringly conceived and beautifully executed autoloaders ever manufactured.

The Mag 10's first trial by fire occurred late in 1973 when a gaggle of gun writers met at Roswell, New Mexico, to try the new gun on high-flying sandhill cranes. Those writers, such as myself, who had past experience with the 10 gauge, were timid about renewing the relationship but, after a shot or two, we realized that the recoil differed little from that of a lightweight 12-gauge gun. Even that isn't a good comparison because the Mag 10 doesn't kick so much as it delivers a hearty shove. Recoil is also kept under control by the Mag 10's robust 11¼-pound weight and oversized grip and forearm, which encourage the shooter's hands and arms to absorb some of the recoil.

Everything about the Ithaca Mag 10 is king size, from the 32-inch barrel to its massive steel receiver. All this adds up to an overall length of some 55 inches, which means it won't fit into most gun

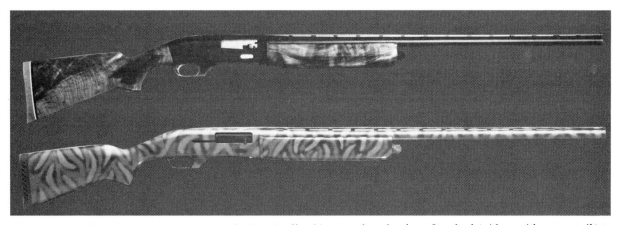

Ithaca Mag 10, the only 10-gauge auto in production, is offered in several grades, from Standard (with or without vent rib) to Presentation Series. Shown at top is Deluxe Grade, with rib and select walnut. Second version pictured is new Camo Seal Mag 10, with Camouflage-pattern Teflon coat from butt to muzzle, making it ideal for waterfowl and turkey hunting. Also available is Mag 10 Deerslayer, with blued or Parkerized finish and 22-inch slug barrel carrying rifle sights.

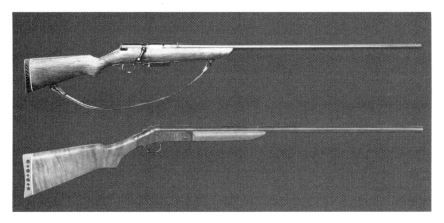

Few manufacturers offer 10-gauge guns, but there is some choice, including economy models. Marlin's 10-gauge Magnum Goose Gun (top) is clip-fed bolt-action with three-shot capacity and relatively low price. Even lower-priced is Harrington & Richardson Model 176 break-action single-shot, available with 32-inch full-choke barrel or 28-inch slug barrel. In addition to these and Ithaca's Mag 10 auto, several 10-gauge Spanish side-by-sides are marketed in U.S.

cases. When you first shoulder a Mag 10, it seems unbalanced, as though almost all the weight was dangling out at arm's length. In fact, this is almost the case, but it is a blessing in disguise because, once the gun is in motion, all that forward weight isn't stopped. This contributes to beautifully smooth swings and follow-throughs. Aside from its long-range advantage, the Mag 10 is one of the easiest guns to hit with I've ever used. You don't jerk and jab it at the target. Rather, you sweep the sky in steady arcs.

As good as all this sounds and is, the announcement of the Mag 10's advent didn't win universal acclaim. One writer, I recall, went to considerable effort to point out why the 10 gauge had no advantage over a modern, three-inch, 12-gauge Magnum. To a large extent, he was correct, even if a bit short-sighted. As he pointed out, development of the 12-gauge shotshell had raced ahead with such improvements as star crimps, plastic cups, shot-sleeves, shot buffering, and ever-heavier shot charges, but the 10-gauge shell was relatively unimproved. The loads we shot at cranes in New Mexico, for instance, were stuffed with old-fashioned fiber wads; there was no shot sleeve or buffering fillers; and the case mouth was closed with an old-style roll crimp. The shot charge was two ounces, only ⅛ ounce heavier than the heaviest 12-gauge loads of that time.

FEDERAL AMMUNITION

However, the gods did indeed smile on Ithaca because, at about that time, the folks at Federal Cartridge were gearing up to produce their revolutionary Premium line of shotshells. What better showcase could there be for their copper-plated shot and state-of-the-art components and loading techniques than a really great Magnum load? When Federal's Premium loads were united with Ithaca's Mag 10 autoloader, the long arm of the 10-gauge Magnum did, at last, reach into the heavens.

How good is the 10-gauge Magnum and how can it be used most effectively? It is, in my opinion, a far better long-range killer than is generally realized. I say without hesitation that it outreaches the 12 gauge by some 20 to 30 yards. Whereas the 12-gauge Magnum is strained to make clean kills at 60 to 65 yards, that is the normal working range for the Big 10, and clean kills out to 80 yards are not all that exceptional.

Of course, that much long-range potential has led to charges that few gunners shoot well enough to utilize the gun's effective range and that it leads to "skybusting." I can't say as how I agree, though I do agree that using a 10-gauge Magnum to its full potential calls for a good measure of boldness on the

shooter's part. Leading a high-flying bird as much as 15 feet is, at first, an adventure into the unknown. But once you get used to the idea, it's as natural as swatting doves at 30 yards.

Though the 10-gauge Magnum is naturally linked to long-range shooting, don't forget its tremendous effect at the closer ranges. After all, the basis of good shotgun performance at *any* range is to kill the game as cleanly as possible. The hammering effect of the 10 gauge at 40 to 60 yards is remarkable. Shooters who have become accustomed to seeing geese and ducks falter and wobble and then plane off in a long fall after being hit with a 12-gauge are overjoyed at the way the Big 10 puts extra pellets in the target that make the difference between clean kills and cripples that get away.

The advantages of the 10-gauge Magnum for goose and duck hunting are, perhaps, even more evident in areas where steel shot is required. Winchester currently offers 10-gauge steel shot loads with 1¾ ounces of BB shot. That makes for an extremely dense pattern.

Here of late, the 10-gauge Magnum shell has also been loaded with a stump-busting 1¾ ounce rifled slug, and Ithaca offers a Mag 10 called the Deerslayer with rifle sights on a 22-inch barrel. But this is a lot of weight to carry through the deer woods, especially when you consider that the range limitation of rifled slugs is accuracy, not foot-pounds. I expect that the best use for the 10-gauge Deerslayer, therefore, is in police work.

The choice in 10-gauge shotguns for waterfowl hunting is limited but sufficient, and the runaway best choice is Ithaca's Mag 10. This gun comes in several grades, ranging from a dull-finished, plain-barreled model up to the Presentation Grade with fancy wood and deluxe finish. The most sensible version for waterfowling and turkey hunting is the Standard Model with ventilated rib. This gun has a low-glare finish and oil-finished stock — a good choice for the waterfowl blind.

Marlin offers a three-shot, bolt-action, clip-fed, 10-gauge Magnum shotgun for less than half the price that you would have to pay for the Mag 10. And for half of what you would pay for the Marlin bolt gun, H&R offers their Model 176 break-action single-shot. The H&R comes in 32-inch full-choke and 28-inch slug-gun versions.

I know of three side-by-side, double-barreled shotguns of 10-gauge persuasion that are currently available in the United States. All are made in Spain. The best known is the Mercury Magnum imported by Tradewinds, Box 1191, Tacoma, WA 984021 (206-272-4887). The other two are the Kassnar/Churchill, imported by Kassnar, Box 6097, Harrisburg, PA 17112 (717-652-6101); and the BGJ Magnum, available from Mandall Shooting Supplies, 3616 N. Scottsdale Rd., Scottsdale, AZ 85251 (602-945-2553). Contact the importers for details and prices.

The Winchester Model 97

Pete Dickey

Unlike its predecessor, the Model 1893, Winchester's Model 1897 had a long and totally successful career. It had all the 1893's good features but none of its shortcomings. It quickly became America's "favorite" shotgun, thus irritating some Europeans who had depended on the U.S. to import rather than make many of its shotguns and/or shotgun barrels.

The British were particularly ill tempered about the 1897, not only because it cut into their double-barrel export business, but because it was so efficient a bird gun. They dismissed all repeating shotguns as "market hunters' guns" and probably had ruder things to say of the 1897 in particular, since it was the repeater that led the pack.

Captain Charles Askins, the premier American shotgunner of his day, apparently had read enough in the foreign press on the subject for, in 1910, he wrote:

"I believe it is true beyond question or dispute that there is more gun, better gun value for the money, in an American repeater than in any other shotgun in the world. It will shoot as well as any, and is equal to two double guns with a man following about to carry one and do the loading — English fashion. The Briton will have none of the repeater on the grounds that it is too deadly and unsportsmanlike, yet he will have the aforesaid two guns carried about so that he can kill game as rapidly as he could with the repeater. An expert can move the slide so fast that he can shoot nearly as rapidly as he could fire two shots from a double gun, while at times he will discharge six shots to the two of the double barreled man.

"The pump gun is the favorite trap gun in America today," Captain Askins continued. "If I am not mistaken, it holds all American records at the trap, the longest run on clay birds, the best annual professional average, and the greatest number of first place wins either amateur or professional. As a trap gun for clay birds under present conditions it is unrivaled. It balances as well as a double arm, shoots more evenly, and will fire five thousand shots for every dollar that it cost and still be ready for business."

At the time of Askins' writing, production of the Winchester pump shotgun was nearing the half-million mark.

This article first appeared in *THE AMERICAN RIFLEMAN*.

(Top) Winchester Repeating Shot Gun, Model 1897. (Bottom) M-1917 Trench gun, with solid frame, saw service in WWI and thereafter. Many are still in use by police.

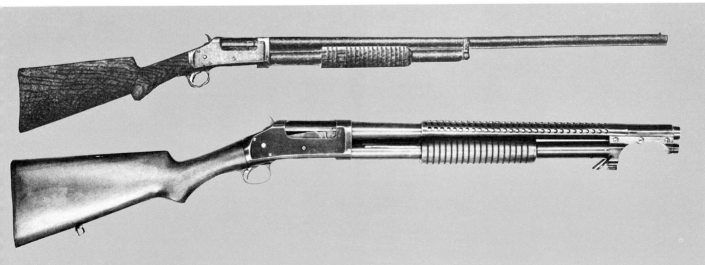

The only direct competition (i.e., an exposed-hammer pump shotgun) was the Marlin Model 1898 and its successors which had reached a total production of around 100,000 at that time. Like the Winchester, the Marlin had a five-shot magazine and was available in solid or takedown versions. However, Remington and Stevens, in their Models 10 and 520, had recently brought out "hammerless" takedown pumps which posed a threat, but a less distinct one than the Browning-designed semi-automatics which were coming into vogue.

Winchester's own self-loader didn't emerge until 1911 and was never to match the 1897's popularity. What Winchester *did* do to hurt the 97's position was to introduce in 1912 a "hammerless" 20-gauge pump and a 12-gauge version in the following year. That was the Model 12 (1912) which, by 1914, was being made in about triple the quantity of the 1897.

Even so, the Model 97 — so called by 1917 — sold remarkably well up to its discontinuance in 1957, when almost a million had been sold. Its detractors today claim it is obsolete by virtue of its exposed hammer. Its manufacturer may have just judged it too expensive at $90 to continue to make and sell at a competitive price.

In 1897, however, it sold for $25, and whether it was its price, its similarities to the 1893, or its differences from it accounted for the Model 1897's instant popularity is arguable, but those differences were significant.

- It was chambered for the newer 2¾-inch smokeless (or blackpowder) 12-gauge shell. It would also handle the 1893's 2⅝-inch shell if the shooter wished. However, Damascus barrels were regularly offered up until 1914, and any guns so barreled cannot be considered "smokeless-powder" guns.

- The lengthened receiver was not scalloped on top but was made with a full-length covering over the ejection port for added strength. The ejection was to the right rather than up and to the right.

- An articulated plate was placed on the right side of the carrier so as to prevent the loss of a shell during loading if the gun were canted.

- The buttstock was lengthened slightly and its drop reduced.

- The firing pin was blocked except when the bolt was closed and the gun ready to fire.

- The locking system was changed from that of the original 1893 so that the slide handle had to be pushed forward a fraction of inch *after* the hammer fell *before* the gun could be unlocked to eject one shell and chamber another.

This, and the full side-ejection, greatly reduced the hangfire danger potential of the 1893. It did not measurably decrease the rapidity of fire if the shells discharged normally, as their recoil automatically threw the forearm forward, permitting the same quick firing sequence of the 1893 with none of its danger.

The Model 97, and the Model 12 which followed, used essentially the same locking system and, when their triggers were depressed and their slides operated smartly, were as fast as any semi-auto.

In its introduction year, and for 20 years thereafter, the Plain Finished solid-frame 97 sold for the same price as the 1893 — $25 — and was first offered with the 1893's general specifications: 30-inch or 32-inch full-choked, rolled-steel barrel; small, quarter-pistol grip; uncheckered stock with grooved forearm; 12-gauge five-shot magazine, and solid frame.

The same optional "extras" of the 1893 were offered: three- or four-blade Damascus barrels; fancy walnut; and checkering of the buttstock. A version equipped with the higher-grade Damascus barrel and the other extras was carried in stock and cataloged as Fancy Finished at $60. Also offered were Trap and Pigeon guns which, with solid frames, were to last in production only until the acceptance of the takedown versions.

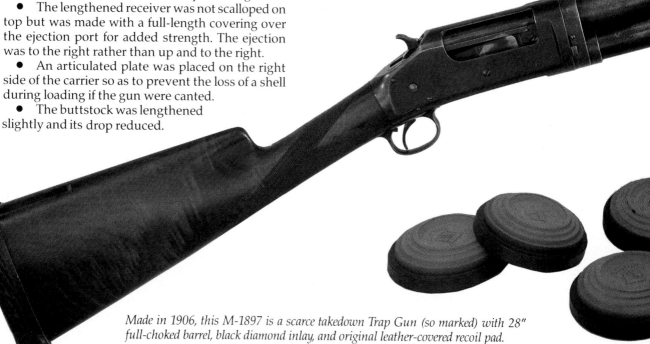

Made in 1906, this M-1897 is a scarce takedown Trap Gun (so marked) with 28" full-choked barrel, black diamond inlay, and original leather-covered recoil pad.

The final, original solid-framed offering was the Brush Gun which had a 26-inch cylinder-bored barrel and a shortened four-shot magazine — the only Model 97 regularly made by the factory with other than a 5+1 shell capacity.

By 1898, the takedown system was adopted. It was welcome, for the assembled gun measured about 52 inches overall and was far from convenient for the then common rail transportation to and from shooting events. When taken down, it fit relatively compactly in a canvas or leather Victoria case. The added cost for the new system, which employed an interrupted-thread adapter and an adjustment for taking up wear, was only $2, and interchangeable barrel/magazine/adapter units soon became available.

The 20-inch-barreled Riot gun also made its appearance in the 1898 catalog, but was first made only in solid frame. It was first seen in takedown style in the 1919 catalog of H&D Folsom Arms Co.

The Trap and Pigeon guns took to the takedown system and stayed with it. The Brush and Plain or Fancy Finished guns were made in both takedown and solid styles, and the takedown Brush gun reverted to the five-shot magazine.

In 1900, the 16-gauge takedown Plain Finished gun, chambered for the 2⅝-inch shell, was introduced. In time, 16-gauge Brush Guns, Pigeon Guns, and several Trap grades (in general "Trap" indicated a grade — not necessarily a shooting discipline) came into being, all in takedown only. The 16-gauge chambering was lengthened to 2¾ inches in 1931 but, by 1950, the 16-gauge, never as popular as the 12-gauge, was dropped entirely. A 20-gauge version never materialized.

The next style to evolve was the $42 Tournament Gun in 12 gauge only. In 1910, like the $52 Trap and $100 Pigeon grades, it was cataloged with straight stock and matted receiver top and barrel. The buttstock was checkered, as was the forearm, but the latter had a simpler pattern than the Trap and Pigeon grades. As opposed to those two, the Tournament was not "made to order" and no free options were offered. The Trap and Pigeon could be made to custom specifications without change in price with the major *catalogued* differences being 30-inch barrel on the Trap and 28-inch barrel on the engraved Pigeon grade.

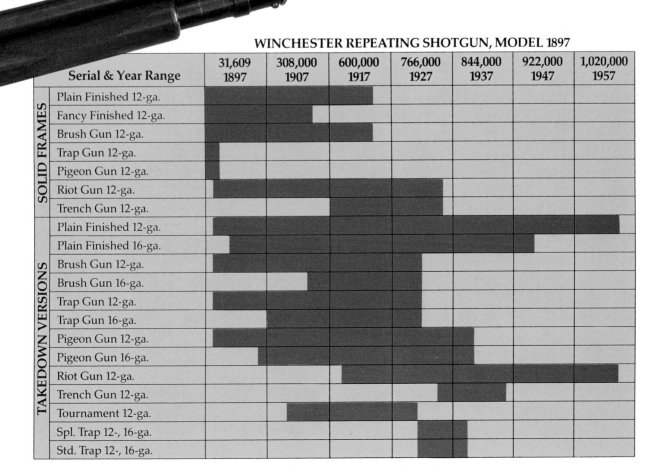

WINCHESTER REPEATING SHOTGUN, MODEL 1897

Serial & Year Range	31,609 1897	308,000 1907	600,000 1917	766,000 1927	844,000 1937	922,000 1947	1,020,000 1957
SOLID FRAMES Plain Finished 12-ga.							
Fancy Finished 12-ga.							
Brush Gun 12-ga.							
Trap Gun 12-ga.							
Pigeon Gun 12-ga.							
Riot Gun 12-ga.							
Trench Gun 12-ga.							
TAKEDOWN VERSIONS Plain Finished 12-ga.							
Plain Finished 16-ga.							
Brush Gun 12-ga.							
Brush Gun 16-ga.							
Trap Gun 12-ga.							
Trap Gun 16-ga.							
Pigeon Gun 12-ga.							
Pigeon Gun 16-ga.							
Riot Gun 12-ga.							
Trench Gun 12-ga.							
Tournament 12-ga.							
Spl. Trap 12-, 16-ga.							
Std. Trap 12-, 16-ga.							

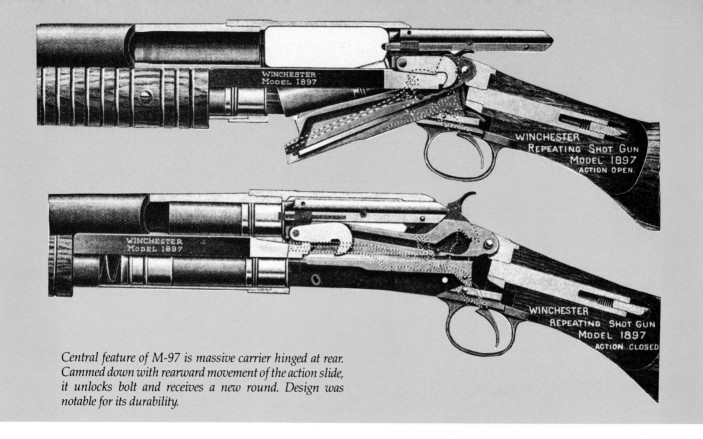

Central feature of M-97 is massive carrier hinged at rear. Cammed down with rearward movement of the action slide, it unlocks bolt and receives a new round. Design was notable for its durability.

All three had diamond-shaped ebony inserts located forward of the checkering on the buttstock which, though not mentioned in most Winchester catalogs, have led to the collector term "Black Diamond Grades."

The Tournament gun was phased out around 1931, and the so-called Special Trap and Standard Trap grades were phased in but lasted only about eight years. Both were made in 12- or 16-gauge, both had checkered buttstocks and forearms, but while the Special had the same straight stock as the previous Tournament gun (with black diamond showing in catalog cuts at least), the Standard had a half-pistol grip (no diamond) as found on the regular field guns of the time. In 1938, just before their discontinuance, the Standard and Special were priced at $48 and $83, respectively, as compared to $33 for the field gun and $190 for the Pigeon grade.

The above covers all the sporting Model 97 styles plus the Riot gun, leaving only the famous M1917 Trench gun with solid frame and its successor built on the takedown frame.

The M1917 was simply a modified Riot gun which had been used extensively by the U.S. armed forces since the Philippine Insurrection. The modification, by Springfield Armory and Winchester, consisted of a bayonet lug, perforated steel handguard, and sling swivels.

General Pershing had learned to appreciate the short shotgun's effectiveness in the Philippines and on the Mexican border prior to World War I, and saw to it that the A.E.F. had as many as Winchester could provide during World War I. This was the birth of the M1917 Trench gun. Fitted with an M1917 Enfield bayonet and M1907 leather sling, it and a few similarly equipped Model 10 Remingtons created enough uproar in the trench warfare in France to prompt an official protest from the Germans. By 1924, the solid-framed Trench gun began to appear in Winchester's commercial literature; by 1935 it had been supplanted by the same gun in takedown configuration, thus ending the production of solid-framed Model 97s altogether.

When World War II arrived, Winchester continued to supply Trench guns (takedowns by now though the bayonet lug and handguard made *quick* takedown impossible), but since trenches were not the modus operandi in the 1940s, the Army referred to the guns as "M97 Guard and Riot Guns." The older solid-framed M1917s and Riot guns lacking the bayonet lug or handguard were called back into service as well.

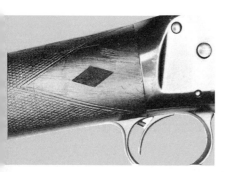

Ebony stock inlays on higher-grade M-97s (and M-12s) have led to the collector classification "Black Diamond."

The Army also used longer-barreled versions of the Model 97 for training. A full page Winchester ad in the July, 1943, AMERICAN RIFLEMAN showed a picture of ballistic engineer M.S. Robinson holding Model 97 No. 128,195 and had this to say about the gun:

"One of many Winchester guns, assigned exclusively to testing millions of Winchester shotshells annually, this particular Model 97 has been fired continuously for 29 years. Now affectionately known as Old Reliable, this veteran of two wars, having already fired 1,247,000 shots, tests the Winchester shells used today in training aerial machine gunners on how to lead fast-moving Axis planes…how to shoot them out of the skies. *Old Reliable has had its firing pin and spring renewed once.*"

The emphasis is ours, and while the author confesses to a bias in favor of the 97, he doubts that all will go the million-round-plus route without more than a firing-pin renewal.

After the war, only the Standard Models (the Plain Finish name had long been dropped) and the Riot guns — all takedowns — remained. By 1958 all, save a few being made from the parts in inventory, were sold.

Some young shooters realize the Model 97 is a bit of history worthy of much respect. Many of their parents say they wish they had bought a 97 before it was discontinued. Some of *their* parents still use theirs, having found nothing better. The few of *their* parents that are still shooting *know* there is nothing better.

While the standard catalog specifications and options of the Model 1897 were fairly easy to comprehend at its introduction, and even simpler at its discontinuance, there were countless changes and options made or offered during its 60-year production span. Some were incorporated at the time of delivery, others were the result of factory retrofitting or parts exchange by outside sources. The following only indicates the vast number of variables that might be of interest to owners or collectors:

ACTIONS

Winchester would *not* convert from solid frame to takedown — nor would it convert from 12- to 16-gauge or vice versa. Matted receiver tops were standard on Trap and Pigeon grades, but could be had on any grade.

BARRELS

Damascus three- or four-blade barrels were made in 12-gauge for solid frames and in 12- or 16-gauge for takedowns until 1914. Steel takedown barrels or interchangeable barrel units were once offered in the customer's choice of 26, 28, 30, or 32 inches for 12- and 16-gauge, plus 32 inches for 12-gauge only. Possible chokes for either gauge were full, improved modified, improved cylinder, No. 1 Skeet, No. 2 Skeet, and cylinder. Winchester's price list in 1946 stated: "Any combination of the foregoing barrel lengths and chokes or bore can be furnished at no extra charge." The 20-inch cylinder-bored barrels were standard on the Riot and Trench guns; 26-inch cylinder barrels were first standard on the Brush guns, but other chokes were later advertised. In the late 1920s and early 1930s, *stainless steel* barrels were offered at extra cost but few were supplied. No barrels were ever listed with three-inch chambers or with raised or ventilated ribs. Matted tops were standard on Trap and Pigeon grades but available on any grade.

BOLTS

"Trap Guns" and "Pigeon Guns" were usually clearly marked on appropriate bolt sides.

BUTTPLATES

Steel, or optional hard rubber, was first offered; soon the standard was hard rubber — steel optional. Rubber recoil pads by Winchester, Silver, Jostam, Hawkins, Goodrich, and others were installed on order. The Winchester pad, at least, could be faced or fully covered with leather. Plastic buttplates were standard by the late 1940s.

ENGRAVING AND FINISHES

Both receiver sides of the Pigeon gun were engraved with bird-shooting scenes, but any amount or style of engraving could be had on any grade to order. The standard finish was blue throughout, but plating was available on request at extra charge.

FOREARMS

Like the stocks, any grade of walnut could be had. In general, the higher the gun grade, the higher the walnut grade — and the price. Grooved forearms were standard on lower grades; checkering was applied to ungrooved higher grades.

STOCKS

Smooth on plain grades, checkered on higher grades. Any degree of checkering available on any grade. Cataloged lengths ranged from 13 to 14 inches, and many different lengths were noted in standard catalog descriptions. Any set of dimensions could be had on any grade. The straight stock was most common on Trap and Pigeon grades, but pistol grips could be had on order. Quarter-pistol grip was standard on field guns for about 10 years, then changed to half-pistol grip until discontinuance, but any style or dimension could be had on any grade at extra cost until the late 1940s.

The generous assistance of George Madis, who checked the data presented herein, is gratefully acknowledged.

PART FOUR

MUZZLELOADERS

Shooting & Hunting with the Small-Bore Muzzleloader

Sam Fadala

Small bores in muzzleloading language mean .40 caliber or less, according to my pigeonholing. Essentially, this range of calibers gives the shooter four over-the-counter caliber choices: .40, .38, .36, and .32, all firing patched balls. While there are many small conical missiles available, especially for the .36 and .32 calibers, it is the patched round ball which will be discussed here. The conicals are good and often useful, but they represent another branch of the sport.

Small-bore blackpowder rifle shooting offers great enjoyment. The rifles are sufficiently accurate for target work, plinking, and small game, with enough power for the larger varmints, wild turkey, and even javelina (peccary). The rifles are generally light, well balanced, and very pleasant to shoot. Because of their narrow barrels, small-bores are generally trim and graceful. Recoil is nil and they are very inexpensive to shoot.

A .40-caliber rifle is right at the juncture between small game and deer and is legal for deer in many areas. My own Ozark Mountain Arms Muskrat rifle in .40 caliber launches a .400-inch round ball weighing 96 grains at more than 1,900 fps. I have taken

antelope with it but do not consider .40 caliber completely adequate for deer. In the hands of a very good shot, a .40 will do. They have taken many, many deer. The .40 may seem to be in a no-man's land, too small for deer hunting in some states, and too large for small game. Nevertheless, the .40 caliber is quite useful: excellent for a local match, plinking, and games. It is less sensitive to wind deflection and adequate for game as large as javelina.

There is only one .38-caliber over-the-counter rifle I know of at the moment: the Richland Arms Plainsman. It fires the same .375-inch round ball of 80 grains weight used in the .36-caliber percussion revolver, offered in swaged form by Hornady and Speer, as well as many other missile makers. Illegal for deer where I live, the .38 is handy to shoot because of its "store-bought" ball, and is more than adequate for the larger varmints and turkey. With head shots the .38 is good for rabbit and squirrel hunting.

The .36 caliber is justifiably popular. It is excellent for small-game hunting with its .350-inch ball

This article first appeared in *RIFLE*.

weighing 65 grains. It is equally useful against most varmints and turkey, as well as large game *if* the marksman is careful about ball placement. The .36 caliber has a wide range of accuracy, but I have had very little success with less than 15 grains of FFFg in my own test guns.

The .36 caliber is more powerful at the muzzle than a .22 Rimfire Magnum, although the shape of the projectile encourages severe velocity/energy loss at long range, shedding more than 50 percent by the 100-yard mark. All the same, blackpowder, small-bore hunting is a stalking game, a true *hunting* game, and I have not found any lack of harvesting power on game as large as wild turkey at 50 to 75 yards using the .36 ball.

The little .32 is the smallest caliber encountered in the gunshop now. Plenty of small muzzleloading rifles have been made over the years, including a .20 caliber which fired a ball about .90 inch, weighing 10 grains. I was not always a fan of the .32, thinking it overly sensitive to wind and on the light side for game of the turkey class. Experience has changed my mind. The 45-grain .310-inch ball is plenty for a turkey at 50 yards — if it's placed properly.

The .32 is wonderfully economical to shoot. It will fire its ball with accuracy and offers plenty of punch for small animals using only 10 grains of FFFg or about eight grains of Pyrodex P. This means 700 shots per pound with FFFg and 875 shots with Pyrodex P — with .22 Long Rifle muzzle velocities. Projectiles can be home-cast of free or low cost lead. One can even make his own percussion caps using the Forster Tap-O-Cap tool, which turns empty aluminum (only) beverage cans into the cap body, using toy caps for the fire. Instructions come with the Tap-O-Cap unit and when followed, a good product is ensured.

Rifle style does not matter at all, since every

Photo by Rick Hacker

Muzzleloading shooter on a squirrel hunt. He's using .32-cal. Tennessee Squirrel Rifle from Dixie Gun Works. Same model also comes in percussion version.

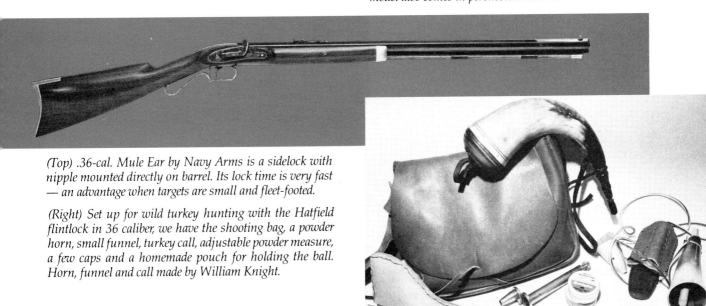

(Top) .36-cal. Mule Ear by Navy Arms is a sidelock with nipple mounted directly on barrel. Its lock time is very fast — an advantage when targets are small and fleet-footed.

(Right) Set up for wild turkey hunting with the Hatfield flintlock in 36 caliber, we have the shooting bag, a powder horn, small funnel, turkey call, adjustable powder measure, a few caps and a homemade pouch for holding the ball. Horn, funnel and call made by William Knight.

small-bore I have tested has performed well. However, there are some choices to be made. The first one is in the ignition. I have both flinter and percussion small-bores and enjoyed both.

A *quality* flintlock will fire with almost perfect reliability, provided it is clean and loaded correctly. My own Hatfield has seldom misfired. The flintlock means no cap purchase, for those looking for utmost shooting economy.

The caplock is more familiar, and we find percussions with bolster, such as the T/C Cherokee .32 or Seneca .36, and with the drum and nipple setup, such as the Muskrat and Dixie Squirrel Rifle possess. There is even a sidelock model, the Mule Ear .36 from Navy Arms, with its very direct ignition and straight line vent from cap to main charge in the breech.

There are no specific loading problems with the small-bores, but the rifling can foul quickly. Although I prefer a paste lube for big-game hunting, with its

good bore protection and lasting power on the patch, I prefer a liquid, such as Moose Milk® or Falkenberry Juice, for the small-bore. The damp patch cleans the bore to some degree as the ball is seated to the breech with loading rod or ramrod. This means more consecutive shots before cleanup. I have fired a .36 caliber 20 times in a row using a liquid lube with no pressure or accuracy problems — and no seating troubles.

In working up a small-game load, I simply shoot for accuracy, starting with the smallest charge that will group. Since revolutions per second (RPS) are a product of the rate of twist plus exit velocity, some squib loads simply do not work in small-bores. As ball mass decreases, more RPS are required to stabilize the missile. That is why my favorite big-bores, .50 caliber and up, have very slow rates of twist, 1:60, 1:70, and even slower. A good round-ball shooter of .32 or .36 caliber may carry a rate of twist of 1:48, or even faster. My own .32s will shoot accurately with

Nancy Fadala draws bead with T/C .32 Cherokee. Easy to manage, the little rifle is just right for the recoil-conscious. About as powerful as a .22 rimfire, it's even cheaper to shoot.

Introducing a lady hunter to blackpowder is best accomplished with a rifle of small caliber. Caplock shown is .32 Mowrey Squirrel Rifle. A charge as small as 10gr. of FFFg is perfectly adequate for most little animals yet recoil is almost absent.

Although .40-cal. balls are considered too light for big game, Gene Thompson used this Muskrat .40 to take his antelope. Long stalk enabled him to get close and place shot very carefully.

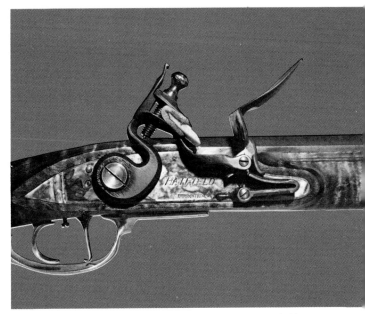

A fine lock makes a big difference in ignition. The Hatfield shown is one of the best. Note how high the touchhole is on barrel flat. It tends to stay free of powder, letting the spark leap from pan to main charge instantaneously, aiding speedy ignition. Lock time is also shortened by double set triggers.

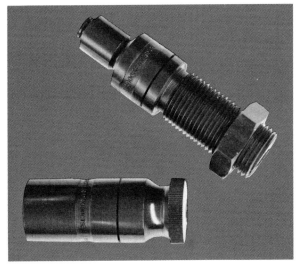

Forster Tap-O-Cap turns toy caps and aluminum cans into percussion caps. This clever tool will pay for itself in no time.

only 10 grains of FFFg, but my .36s seem to require 15 grains as a minimum. Naturally, bores vary and the shooter should start around 10 grains in his own .36 to see if accuracy is available, because small-game power will be possible with that charge.

Accuracy itself is, of course, commensurate with the quality of the barrel, load, and overall condition of the rifle. Good patches mean strong patches, but not always thick ones. I use a .012- to .013-inch patch of the tightest weave with most of my small-bores. Ball fit is another accuracy-related problem. In my own .40-caliber Muskrat, which I determine to have a 1:48 rate of twist (advertised as 1:40), a .400-inch ball is best. A .350 works well in the .36s, and a ball of .310 to .315 inch seems right for .32 caliber.

Trajectory for the smaller round balls is good enough for small-game hunting, most target work, plinking, and an occasional varmint. For example, .32- or .36-caliber rifles can be sighted dead on at 50 yards. This will put the ball an inch high at 25 and about two inches low at 75 — flat enough to omit holding over or under at normal small-bore ranges. This trajectory is based on a muzzle velocity of only 1,500 fps, a very mild load.

As for drift, any round ball is extremely susceptible to wind. As the diameter of the ball decreases, mass falls off way out of proportion. A .310-inch ball weighs only 45 grains, while a ball twice that diameter will go 562.

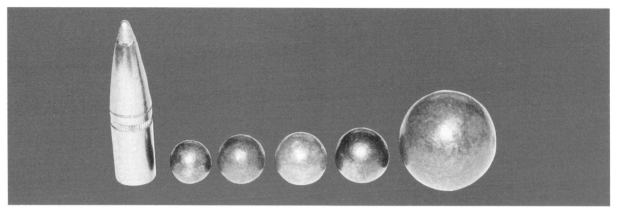

180-gr. .30-cal. spitzer flanked by round balls of various sizes. (L-R) .310" (.32 cal.), .350" (.36 cal.), .375" (.38 cal.), .395" (.40 cal.). (Far R) .690 ball weighing 494gr. Compare it with the little 45-gr. .310" sphere.

In the field, I have not found drift a real problem, even with a .32 caliber. Home-cast and factory-swaged balls for small-bores usually prove quite uniform, which aids accuracy and means that doping the wind can be calculated with some field sense tossed in for the right Arkansas windage.

Sights for most small-bores are quite good. A person with an eye problem could have a scope attached to his frontloaders, but I enjoy open sights on my own models. Adjustment is generally made by drifting the rear sight for windage. For elevation, the front sight is filed down to raise point of impact, or a taller sight is used to drop point of impact. There are also many small-bores offered with adjustable sights, such as the T/C Cherokee, Richland Arms Plainsman, Navy Arms Mule Ear, and others. With the first, I managed to get half-inch three-shot groups at 25 yards in one benchrest shoot.

Economical, enjoyable, accurate, capable of putting game in the pot or varmints in the minus column, the small-bore, blackpowder rifle is on the rise in popularity. A shooter with do-it-yourself interests can squeeze the most from a small-bore, working up the most accurate load for the smallest cost. No blackpowder or Pyrodex battery is complete without at least one sub-caliber in the rack.

EXAMPLE OF SMALL-BORE BALL UNIFORMITY

As an example of small-bore ball uniformity, ten .310-inch lead balls were selected at random from a box of Hornady swaged projectiles. Here is how they weighed:

(1) 44.7 grains	(6) 44.7 grains
(2) 44.6 grains	(7) 44.7 grains
(3) 44.7 grains	(8) 44.6 grains
(4) 44.7 grains	(9) 44.9 grains
(5) 44.7 grains	(10) 44.7 grains

The spread between the highest and lowest weight is but .3 grain. Both the mode and the mean are 44.7 grains. Obviously, such uniformity is very important to small-bore shooting because a one-grain variation in a 50-grain ball is a full two percent difference.

SAMPLE BALLISTICS FOR SELECTED SMALL-BORES

Charge (grains)	Muzzle Velocity (fps)	Muzzle Energy (ft/lb)	100-Yards Velocity (fps)	Energy (ft/lb)
Ozark Mountain Muskrat .40-Caliber Rifle (36" barrel)				
.395" test ball, 93-gr. weight				
20 FFFg	1,294	346	828	142
30 FFFg	1,584	518	927	177
40 FFFg	1,813	679	981	199
50 FFFg	1,993	820	1,017	214
Richland Arms Plainsman .38-Caliber Rifle (37" barrel)				
.375" test ball, 80-gr. weight				
20 FFFg	1,418	357	851	129
30 FFFg	1,686	505	944	158
40 FFFg	1,876	625	1,013	182
50 FFFg	1,930	662	1,051	196
Hatfield .36-Caliber Flintlock Rifle (39.5" barrel)				
.350" test ball, 65-gr. weight				
20 FFFg	1,471	312	794	92
25 FFFg	1,653	394	851	105
30 FFFg	1,799	467	882	112
40 FFFg	2,023	591	956	132
Thompson/Center .32-Caliber Cherokee Rifle (25" barrel, including breech plug)				
.310" test ball, 45-gr. weight				
10 FFFg	1,120	125	538	29
20 FFFg	1,649	271	775	60
30 FFFg	1,871	350	879	77

Blue Steel & Gray Smoke

Toby Bridges

While many historians often refer to the great American Civil War as the first "modern" war, the era could just as easily come to be known as the last of the "old" wars. With the outbreak of fighting between North and South, arms producers found themselves hard pressed to keep up with the demand for quality, serviceable arms.

Sophisticated new machinery and new manufacturing techniques were quickly developed and the resulting arms produced by both government arsenals and private contractors were some of the finest military arms the world has ever known.

The war also proved to be the testing ground for newly developed metallic-cartridge, breechloading arms, which in turn greatly changed some military tactics of the time. By the end of the war, the breechloader had established its superiority over the slow and cumbersome muzzleloading rifle-musket and left little doubt that it was destined to become the military arm of the future.

More than 1.5 million government-pattern .58 caliber percussion rifle-muskets were made at Springfield Armory and by a number of private contractors. Of the two Springfield Armory-designed models, the Model 1861 saw the greatest production and is generally considered the standard arm of the Civil War.

Actually, there are only a few distinguishing differences between this model and the later Model 1863. Perhaps the easiest to recognize difference is the carry-over of the oddly shaped Model 1855 hammer. Another distinguishable feature of the Model 1861 is the use of spring-shaped flat iron barrel bands.

Both the Model 1861 and Model 1863 Springfield featured a tapered round 40-inch barrel. The folding rear sight offered flip-up sight leaves for 100-, 300-, and 500-yard shooting. The standard service load was about 60 grains of FFg blackpowder and a huge 500-grain hollow-based Minie bullet. Getting such a heavy bullet to a target at 500 yards required quite an angled trajectory. Both models featured rifling of three wide lands and grooves with one-turn-in-72-inch rate of twist.

Although the two Springfield models enjoyed considerable parts interchangeability, the very similar-looking Special Model 1861 Contract rifle-musket did not enjoy this compatability. This 40-inch-barreled .58-caliber percussion rifle-musket was produced entirely by private contractors. Although the design of the musket has been attributed to Colt, the firms of Amoskeag Manufacturing Co. and Lamson, Goodnow & Yale Co. accounted for approximately half of the more than 177,000 Special Model 1861s produced from 1861 to 1865.

Many muzzleloading firearms authorities consider the Special Model 1861 rifle-musket to be the finest arm of its type ever produced. Surviving originals reveal some of the highest degree of military armsmaking from the Civil War years. The barrels of the Colt, Amoskeag, and L.G. & Y. produced guns are flawlessly machined without noticeable waves in the machining or polishing.

The three-groove rifling tapered from around .015-inch deep at the breech to .005-inch at the

This article first appeared in THE AMERICAN RIFLEMAN.

muzzle, an idea borrowed from the British Enfield rifle-musket. Even on original muskets in poor condition, the locks remain crisp and positive and inletting of the American black walnut stock precise. The Special Model 1861 muskets displayed quality more commonly found only in high-grade sporting arms.

Though American arms manufacturers made many technical advances during the early years of the Civil War, they still couldn't quite meet the demand for military arms. To supplement the arms produced by American makers, the U.S. government purchased more than a million arms from French, Belgian, Austrian, Prussian, and British makers.

Most of these arms were considered inferior to the American-made muskets, except for one — the .577-caliber Pattern 1853 Enfield. More than 425,000 Enfield rifle-muskets were carried by U.S. troops during the war; the accuracy and reliability of the British-produced muskets were on a par with any American-produced percussion long gun.

The Enfield Pattern 1853 rifle-musket had a lengthy 39-inch barrel. Designed expressly for shooting the hollow-based Minie-type bullet, the Enfield musket was rifled with three lands and grooves, the latter tapering from around .015-inch deep at the breech to .005-inch at the muzzle.

This type rifling loaded easily with the Minie bullet and produced very acceptable accuracy with the big slugs. Except for the slightly slower one-in-78-inch rate of twist, the rifling is practically the same as found in the Special Model 1861 rifle-musket.

As testimony to the quality of the percussion Civil War muskets, thousands are still in use today by muzzleloading competitors, especially among members of the North/South Skirmish Association. A shootable original Springfield, Special Model 1861 or British Enfield is becoming harder and harder to find.

Most really prime specimens are now either in antique arms collections, destined never to be shot again, or already in the hands of a dedicated blackpowder shooter who knows how difficult it would be to replace his prized old shooter. Even if a solid, serviceable musket with a good bore could be located, discretion should be used before subjecting a piece of 120-year-old American heritage to the rigors of every-day shooting.

Fortunately for those blackpowder burners with a strong desire to own and shoot these colorful military arms, there are now a number of extremely high quality, entirely modern reproductions of these well-built Civil War long guns. The attention to detail and quality of some make them more appropriately recreations of the real thing!

Navy Arms' copy of the Springfield Model 1863 has been around since the mid-1970s. When first introduced, the gun was being produced in Japan. Today, the gun is manufactured entirely in the

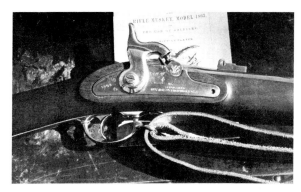

Navy Arms 1863 musket closely matches original arm, but lock markings ensure that it won't be mistaken for real thing.

United States at Navy Arms' manufacturing facility in Union City, New Jersey.

It sports a 40-inch, 50-caliber barrel fitted with the regulation folding-leaf rifle-musket rear sight with notches for 100-, 300-, and 500-yard shooting. The bore has three wide lands and grooves, the latter running right at .005-inch deep at the muzzle. The rate of twist in the new barrel is closer to one in 66 inches than one in 72 inches. The slightly faster rate of twist is much better suited for shooting some of today's improved Minie designs.

Current production muskets are stocked with a very good grade of straight-grained American walnut and authentically oil finished. The finish has been buffed to a satin sheen. All contours of the stock are sharp and clean, inletting well executed.

Metal finish on original Model 1863 muskets often varied, with the front and rear sight, barrel bands, and occasionally other parts blued. However, except for the case-hardened lock plate and hammer that were pretty well standard on this model, most other metal parts were generally polished bright and left in the white.

Typical Enfield type rear sight.

All metal parts, including the lock plate and hammer, have received this treatment on the Navy Arms rifle-musket. Unless a shooter wants to keep these parts bright and purposely polishes them constantly, the unfinished metal will take on a natural light brown patina after several months of use, especially the more the musket is handled with blackpowder-soiled hands.

The massive musket hammer of the lock is powered by a beefy mainspring that insures ignition with the big winged musket caps used to fire the new Model 1863. The heavy, bevel-edged lock plate is marked with an eagle just forward of the hammer, along with "U.S." and "Springfield" over the Navy Arms name. To the rear of the hammer is stamped the date "1863." The only other markings found on metal parts are the serial number on the left side of the barrel and the Navy Arms name and address on top of the barrel, just behind the rear sight. The left side of the walnut stock, just to the rear of the back sidelock screw, bears the cartouche "VAB," done in the manner of the ESA (Erskine S. Allin) inspector's cartouche found on original Model 1863 muskets.

Navy Arms' copy of this historic Civil War musket displays excellent, very authentic lines. However, the reproduction is actually a composite copy of two slightly different variations of the same model. The first type Model 1863 was built without the barrel band springs found on the earlier Model 1861. The upper and lower barrel bands were split and fastened in place by a screw through the bottom.

The second type was built with solid upper and lower bands and once again relied on band springs to hold these in place. On both, the middle band was split at the bottom to fit the upper sling swivel. The Navy Arms reproduction features the split lower band of the first type and the solid upper band of the second type, all still retained by band springs.

This well-built American-made Civil War long gun reproduction is available from Navy Arms Co., 689 Bergen Blvd., Ridgefield, NJ 07657. At this writing the suggested retail price is $380 for the factory-finished gun and $310 for a fully inletted kit.

Springfield Firearms Corp. of Springfield, Massachusetts, currently produces what has to be the ultimate reproduction Civil War rifle-musket. The modern copy of the Special Model 1861 contract musket produced by this relatively new armsmaking firm is so close to the original that practically all parts will interchange with a Colt, Amoskeag or L.G. & Y. Special Model 1861 that was produced during the Civil War. The Springfield Firearms Corp. reproduction of the Special Model 1861 is such an authentic copy of this gun that about the only things missing are the inspector's marks that would distinguish the gun as original!

The lock of an original L.G. & Y.-produced Special Model 1861 will often readily interchange with the lock of the modern reproduction. The lock plates are an exact match and with either lock in either mortise, the fit is perfect. The internal parts of the new lock will also fit right onto the original plate, with the exception of the bridle and sear screws. These screws from the old lock will fit the new-made plate, but the new screws seem to be just a little too large in diameter to fit the holes in the L.G. & Y. lock plate.

All other parts of the Springfield Firearms Corp.-produced rifle-musket are of the same high quality and display the same closeness with parts from an original. The steel barrel bands, of the split type tightened in place with a screw, are even stamped with the "U" also found on the bands of the L.G. & Y.-produced musket. Other authentic markings found on the new gun include the eagle stamping on the side of the bolster of the breech and the "U.S." stamping on the tang of the buttplate.

The "U.S." over "Springfield Firearms Corp." and "Springfield Mass" forward of the hammer help distinguish the modern copy as just that. The "SFC" stamped at the left rear of the barrel and the

Dixie Gun Works' modern copy of the British Enfield rifled-musket shown with a variety of accessories also currently available.

"SF" stamped into the left side of the stock between the two sidelock screws are also markings common only to the modern reproduction. Other than these slight differences, cosmetically the new musket is a dead ringer for the original.

H&H Barrel Works makes the barrels for the Springfield Firearms Corp. rifle-musket, and like all the muzzleloading barrels produced by this maker, the barrel is strictly first-class. The bore features the three wide lands and grooves designed for shooting the hollow-based Minie bullet. Like the original Special Model 1861 musket, the barrel features rifling that starts out at .015-inch deep at the breech end of the tapered round barrel and decreases to just .005-inch deep at the muzzle.

The rear sight is the regulation U.S. musket type rear sight with folding sight leaves graduated for 100-, 300-, and 500-yard shooting. The front sight of the reproduction is the same square lug post that doubles for attachment of a bayonet, but instead of being silver-soldered to the barrel as on the original,

the sight on the modern-made musket has been fitted with a dove-tailed base, allowing some windage adjustment. The sights are the only metal parts that are blued, all other parts have been buffed bright and left in the white, just as were the original muskets.

The modern copy has been rifled with one-in-63-inch twist, which is a little faster than the twist found in Civil War barrels. The faster twist offers better accuracy with the improved Minie bullet designs, which have a shorter ogive than the traditional Civil War bullet. Hoppy Hopkins, president of H&H Barrel Works, used one of the Springfield Firearms Corp. Special Model 1861 muskets during an invitational international muzzleloading match in 1982 and won a gold medal shooting one of the wadcutter-design hollow-based target Minies.

From its H&H barrel to its one-piece Reinhard Fajen-turned American black walnut stock and authentically reproduced parts, here is a superb reproduction of the Special Model 1861 rifle-musket that should receive approval from even the most discriminating shooter. As can be expected, such quality and attention to detail doesn't come cheap. Current suggested retail of the Special Model 1861 reproduction is $550, from Springfield Firearms Corp., 604 Cottage St., Springfield, MA 01104.

Dixie Gun Works, of Union City, Tennessee, currently offers a very good copy of the British Pattern 1853 Enfield rifle-musket. The originals of this arm saw extensive use by both North and South during the Civil War. In addition to the more than 400,000 Enfields purchased by the U.S. government, the Confederacy may have purchased as many as 700,000 of the British-built muskets, which would make the Enfield the most widely used arm of the American Civil War.

Dixie's Italian-made copy of the P-1853 Enfield (Dixie designates it the 1862) rifle-musket sports a 39-inch tapered round barrel that comes rifled with the standard three-groove rifling for shooting the Minie bullets. Instead of the slow one-in-78-inch twist found in the original Enfield barrel, the Italian manufacturer of this musket has elected to rifle the bore with a much faster one-in-48-inch twist. Rifling depth runs right at .007-inch.

The rear sight of the Dixie three-band Enfield rifle-musket closely follows the design of the original. With the sight in the folded-down position, the musket should be on target at about 100 yards. A sliding elevator raises the rear notch by fitting into steps along each side of the arrangement and is calibrated for 200, 300, and 400 yards.

With the sight bar flipped all the way up, a notch on the sliding elevator can be adjusted for 500-, 600-, 700-, and 800-yard shooting, while another notch atop the sight bar is supposed to have the musket hitting on at 900 yards! The front sight is a simple

Capital "U" on barrel band of Springfield Firearms Corp.'s rifled musket reflects authentic detailing.

Springfield Firearms Corp.'s name on lockplate is the only significant difference between modern-made arm and original Springfield Special M-1861. Maker also stamps its letter codes on both stock and barrel.

bladed lug that doubles to hold the bayonet in place.

Compared to most American-produced Civil War arms, the British Enfields were highly finished, with a deeply blued barrel and barrel bands, case-hardened lock plate and hammer, and polished brass buttplate, trigger guard, and nose cap.

Comparing Dixie's modern copy to the Springfield Model 1863 and Special Model 1861 reproductions, the same is still true. The only real deviation from the original is found with the barrel bands. On the original Enfield rifle-musket, the three screw-retained bands were made of blue steel. Dixie's modern version sports brass bands that have been anodized with a hard, scratch-proof black finish.

The Pattern 1853 Enfield rifle-musket available from Dixie Gun Works should appeal to the Civil War arms fan with a limited budget. This top-quality reproduction represents something of a bargain at just $285. It's available from Dixie Gun Works, Inc., Gunpowder Lane, Union City, TN 38261.

All three rifles have been approved for competition by the North/South Skirmish Association. Of the three, the Navy Arms Model 1863 proved to be less choosy about its loading during test firing. Lyman's No. 575213-OS 460-grain "Old-Style" Minie ahead of the standard 60-grain service charge of FFg blackpowder consistently turned in the best performance in this musket. With the bullets as cast by the mold, four-inch groups at 100 yards were fairly common. By running the big slug through one of Dixie Gun Works' .58-caliber sizing dies, a perfect .575 diameter was guaranteed and accuracy with the same load tightened to around three inches at 100 yards.

Without prior sizing, the Lyman bullet wouldn't even begin to fit into the muzzles of the Springfield Firearms Corp. musket or the Dixie Enfield. Once sized, the bullet slipped right in and seated easily over the powder charge. In fact, all bullets fired in these two rifle-musket reproductions required sizing before they could be loaded, including several of the Lee Precision bullet designs.

Ahead of the 60-grain service charge of FFg blackpowder, the Lyman "Old Style" Minie gave only mediocre accuracy in the reproduction Special Model 1861. The best five-shot groups fired at 100 yards still measured around five inches across. The .575/472M Lee Precision improved traditional Minie ahead of the same powder charge shrank average group size to a little over three inches, while the Lee .578/476M modern target (wadcutter) Minie punched neat little clusters at 100 yards that measured just barely over 2½ inches. The latter was the best accuracy obtained with any of the three muskets tested, which is pretty darn impressive for such a large-bored gun and big bullet.

Dixie's Enfield reproduction held its own with the Model 1863 and Special Model 1861 reproduc-

A good selection of modern reproduction rifled-muskets allow today's black powder shooter/historian to experience shooting the big bored Civil War muskets.

tions, and turned in a number of three- to four-inch groups with the Lyman "Old Style" Minie. Like the Springfield Firearms Corp. musket, the Italian-made Enfield showed a preference for the Lee Precision bullets, especially the wadcutter-styled Minie. Ahead of the 60-grain charge of FFg, the bullet could be counted on to punch three- to four-inch groups. With a slightly lighter 50-grain charge of FFg, most groups with the target Minie were consistently closer to three inches.

As crude as the sighting arrangements of all three muskets appeared, all surprisingly hit fairly well on at 100 yards. The Springfield Firearms Corp. Special Model 1861 would keep most of its hits inside the six-inch black bull used during test firing, while the Navy Arms Model 1863 impacted about three inches low and the Dixie Enfield rifle-musket punched the target paper about that distance above point of aim with the 60-grain powder charge.

Colonel LeMat's Grapeshot Revolver

Phil Spangenberger

War often fosters invention, and the American Civil War, considered by many to be our first modern war, saw more revolutionary ideas in firearms than almost any other conflict. One of the most interesting and romanticized handguns — although little hard fact is known about it — is the LeMat revolver. This unique Rebel revolver was the highly prized personal sidearm of cavalrymen in gray, Southern sailors, and such heroic Confederate leaders as General James Ewell Brown ("Jeb") Stuart and General P.G.T. Beauregard. Its unique design, sleek looks, and battle load of nine pistol shots, plus a hefty load of buckshot, made it a formidable arm by anyone's standards!

The LeMat was the result of the inventive genius of a New Orleans Frenchman, Dr. Jean Alexander Francois LeMat, a devout Confederate who gave up his medical practice in order to pursue supplying the Southern cause with his extraordinary revolver. Actually, Dr. LeMat had been working on the idea for this arm for several years before the War between the States, and it was granted patent number 15925 from the U.S. Patent Office on October 21, 1856. For the next couple of years, it is believed that Dr. LeMat continued with his medical career while he promoted his unusual revolver.

On March 2, 1859, a trial board comprised of prominent members of the military and the political world was held. The board, held in New Orleans, included such distinguished names as Lieutenant Colonel Braxton Bragg (who was recently retired from the U.S. Army and was later to become a Confederate general) and Major Pierre Gustave Toutant Beauregard. (Then an army Engineer officer and later to become one of the Confederacy's foremost generals, Beauregard was also soon to enter a partnership with LeMat for production of his revolver.) The board overwhelmingly favored the adoption of the LeMat for the armed services, especially the cavalry. Part of their report stated: "...We consider this arm far superior to any we have seen for the use of cavalry against Indians or when charg-

ing on a square of infantry or a battery of field pieces. It is also indispensable for artillerists in defending their pieces against such a charge, and for infantry defending a breach...Its advantages in the naval service in boarding or repelling boarders is too obvious to require anything but passing notice...

"It is more than probable that the introduction and use of this pistol in the cavalry service would give to the latter the preponderance over the infantry, if not armed in like manner, for what would become of a line or square of infantry after its fire should have been drawn by the cavalry when the latter coming up to within a few paces would pour 10 shots into their very faces..."

A little over a month later, on April 4, Major P.G.T. Beauregard officially became Dr. LeMat's partner. According to the contract agreed upon by both men, one fourth of LeMat's patent rights would go to Beauregard in exchange for a financial investment and favors which the army major was able to procure.

In May of that same year, another trial board was convened, this time in Washington, D.C., and it was this board's recommendation that the LeMat revolver "be subjected to trial in the hands of troops that are in actual service in the field." Although this board was staffed by such military notables as Lieutenant Colonel Joseph E. Johnston of the First U.S. Cavalry (later to become a Confederate General) and Brevet Major and Captain of Ordnance, T.T.S. Laidley (who later designed the U.S. Army's rifle targeting system which promoted accurate shooting by the private soldier), no government field trials were ever actually held.

However, inspired by the Washington, D.C. board's favorable comments, Dr. LeMat patented and improved the hammer for his "grapeshot" revolver, then traveled abroad, spending the next several months securing patents on his handgun in England, Belgium, Russia, Spain, Prussia, and

This article first appeared in *GUNS & AMMO*.

Navy Arms LeMat looks right at home with original London-made "LeMat & Girard" revolver. Also displayed are southern-produced officer's sword, Rebel Zouave officer's jacket from the Chichester's Zouaves (South Carolina volunteer unit of Hampton's Legion), 1860s pocket watch, South Carolina kepi, and Confederate currency.

Original LeMat revolver and Confederate items from the collection of Bob Lewis

Photo by Pat Brollier

Saxony. It is also believed that he made the necessary arrangements for the manufacture of his LeMat revolver during this trip.

While abroad, LeMat employed a Dr. Charles F. Girard as a "special agent" in Europe. Girard was soon to become a full-fledged partner, owning a three-quarter interest in LeMat's patent rights! In April of 1860, Major Beauregard sold his interest in LeMat's patent rights back to the inventor. By July of that year, the new partnership with Dr. Girard was agreed upon and the firm of C. Girard & Co. was established. Apparently, LeMat himself was content to stay in the background working on improvements and new models of his revolver, along with pursuing possible sales, for a one-fourth interest.

By the spring of 1861, the bitterness between the North and South erupted into the secession of the Southern states from the Union. Knowing that the new Southern Confederacy would need arms and equipment for a war that statesmen on both sides predicted was forthcoming, Dr. LeMat traveled to Montgomery, Alabama where the Confederate government was being formed. It was also around this time that Dr. LeMat became Colonel LeMat, evidently taking advantage of a complimentary title bestowed on him by the Louisiana governor. In 1859, "Colonel" LeMat served on the governor's

LeMat's smoothbore barrel nipple is found in frame, under the hammer, rather than on cylinder.

staff as aide-de-camp. As a result of his presence, he procured a contract to supply 5,000 grapeshot revolvers to the Confederate Army. Another order for 3,000 LeMats was soon obtained from the Southern Navy and production of these guns was set up in France.

Recent research has revealed that there was no LeMat factory as such. Rather, these arms were produced in a "cottage industry" arrangement; different parts of the LeMat were produced by small shops capable of making individual components, instead of having the entire gun turned out in a

Gen. Beauregard (L) and Gen. Jeb Stuart (R) favored the LeMat grapeshot revolver over all others as personal sidearms.

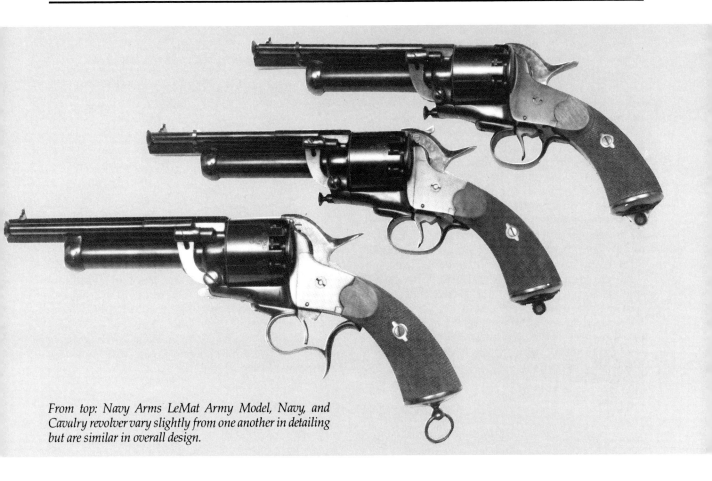

From top: Navy Arms LeMat Army Model, Navy, and Cavalry revolver vary slightly from one another in detailing but are similar in overall design.

single factory. This is sometimes known as a "wheelbarrow factory," in that quantities of completed parts would be loaded in a wheelbarrow, or small cart, and transported to the next stage of operation, until the handguns were completed.

These first army revolvers were percussion arms, made with .42-caliber, nine-shot cylinders that rotated around a five-inch smoothbore barrel of .63 caliber for firing buckshot or a larger, specially designed disintegrating ball load. However, due to problems with the Confederate purchasing agent in France, and the rapid devaluation of Southern currency, only around 900 pistols appear to have been delivered to the Rebel army and about 600 LeMats to the Confederate Navy during the war.

Problems resulting from the use of malleable cast iron in the LeMat's frame, barrel, and cylinder plagued both C. Girard & Co. and the Confederate government throughout the entire conflict. Finished LeMats were first shipped directly to the Confederacy where they were inspected, and either accepted or rejected. Those revolvers that did not meet the Southerners' standards were offered for private sale in the South.

Ironically, despite these problems, the Confederate government, in 1864, placed yet a third contract for 2,000 pistols of the modified "Baby LeMat" pat-

tern, which (briefly) was a smaller version offered with a nine-shot, .32-caliber cylinder with a 4½-inch barrel and a .41-caliber smoothbore underbarrel which measured a scant 2¾ inches. These Baby

Civil War cavalrymen who used the LeMat found it to be a reliable and effective sidearm.

LeMats (as was true of their larger brothers) were by now required to be made in France, but were shipped to London, England, for inspection and proving. Although this process saved some time for the ill-fated Confederacy, it proved too costly and time consuming for the Girard firm, and the production of all LeMat revolvers was moved to Birmingham, England's gunmaking center.

By the end of the war, only about 100 of these smaller LeMats were completed and ready for inspection. None ever reached the Confederate States. It appears that the production of the LeMat revolver ceased shortly after the War between the States ended. A few pinfire versions were produced, but for all practical purposes, manufacture and sales of any LeMats, percussion or pinfire, ended soon after Appomattox. It is estimated that less than 3,000 percussion revolvers and only a handful of pinfires were ever turned out. Nonetheless, those that did make their way to southern shores were favored sidearms, as they offered the fighting man a fierce handgun with the potential of 10 successive shots without reloading — including a formidable buckshot charge.

Navy Arms replicas are marked at top of barrel in a variation of original LeMats.

Val Forgette, often referred to as the "Father of Modern Blackpowder" for his introduction nearly 30 years ago of affordable and shootable reproductions of Civil War-era revolvers and long arms, can now add the colorful LeMat replica to his muzzle-loading laurels.

Val's firm, Navy Arms Co., is offering three models of the LeMat grapeshot revolver which they term the Army Model, the Navy Model, and the

Cavalry Model, which author found easiest to disassemble, takes down by (1&2) lowering lever located at base of frame. Next, unscrew barrel assembly (3&4) lift it from smoothbore barrel —which also serves as cylinder axis. Cylinder can now be removed from its position (5) and basic disassembly is complete. It is estimated that only around 3,000 percussion LeMat revolvers and only a handful of pinfire models were ever produced.

(L) Army and Cavalry Model LeMats share same swivel system of two small pins on both sides of hammer nose to lower smooth-bore barrel's hammer. (R) Navy Model uses stud found at top of hammer.

Cavalry Model. Each of these guns features minor variations found in original LeMats of the last century. Externally, these handguns are fit and finished beautifully. They feature highly-polished blue octagon rifled pistol barrels that measure 6¾ inches long with a 4⅞-inch-long .65-caliber smoothbore tube underneath. The nine-shot, .44-caliber cylinder, the loading-lever assembly, frame, trigger guard, and backstrap are all blued and polished as well. The guns' triggers and hammers are nicely color casehardened, and the two-piece walnut stocks are handsomely cut checkered about 18 lines to the inch, with a blued-escutcheon plate neatly inset on each side.

Additionally, each model's cylinder sports a bit of floral embellishment around the outer surface by the cone (nipple) of each chamber. This decoration, along with a border of tiny dots encircling the forward section of the cylinder, appears to be roll-engraved, or etched in — whichever method was used, it serves the revolver well and does enhance the overall look of the LeMat. As well, the top of each model's barrel is stamped with the name, "Colonel LeMat," framed within a fancy Victorian filigree-styled border. The front sight is a blued dovetailed wide-based bead, and while the rear sight is nothing more than a notch in the hammer in the manner of the percussion Colts, for all practical purposes, it is non-existent. The LeMat is a fistful of firepower, weighing in at three pounds, seven ounces, and measuring a full 13 inches from stem to stern.

During the photography session for this article, we had the opportunity to compare a Navy Arms LeMat replica with an original percussion arm from longtime Confederate arms collector Bob Lewis. All hands present were impressed with the attention to detail shown on Val Forgette's copy — including Bob who like most collectors is a real stickler for authenticity!

As far as variations are concerned, the Army and Navy Model LeMats share the same lanyard ring extension at the base of the grip. Their loading assemblies are held in position in a similar manner

— a cradle arm, which is screwed into the under portion of the pistol barrel, and a ramrod head indentation holding it in place at the muzzle. These two revolvers both utilize the same frame-disassembly pin system. The major distinction between the two is the method used to fire the grapeshot underbarrel. All three LeMats are made with the smoothbore barrel's cone built into the upper-rear section of the gun's frame. This barrel is fired by manually switching the spring-loaded pivoting underbarrel hammer nose downward into firing position. To shift the Navy model's underbarrel hammer into firing position, simply push forward on the protruding lever found at the top of the hammer. The Army and Cavalry models utilize small pins found on each side of the revolver's hammers. By merely pushing the pins downward, the underbarrel hammers are moved into firing position.

Loading-lever assembly of Navy Arms reproduction is located on revolver's left side, as are some on Civil War LeMats.

My personal favorite LeMat is the Cavalry model. This is almost identical to the actual revolver used by General "Jeb" Stuart during the Great Rebellion. Stuart was the epitome of the Southern Cavalryman and literally rode circles around the Yankee army! This version has the spur trigger guard, which was originally designed to aid mounted troopers in holding their handguns steady while handling a plunging or bolting cavalry steed. I think the spur addition to the trigger guard adds class to the gun and lends a certain raciness to it. Two other features I prefer on the Cavalry LeMat are the loading-lever assembly's simple muzzle indentation (a means of holding it in place), and the lever system employed for breaking down the barrel assembly from the frame. Both GUNSMITH editor Garry James and I found this to be easier and faster to operate than the pin system of the Army and Navy Models.

Four non-firing prototypes were sent to us for examination — two Cavalry Models, one Army, and one Navy Model — so we restricted ourselves to visual scrutiny along with basic disassembly of each version. As handsome as these arms were externally, both Garry and I felt that their internal workings could have been finished better. However, since both of us are blackpowder addicts, it is not surprising that we are eagerly awaiting the arrival of a shooting version of the Navy Arms LeMat. What *is* surprising is that several of our non-muzzleloader associates are equally excited about the LeMat replicas and are even considering adding one of them to their personal batteries. What better testimonial is there than that? As of this writing, production of the LeMat is under way, and a finished shooting LeMat will be available by the time you read this. They are scheduled to retail for about $500 per copy, and due to cost of manufacturing, will be made in a limited run only.

Navy Arms will also offer a deluxe set which will feature a LeMat engraved in the same manner as General P.G.T. Beauregard's personal sidearm. This revolver will be cased, along with a copy of a book co-authored by Val Forgette and Alan Serpette on the history of the LeMat. This volume promises to reveal some new insight into the firearm's past, along with many interesting photos of original guns. This deluxe set will sell for $1,000. If you are like me, and your pulse quickens when you see a gun like the rare and exciting LeMat being offered, then you'll definitely want to own a Navy Arms LeMat replica. For further information on the availability of the LeMat reproduction, write to Navy Arms Co., Inc., 689 Bergen Blvd., Ridgefield, NJ 07957.

Above: Rammer for use in tamping down load in smoothbore tube, is snugly fitted into LeMat's loading lever. (R) To use it, simply withdraw it from lever, invert it, and tamp down under-barrel's charge.

PART FIVE

AIR GUNS

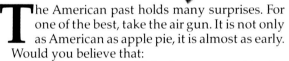

The Air Gun of Lewis & Clark

Ashley Halsey, Jr.

The American past holds many surprises. For one of the best, take the air gun. It is not only as American as apple pie, it is almost as early. Would you believe that:

— The air gun was widely demonstrated in the United States first to Indians, not whites?

— These demonstrations took place not in the settled East but in the untamed, unmapped West?

— Between 1804 and 1806 the air gun was used as a diplomatic means of impressing the Indians to be peaceful and cooperative?

— The rare air gun actually used still exists and is no mere BB gun but a powerful .31-caliber poly-groove rifle?

This uniquely historical arm was carried across the young nation and back on the first major government exploration of the West. The U.S., having acquired the vast expanse of land beyond the Mississippi River by the Louisiana Purchase, was curious to learn exactly what lay out there. President Thomas Jefferson ordered two young army officers, Captains Meriwether Lewis and William Clark, to lead a mapping exploration to the

Pacific coast. They were to traverse areas never before seen by white men. In terms of high adventure and deadly risk, the expedition in its day and time compares with the first human ventures into space. Nobody knew precisely where they were going or whether they would ever get back.

Everyone from President Jefferson down wanted the intrepid little band of soldiers and frontiersmen to have the best arms. They were issued the very latest: U.S. Model 1803 half-stock flintlock rifles, .54 caliber, newly made at Harpers Ferry Armory. Lewis took a further step to equip himself.

Air guns, far from having been perfected by Daisy in the present century as many Americans assume, date back in sophisticated forms to the 1600s and earlier in Europe. As with the wheellocks of the 1400s and 1500s, hand-production from mediocre materials severely limited the quantity of air guns. But Lewis located one made relatively recently in America. In his diary, he referred to "my air gun which I had purchased." Quaintly, he termed it

This article first appeared in *THE AMERICAN RIFLEMAN.*

"she" and "herself" as if it were feminine. Oddly and unfortunately, the gun's first victim was.

The expedition set out by boat down the Ohio River from Pittsburgh, Pennsylvania, on November 19, 1803. It paused at a riverside gathering only three miles downstream because of shoal water and possibly for refreshments. Lewis tells how, being invited to demonstrate the air rifle (and probably requiring little urging), he "fired myself seven times at 55 yards with pretty good success." Then a local gentleman undertook to test the unfamiliar gun. He accidentally zipped a ball "through the hat of a woman about 40 yards distant, cutting her temple

Lewis air rifle (top) and another made by Lukens resemble flintlocks except for air-valve strikers above their locks.

about a fourth the diameter of the ball." The woman fell, gushing blood. The wound proved "by no means mortal or even dangerous," however, and the little expedition paddled on to glory.

Nearly every literate Lewis & Clark party member kept a diary, and many mention the air gun. The official record cites its use 18 or 19 times. Although apparently an excellent weapon for taking small game and deer quietly, the air gun figured largely as "strong medicine" to impress the Indians. Many of them never had seen a paleface, but flintlock trade muskets had reached their hands from other tribes. Flintlocks meant sparks, smoke, and thunder-clap noise. Enter, by contrast, "Big Magic" in the form of a smokeless, soundless rifle.

Near where Sioux City, Iowa, now stands, Sergeant John Ordway recorded how the Indians swarmed around asking for gunpowder and "our Great Father's milk," meaning whiskey. Ordway noted, "the Commanding Officer shewed [sic] them the air gun…which pleased them very much." On another occasion when Lewis fired the rifle, "They appeared to be astonished at the sight of it and the execution it would do." The target performances continued across what are now six or seven western states. After one, Ordway recorded, the Indians returned to their village and respectfully raised a U.S. flag that had been given to them.

The amazing air gun that Meriwether Lewis sometimes waved about like a magician's wand was indeed calculated to make an impression. Its 34-inch octagon barrel was entirely brass, full-stocked to the muzzle. The muzzle was ornamented with small circles like a Pennsylvania or Kentucky rifle. The Kentucky-style trigger guard and fittings consisted of silver or German silver.

The .31-caliber lead balls were loaded singly through the muzzle, although a few advanced air guns of the type had gravity-fed breech magazines. The typical rifle ramrod appears to have been seldom used. Relatively fine, shallow 15-groove rifling, differing from the usual six or seven deep grooves of Kentucky rifles, gave the bullet a snug fit that rendered the customary patching and ramming unnecessary.

Instead of a wood buttstock, the rifle had a pneumatic butt reservoir scarcely distinguishable from a regular butt, although it was actually a sheet-metal flask welded strongly to hold pressurized air. To pump up the flask, it was detached from the frame or receiver. A plunger-type piston pump fitted with two internal piston rings enabled the shooter to raise air pressure up to 900 psi — about 30 times that of a modern car tire. The butt reservoir, once pumped up with as many as 1,000 strokes, retained enough air for 40 shots.

The pump incorporated an ingenious labor-savor. Most air-gun pumps of the period included a cross bar at the far end from the coupling with the butt reservoir. They were laboriously operated either by putting the bar under the feet and pushing down or by using the bar as a handle. The far end of the Lewis rifle pump, by contrast, consisted of a large screw that could be screwed into a tree or wooden building. The pumper then simply put his shoulder to the butt and rocked back and forth until done.

At first glance the firing mechanism appeared to be a typical flintlock. But the jaws of the hammer clasped a horizontal metal bar instead of a flint. When the rifle was cocked and the trigger pulled, this bar hit and released a vertical striker protruding above the breech. That in turn actuated a lever inside the lock inlet. The lever moved just enough to release a measured charge of air into the chamber of the rifle. In discharging at considerable velocity without smoke or sound, the air rifle represented a phenomenon in its time.

Only once, as far as records reveal, did Lewis consider using the air rifle as a weapon. This was August 11, 1806, while hunting elk in thick brush along a river bottom with several of his party. Out of

Air gun's lock had a conventional look, but its jaws held an iron lug.

nowhere, a bullet caught him in the thigh. Hostile Indians were immediately suspected. Lewis dragged himself back to his boat but could go no farther. So, he related, [I] "prepared myself with a pistol, my rifle and my air gun, being determined as a retreat was impractical to sell my life as deerly [sic] as possible." But no attack materialized. The wound, it turned out, was inflicted by a stray bullet fired by one of his own party.

The expedition got back with the loss of only one man through illness and was hailed for its notable success. It brought home not only some of the first field maps of the Great West but specimens of its animals, birds, plants, and minerals. The fabulous air rifle presumably was shipped to Washington with the maps and specimens. There it disappeared without a trace. Twentieth century arms collectors and historians searched and quested for it in vain. At one point it was believed found, but the supposed discovery turned out to date much too late to be the right gun.

Soon the collectors' search took on the intensity and mystery of a detective drama. By then the Lewis rifle had been missing for nearly 140 years. If not located and positively identified soon, it might sink into obscurity for all time.

Into the situation stepped a collector already distinguished for his antique arms sleuthing and powers of deduction — Henry M. Stewart, Jr., of Philadelphia. Also by chance, the missing rifle happened to have been made in Philadelphia. Stewart stood on its home ground, a handy place to begin his search. Further, he was knowledgeable concerning early guns and had already begun collecting them.

Henry Stewart's first air gun was a two-barrel over-under rifle that could easily be mistaken at first glance for a true Pennsylvania or Kentucky rifle. The resemblance was hardly surprising. It had been made by Jacob Kunz, a Philadelphia gunsmith celebrated for his Kentucky-type arms. This one was different. One barrel was discharged by conventional percussion ignition. But on the other barrel functioned as an air rifle, drawing its power

Lateral lug in hammer jaws hits striker, releasing air charge.

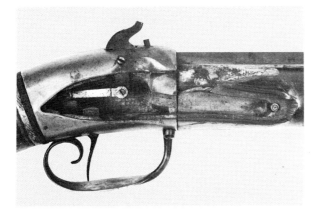

Striker was attached to an arm which extended back to air chamber in butt.

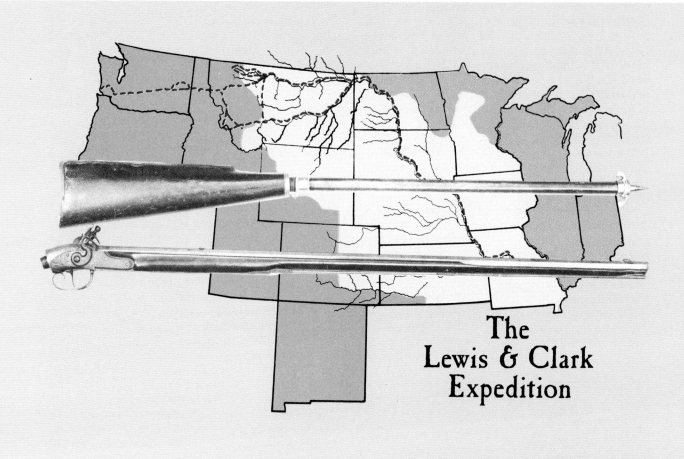

Expedition route is marked in red. U.S.-owned territory is shaded brown, the Purchase in blue, and unexplored or Spanish land olive. Dismantled air gun illustrates pump attachment.

from air compressed in a buttstock reservoir. Cased with the rifle was its air pump. Stewart acquired it at a sealed-bid auction.

Possessing the Kunz air rifle sent the collector off in pursuit of others. No narrow researcher, he also sought to find out all he could about the gunsmith and his contemporaries. He learned that one influential patron and colleague of Kunz was Isaiah Lukens, a prominent Philadelphian who, among other things, made the big tower clock for Independence Hall and founded the prestigious American Philosophical Society. Lukens, with his avid scientific mind, knew much about early guns. Stewart concluded that Lukens prompted Kunz to go to work building them. But what did that have to do with the missing Meriwether Lewis gun?

Back in the early 1800s, there were not many places to turn to buy an air gun. Philadelphia, with its industrious Mr. Kunz, obviously was one. Stewart

fine-combed the contacts of both Kunz and Lukens. One of Lukens' friends was Charles Willson Peale, a noted portrait painter who also conducted a natural history museum in Independence Hall. In the museum were the bones of a mastodon, specimens of other animals, and Indian artifacts from the West. And where might Peale have gotten those?

"It was my educated guess that the skeletal remains and artifacts collected by the expedition and shipped east from its base at St. Louis to Washington," Stewart says, "had gone to Philadelphia by courtesy of President Jefferson. Supposedly they were sent to Monticello, Jefferson's home, for further study but that does not seem to have been the case."

As a quantity of the expedition's finds and gear had been shipped to Philadelphia, possibly including military items originally drawn from the Schuylkill Arsenal there, might not the fabulous missing air gun have been among them? Might it still be in the Philadelphia area?

Keeping in mind the close Kunz-Lukens-Peale connection, Stewart delved further. A major center for historical science is the Franklin Institute in Philadelphia. In the clock section of its library, Stewart found an old printed catalog for an auction of "town clocks, gold chronometers," lathes, machinery and, in smaller print, "air guns." They were part of the estate of none other than Isaiah Lukens. Item 95 of the inventory read: "1 large air gun made for and used by Messrs. Lewis & Clark in their exploring expeditions. *A great curiosity.*" (Italics original).

Although delighted to have guessed right, Stewart still faced a huge question mark. The auction had been held more than 100 years earlier — January 4, 1847, to be exact. The catalog listing established that the expedition rifle was returned to Philadelphia. But beyond that, the scent was cold. Where to turn next? Fate spoke up from Milwaukee, Wisconsin, of all places.

In Milwaukee there lived and researched an advanced collector of air guns, one of the few of the breed in the country at the time. This man, Charter Harrison, collected widely. Studying his collection, he concluded that the long-lost expedition rifle rested right in his gun rack. Then, having announced his great find with a flourish, he second-guessed himself. He said the expedition arm was not the one he first thought but another antique air gun in his collection. He presented the second piece to the Smithsonian Institution. Curators there quickly dated it as having been made about 20 years after the expedition. Meanwhile Harrison offered the first piece for sale. Henry Stewart, hot on the trail, acquired it.

During the intervening years, the expedition rifle apparently had shuttled between Washington, Philadelphia, and points west. At the 1847 auction of the Lukens estate, it may well have been sold to Joseph Saxton, a prominent Philadelphia friend of Lukens. Certainly Saxton acquired many items from the Lukens estate, including air canes that fired bullets. A descendant, Joseph Saxton Pendleton, lent some of this memorabilia to the Smithsonian in the early 1900s, according to old records checked in recent years by Craddock Goins, then the Smithsonian's curator of military history. Later these loan items were sent back to Philadelphia to the Franklin Institute. Subsequently the rifle and other items turned up in the Charter Harrison collection in Milwaukee, possibly by trade or other acquisition from Saxton's descendants.

One confirmation of the rifle's identity and authenticity was soon forthcoming. The expedition's official journal reported that the rifle's mainspring had been broken and repaired or replaced in 1806. In the presence of officials of the

Lewis & Clark Heritage Foundation, Stewart, an engineer by education and an antique arms gunsmith of high caliber by self-training, opened up and examined the rifle's lock. Sure enough, he found what he termed "an identical mainspring in tempered blue showing little or no exposure or wear." As the replacement was made near the close of the expedition, it should be noted that no visible wear or rusting could have taken place before the gun was retired.

The original hammer was of the goose-neck type typical of the flintlock period, Stewart reports. It was broken or lost and, he adds: "either Isaiah Lukens or an equally knowledgeable person replaced it with an 1836 double-neck hammer correctly fitted with trip lever and spring.

"I have found myself fascinated by air guns," Stewart says. "Except for early manufacturing problems which sharply restricted their production prior to the Industrial Age, they possessed many advantages over blackpowder arms and even modern cartridge arms. Among these are silence, smokelessness, cleanliness and, back in the days of single-shot firearms, a capacity for repeater or rapid fire."

The expedition rifle stands as the most noteworthy specimen in the Stewart collection of eight long arms powered by compressed air. All eight of the arms are rifled. Five have brass barrels, a popular material centuries ago before smokeless powder raised breech pressures. Barrels of the other three are of iron.

Like all air guns operating on compressed air, they must have chambers to contain the air. Some are in the buttstocks, others are ball-shaped reservoirs above or below the barrel.

Four guns in the Stewart collection were manufactured by Jacob Kunz and/or Isaiah Lukens. (The "and/or" is necessary because the two men collaborated closely and just who did what is not clear to this day.) Two of the guns bear Kunz's name and two are signed Lukens. All four are similar.

Stewart believes that the two Philadelphians evolved an American school of air gun design distinct in some ways from the European. "I have deliberately searched the records and purchased many air weapons for study," he says, "before concluding that the outside striker developed around a regular flintlock hammer to release the measured amount of air from a pneumatic butt reservoir is unique to Lukens' design."

Some earlier European air guns employed outside strikers developed around external cocking levers, he points out, but none closely duplicated the flintlock hammer in appearance and operation. What Lukens and Kunz produced, in short, was an air rifle that could pass as a flintlock of the period. That was what enabled Lewis to surprise and awe the Indians with "Big Magic."

Surveying the Air Gun Alternative

Kerry Watkins

Every once in a while, a story comes along that is not only interesting but is also fun to do. AMERICAN SHOTGUNNER's first survey of air guns is just that type of story. But what made this survey so special was its broad appeal. During the course of the testing, several women on the staff who are not regular shooters gave the air guns a workout. At least two of them proved remarkably good and soon developed an interest in shooting where none existed before.

Many pounds of pellets were sacrificed during the course of testing. Throughout it all, we were constantly amazed at the accuracy potential of these air guns. The major advantage of using an air gun is, of course, the cost. But there are a half-dozen other advantages which make a quality air gun worthy of inclusion in any serious shooter's collection.

Air-gun competition is more popular on a per capita basis in Europe than in the U.S., but America is catching up. International air-gun competition among U.S. shooters was given a big boost in the summer of 1984 when Pat Spurgin of Billings, Montana, captured the Olympic gold medal in the very first women's air-rifle Olympic competition. Spurgin, who has been a small-bore and air-gun competitor for many years, was featured on ABC's television coverage of the Summer Games in Los Angeles. This was the first mass exposure this serious sport has received in this country.

Two of the major reasons why air guns are more popular in Europe than here are the limited number of organized ranges overseas and the restrictions placed upon firearms and their use. Air guns can safely be shot indoors in controlled situations. The international course of fire is set at 10 meters (approximately 33 feet). Since air guns do not produce the loud report or burning powder fumes of firearms, just about any area where traffic can be restricted can be used as a range, with preference being given to indoor ranges with their absence or group-spreading winds. Since nearly all matches and practicing take place indoors, air-gun competition is a year-round possibility regardless of location. The 10-ring in air-gun competition is not a ring at all, but rather a spot 1mm (approximately 1/25-

This article first appeared in *THE AMERICAN SHOTGUNNER.*

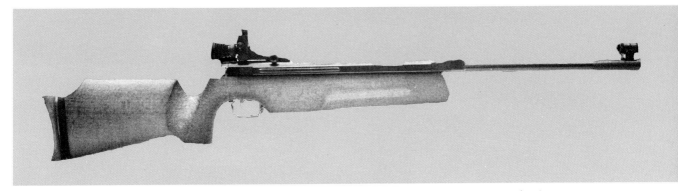

Gamo 126 Super Match received from Daisy quickly became the favorite rifle of two male shooters on evaluation team.

inch) in diameter. Accuracy of the highest order is required of both guns and shooters. As a result, air guns for world-class competition are among the most accurate of arms.

In the U.S., one of the most popular shooting sports is metallic silhouette shooting, and a course of fire has been scaled down for air-gun competition. This form of air-gun competition is gaining popularity. The silhouette course involves firing at tiny steel animal silhouettes: a chicken at 20 meters, a pig at 30 meters, a turkey at 38.5 meters, and a ram at 50 meters. Since this represents a standard NRA rifle course in 1/10 scale, obviously the targets are also on the same scale. The ram is the largest target measuring a whopping 2.8 inches tall. Since silhouette shooting is done outdoors, the winds and climatic conditions add to the difficulty of the varying ranges. And since the targets have to be knocked down, an air gun of sufficient power and accuracy is needed.

While most air-gun competition is challenging and fun, one need not shoot in competition to enjoy air guns. Certainly more lower-level air guns than world-class models are sold in the U.S. The less expensive models can provide a great deal of pleasure at very low cost. Many are surprisingly accurate and have sufficient power to justify their use in the elimination of small pests up to rat size with the proper pellets. Air guns used for pest elimination kill by penetration alone. Since the pellet is small and doesn't penetrate far, hitting a vital area is important. While shooting game birds with an air gun is certainly feasible, it is not legal to do so. Nor should air guns be used for hunting rabbits or chasing away the neighbor's dog.

Wounding rabbit-sized game is a cruel sport. Shooting the neighbor's dog with a pellet gun could make you the focus of much adverse attention, a potential lawsuit, and possibly criminal charges as well. Air guns have their place. By realizing their potential and limitations, you too can enjoy this rapidly growing sport.

Twenty-nine air guns were received for our survey from 11 manufacturers and importers. Of this total, 16 were rifles and 13 were handguns. We divided this group into two basic categories: hunter/plinkers and target models. To make the target category, an air gun had to exhibit not only world-class accuracy, but it also had to have extremely fine adjustable sights. It was a relatively easy matter to separate the target and plinker handguns, but the rifles were another matter. Some of the plinker rifles exhibited amazing accuracy and had fine sights despite costing much less than the obvious match rifles. Those that exhibited target accuracy could be used by beginners for competition, but if the interest level increases, a heavier match rifle is of benefit as it allows a steadier hold which results in tighter groups. The triggers on the pure match rifles are also superior in their letoff.

So without further delay, here are the air guns recommended by AMERICAN SHOTGUNNER, beginning with the match-quality rifles and working down to the less expensive models. See charts for more detailed specifications on various models.

MATCH-GRADE AIR GUNS

Four match-grade rifles were tested. These included an RWS Model 75 T01, a Gamo Model 126 Super Match, a Haenel Model 312-1, and a Haenel Model 303-8, all in .177 caliber, the standard for U.I.T. (Union Internationale de Tir, more commonly referred to as the International Shooting Union in English-speaking countries) international competition.

Of these four rifles, all but the Haenel 303-8 were side-lever designs with barrels fixed to the receivers. The Haenel 303-8 is a barrel-cocking design which presents a slight problem since its rear sight is mounted on the rear of the receiver, not on the end of the barrel as in other barrel-cocking designs. The longer sight radius afforded by having micrometer sights at the end of the receiver is an aid

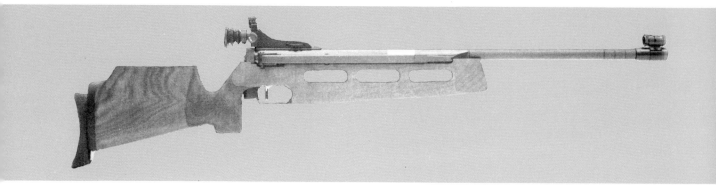

Author favored RWS M-75 T 01. It was easier to cock and load than some of the other match rifles.

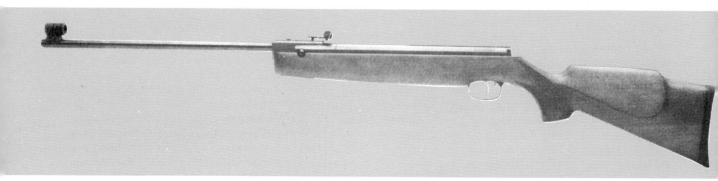

Beeman R8 represents good value in intermediate-velocity air rifle.

to accuracy. Fortunately the 303-8 has a very solid lock-up and we didn't notice any great shift in group patterns after several hundred rounds through this rifle. However, extended wear on the locking mechanism of a barrel-cocking rifle with receiver sights will eventually result in a shift in the point of aim. The 303-8 did have one nice feature — its rear sight had six apertures on a rotating disk — but its elevation and windage adjustments were not marked for direction. But for an interested newcomer to the sport, the East German-produced Haenel 303-8 at $249 isn't too bad.

The larger Haenel 312-1 was superior in just about every way to its little brother, with better sights, stock, trigger, and groups. The receiver end of the barrel had a cutout which allowed a pellet to be placed into the barrel easily, a worthy feature considering this model had a rather cavernous chamber area where a dropped pellet could take awhile to extricate. Neither of the Haenel models was of the recoilless design which is now considered standard among match air rifles. The extra noise and kick of these rifles could get a bit tiring in the long run.

Probably the best deal among the match rifles was the Spanish-made Gamo 126 Super Match marketed in this country by Daisy. With a suggested retail price in the $300 area, this model had an excellent set of micrometer sights (with English

direction markings, we might add), a fine adjustable trigger, an adjustable buttplate, a rail for mounting a palm rest or hand stop, and a well-proportioned and stippled match stock with Wundhammer pistol grip. The receiver is also tapped for scope mounting in case you want to use this model for the increasingly popular running-boar competition. One slight disadvantage of the Gamo 126 Super Match is its chamber which requires a separate action to open after pulling back the cocking lever. The loading action has to be done in the proper order or else closing the side-cocking lever will not compress the spring and piston.

The RWS Model 75 T01 is the base world-class model from this famous West German firm which also makes this model with adjustable stock and with a scope for the running-boar game. It was the easiest of the match rifles to operate and had the best-fitting stock and by far the best trigger.

HUNTER AND PLINKER MODELS

It is almost unfair not to include the following five rifles in the match category because they are capable of extreme accuracy if fired from a bench rest. What makes the difference here is the shorter sight radius and open, blade-type rear sights used on

Beeman's new P1 Mag. air pistol has two power levels, one reaching 600 fps, the highest of any current pistol.

these barrel-cocking guns. The stocks are of a standard pistol-grip rather than heavy match type, and the triggers are not as light as those on the pure match rifles. They do not have recoilless mechanisms either.

The five rifles in this hunter/plinker/target category include: Beeman's R1 (the world's highest-velocity air rifle at 940 fps with standard match pellets), Beeman's R8, Crosman Model 6500 (made by Anschutz), RWS Model 45, and the BSA Mercury S. Any of these rifles would be an excellent choice for a beginning target shooter who might also want to use his rifle for more informal pursuits. The Beeman rifles and the Crosman featured Monte Carlo stocks with raised cheekpieces. All the rifles had rubber buttplates. The Beeman and RWS models had cut checkering, the others pressed checkering. All but the BSA had globe front sights with interchangeable posts and/or center spots. The BSA did have a counter-bored muzzle which protects the rifling at the muzzle but makes proper cleaning a little more difficult.

PLINKER RIFLES

For just plain fun on a shoestring budget, any of the following models should suffice. There is a wide range of quality and design to consider. Three models in this group were imported barrel-cocking designs: the Marathon AR 50 and AR 200 from Spain, and the West German RWS Model 24. The AR 50 is a special model made for junior shooters. Its stock was about 3½ inches shorter than a standard stock, but the prototype model we received had a full-length barrel whereas the production model is scheduled to have a shortened barrel.

The name Daisy will often pop up when shooters are asked to name their first gun. The famous American company is most often associated with BB guns, but they have an extensive lineup of air guns, too. We received two pump pneumatic rifle models: the Powerline 860 with plastic stock and open sights, and the Powerline 953 with wooden stock and match-type sights. Both had rifled steel barrels designed for pellets. The 860 is a multipump design

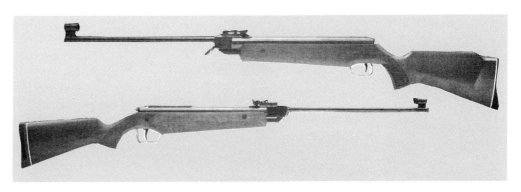

(Top) M-6500 made in Germany for the American Crosman Co.

(Bottom) RWS M-45, another Mag.-power air rifle that would make an excellent hunting rifle for pests and small game.

which can push a standard pellet along at more than 600 fps with 10 pumps. The Model 953, a single-pump model, had a sticker on the box touting its Lothar Walther precision barrel. It also included a nylon arm strap for position shooting. With a price in the $125 to $150 range, the 953 could well serve as a target trainer.

Our final two rifles are also American-produced pneumatics with familiar names: Benjamin and Sheridan. Both are multipump designs. These rifles (and the pistols from the same companies) arrived too late for a full range of tests. In last-minute informal shooting on the indoor range, both proved accurate and powerful. The Sheridan is the only air rifle that did not use standard .177 (4.5mm) pellets. After hunting around at several stores, we scrounged up a tin of Sheridan 5mm full-skirted pellets. The Sheridan rifle had a Williams peep sight, but not the type with micrometer click knobs. Rather, it had to be adjusted with a screwdriver. It proved more accurate with less than the maximum number of pumps.

Unfortunately, the 5mm pellets, while widely used in the U.S. by Sheridan shooters, are just now becoming popular among international shooters. The number and design of 5mm pellets is limited at present.

MATCH-QUALITY AIR PISTOLS

Five world-class air pistols were received as samples for evaluation. The difference between the match air pistols and the plinkers was more clear-cut than in the rifles. But still, there were two plinker pistols that could serve the needs of beginning target shooters.

The five match models included the Feinwerkbau Model 65 Mark II, the CO_2-powered Walther Model CP2, the Air Match Model 600, the Fiocchi Model P10, and America's first world-class air pistol, the Daisy Powerline 777. All the match pistols have anatomical grips with adjustable tables except for the Daisy, which has a fixed table suitable for small to medium hands. Shooters with large hands will have to whittle the Daisy's stocks a bit for a custom fit. All but the Daisy had broad rear-sight blades which were either interchangeable or adjustable for slot width. The Daisy's rear sight was not as wide nor was it adjustable for width. In addition, the Feinwerkbau, Air Match, and Fiocchi had changeable front sight posts.

The Daisy, Air Match, and Feinwerkbau were all side-lever (left side) recoilless models; the Fiocchi had a very easy-to-operate bottom lever which could be operated without any shift in grip by the shooting hand; and, of course, the Walther had only a small lever to open the chamber since its CO_2 operation doesn't require any cocking of a spring piston.

To be painfully honest, all of the match-grade pistols were far better shooters than were the folks who tested them. I purchased the Feinwerkbau Model 65 as a training aid for my metallic silhouette handgun shooting because it offered two trigger-pull weights and either recoil or recoilless operation.

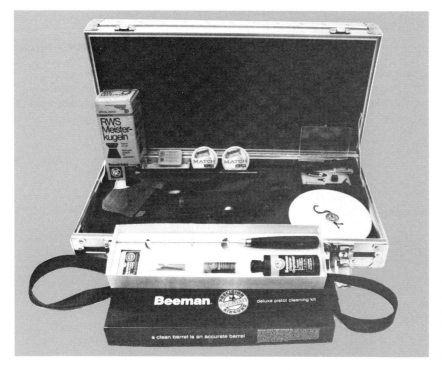

Author's outfit includes FWB 65 Mark II, Apollo 20X50 spotting scope, Beeman accessories, and RWS and H&N match pellets Wilson Magnum Line pistol case offers superb protection.

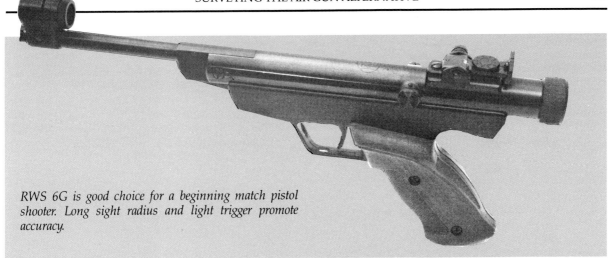

RWS 6G is good choice for a beginning match pistol shooter. Long sight radius and light trigger promote accuracy.

I soon found myself so engrossed in shooting the tiniest possible groups with my air gun that I neglected shooting big-bore silhouettes at all. My most memorable group of three shots measured just slightly more than .181 inch using sized RWS match pellets. This equates to a center-to-center spread of a mere 25 thousandths of an inch! It was fired from a Creedmore position left-handed over a range of eight meters.

Three pistol models offered excellent accuracy despite the fact they didn't have the features standard on pure match pistols. These models included the Beeman P1 Magnum, a new model boasting the highest velocity for any air pistol and looking much like a Colt, an interesting design which allows two power settings which are selected while cocking the barrel. The barrel and sights are fixed into the top of the simulated slide. The barrel is released by cocking the pistol's hammer. Velocities in the 600 fps range are possible with light pellets. While the grip panels and general styling are similar to the Colt .45 automatic, the trigger action is not. The trigger is top-pivoted, not a straight-back push.

The RWS and BSA are both barrel-cocking designs with anatomical molded stocks and finely adjustable rear sights. The RWS is a much superior model additionally having an adjustable trigger, globe front sight with interchangeable inserts, a choice of four rear-sight notches, and recoilless operation.

Crosman's 357 Eight Sharpshooter's Kit came complete with 1.5X scope, scope mount, ram silhouette target, spare cylinder, and cleaning rod.

PLINKER PISTOLS

Crosman sent us a Colt Python Hunter clone called the .357 Eight Sharpshooter's Set. The set included a 1.5X15mm scope and barrel mount, cleaning rod, ram metallic silhouette, and a spare cylinder. This top-break pistol can fire six shots in either single- or double-action thanks to its being powered by CO_2

Powerlets. The scope is a great aid in keeping targets in focus, and we had a great time shooting silhouettes with this revolver.

Sheridan and Benjamin sent us two pump-up pistols which are extremely similar in appearance. The Sheridan used 5mm pellets (.20 caliber) while the Benjamin needed .22 pellets. These pistols were received too late for the full evaluation. Both were

AIR GUN ACCESSORIES FOR SERIOUS SHOOTERS

Although air guns are not true firearms, they do "fire" projectiles, often at velocities exceeding that of some centerfire ammunition. These projectiles are known as BBs, pellets, or darts. At present, three main calibers are used in popular air guns: .177 (4.5mm), .20 (5mm), and .22 (5.5mm). The ranking in terms of popularity from top to bottom is .177, .22, and .20. The .20 is increasing in popularity now that some top German rifles are being manufactured in this caliber.

.177-CALIBER PELLETS

The .177 caliber is the standard caliber for international air-gun competition. This caliber also attains the highest velocities, in excess of 900 fps in Magnum-power rifles and nearly 600 fps in Magnum pistols. At these extreme velocities, it is easy to see that pellets have the potential to inflict serious injury. Pointed pellets are used for hunting and kill by penetration that is effected by mass and velocity. The .177 pellets have the least mass but the greatest velocity. It is believed they offer the greatest penetration at short distances and the highest degree of accuracy.

.20-CALIBER PELLETS

The .20-caliber pellets were formerly available only for the American-produced Sheridan pump pneumatic air rifles. The Sheridan rifles used a pointed, full-skirted pellet which sealed in the bore well but didn't offer maximum velocity because of its high friction coefficient. Now that the Germans are producing quality air guns in this caliber, the pellet manufacturers have come up with a series of waisted pellets which allow greater velocity and accuracy as well. This caliber is becoming increasingly popular because it offers a compromise in the velocity and mass departments.

.22-CALIBER PELLETS

The .22 caliber pellets will probably wane in popularity as more and more .20-caliber guns become available. The .22 pellets offer the greatest mass but their velocities are much lower. Since air guns shouldn't be used for hunting pot-sized game, mass is not as important a factor as velocity.

BB AND PELLET TYPES

The types of BB's and pellets offered fall into six major categories. Round lead balls and steel BBs have the greatest mass for their size, but they lose energy fairly rapidly due to their lower ballistic coefficients. Steel BBs should never be used in quality rifled barrels designed for pellet use. They will gradually destroy the precision rifling which will result in a loss of velocity and accuracy when used for pellets.

The most popular type of pellet is the waisted diabolo shape which can be subdivided into five categories. The flat-headed version is referred to as a wadcutter design and most match pellets fall into this category. The wadcutter diabolo pellets cut clean holes that are easy to score on paper targets. The RWS Meisterkugeln and H&N (Haendler & Natermann) match pellets are presently the most popular brands among serious competition airgunners. Match pellets weigh 7.25 to 8.6 grains with extremely small variance between pellets. The lighter ones are used for match pistols, the heavier versions for match rifles.

The round-headed diabolo pellets come in two versions, one thin-walled and extremely light for the highest attainable velocities. The thicker-walled and more solid round-headed pellets offer high ballistic coefficients and retain energy for long-range sports such as metallic silhouette where the ram target is placed at 50 meters (164.1 feet). The RWS Hobby and the Beeman Laser are good examples of seven-grain (in .177 caliber) high-velocity diabolo pellets. The Beeman Ram Jet is one of the better heavy (9.8 grains in .177) round-headed pellets.

The last general category of pellets is composed of those designed for maximum penetration and killing power. These diabolo designs are either pointed or have a hollow point to induce expansion. The Beeman Silver Jet and Silver Sting and the RWS Superpoint (8.39/15.45, 8.61/15.74, 7.7/11.7 grains in .177/.22 calibers, respectively) are good examples of pointed pellets. The Beeman Silver Bear (7.1/12.65 grains in .177/.22) is a good hollow-point design. The Beeman Kodiak, a semipointed diabolo design, is available only in .22 caliber and is the heavyweight champ at a massive 21.1 grains.

IMPRESSIVE ACCESSORIES

A couple of accessories to insure you get the most out of your pellets are marketed by Beeman. The first is the Pell-Size, a precision plunger which centers and sizes .177 pellets to match various bore sizes. The Pell-Size comes with the optimum .1785 die, but additional dies in .178, .179, and .180 are available. The use of this handy accessory can lead to smaller groups. The second, the

reasonably accurate despite rather crude rear sights. Both had plastic stocks but wooden handles for the underlever pump arms, an unusual mix.

Daisy sent a CO_2-powered BB repeater called the Powerline 1200. The plastic stocks were anatomical for right-handed shooters and still usable by left-handers. The pistol's styling is reminiscent of a High Standard target .22 pistol. The plastic rear sight is adjustable for windage and elevation.

Daisy also sent a Luger look-alike which is but one model in their new Softair line. This model fires 6mm plastic spheres that look much like pearls. The pellets are inserted into dummy 9mm cartridges, loaded into a magazine, and chambered just like in a real Luger.

Wide variety of match, hunting, and plinking pellets were used during six weeks of air-gun testing.

companion tool to the Pell-Size, is a pellet-seating tool called the Pell-Seat (Beeman product names are quite self-explanatory). Inserting the pellet into the barrel, the Pell-Seat gently flares the skirt of the pellet to eliminate blow-by, escaped air which causes variances in velocity and accuracy.

Now that we have covered the guns and pellets, the next items most affecting accuracy in air guns are a clean bore and quality sights. Both Beeman and RWS market quality cleaning kits specially designed for air guns. The Beeman model even includes a special plastic muzzle bushing to prevent damage to the rifling in the critical area near the muzzle. Both companies also sell felt cleaning pellets which can be used during a match for a quick cleaning. If you shoot a spring-piston air gun, use two cleaning pellets since using only one may not give enough resistance to prevent the piston from slamming home, thereby damaging the critical seal.

It is especially important for competition shooters to have spare parts and seals for their match guns. Not having them could be very costly for many reasons. Air-gun compression chambers require special lubricants that are free of petroleum byproducts. Proper tools for disassembling your air gun are also needed. You may even want to add a UIT- or NRA-approved scoring gauge to your kit for accurate scoring of your practice shots, a way of obtaining consistent performance.

If you plan to compete in the running-boar competition or take your rifle afield for hunting small pests or game, a scope and mount will greatly improve your chances of success. Beeman, RWS, and others offer a great variety of scopes to meet various needs. The major advantage of using a scope is in keeping the target in sharp focus. Also, scopes generally offer slightly finer adjustments than do standard air rifle sights. The scope we tried on the Crosman .357-Eight revolver greatly increased silhouette scores (over a shortened course) over using the same pistol with only its open sights.

OTHER GOOD CHOICES

There are hundreds of other accessories that will benefit match shooters: Ultra-precision micrometer rear sights with replaceable apertures, matching globe-type front sights, palm rests, barrel weights, benchrest pads, rifle tripod rests, pellet holders and trays, trigger shoes, slings and sling swivels, cases, spotting scopes, pellet traps, targets, adjustable stocks and buttplates, specialized shooting glasses, and much more.

Serious match shooters would also do well to acquire *TARGET RIFLE SHOOTING,* by David Parish and John Anthony, and *COMPETITIVE PISTOL SHOOTING,* by Dr. Laslo Anatal. The National Rifle Association also offers several pamphlets on air-gun competition. Contact the NRA at 1600 Rhode Island Ave., NW, Washington, D.C. 20036, and direct your letter to Margaret Schoap-Maurer, Director of Air Gun Division. She can also be reached by calling (202)828-6154.

Competitive air-gunning, although deceptively simple-looking due to the short range involved, is very challenging. The practice and good shooting habits you may develop with sport air-gun shooting will benefit you in other forms of competition and during your hunting trips, too. Give air guns a try. Set up a range at home and get the whole family involved in this fascinating sport.

AIR GUN SPECIFICATIONS

Make & Model	Action Type	Caliber	Sights	Barrel
Beeman R1 rifle	Barrel cocking, spring piston	.177	Adjustable for W & E	19.6″
Beeman R8 rifle	Barrel cocking, spring piston	.177	Adjustable for W & E	18.3″
Beeman P1 Mag. pistol	Barrel cocking, spring piston	.177	Adjustable for W & E	7″
Beeman/Feinwerkbau 65 MK II pistol	Sidelever cocking, spring piston	.177	Micro adj. for W & E	6.1″
Benjamin/Sheridan Benjamin M-347	Underbarrel multi-pump pneumatic	.177	Course for E only	15.8″
Benjamin/Sheridan Sheridan CBW rifle	Underbarrel multi-pump pneumatic	.20	Adjustable for W & E	19″
Benjamin/Sheridan Benjamin M-232	Underbarrel multi-pump pneumatic	.22	Course for W & E	8.5″
Crosman Anschutz 6500	Barrel cocking, spring piston	.177	Adjustable for W & E	18.5″
Crosman 357 Eight Shooter's Set	CO2-powered six-shot revolver with 1.5X scope	.177	Micro adj. for W & E	8″
Daisy/Gamo 126 Super Match	Sidelever cocking, spring piston	.177	Micro adj. for W & E	17.7″
Daisy Power Line M-953 rifle	Underlever single-pump pneumatic	.177	Adjustable for W & E	20.5″
Daisy Power Line M-860 rifle	Underlever multi-pump pneumatic	.177	Course for W & E	20″
Daisy Power Line 777 Match pistol	Sidelever single-pump pneumatic	.177	Adjustable for W & E	9″
Daisy Power Line 1200 BB pistol	CO2-powered repeater	BB	Course adj. for W & E	8.18″
Daisy SoftAir M-08	Manual cocking	.25	Fixed	4.2″
Dynamit Nobel 75 T 01 rifle	Sidelever cocking, spring piston	.177	Micro adj. for W & E	18.9″
Dynamit Nobel RWS M-45	Barrel cocking, spring piston	.177	Adjustable for W & E	20.5″
Dynamit Nobel RWS M-24	Barrel cocking, spring piston	.177	Adjustable for W & E	17″
Dynamit Nobel RWS M-6G	Barrel cocking, spring piston	.177	Adjustable for W & E	7″
Flocchi P10 Match pistol	Underlever single-pump pneumatic	.177	Adjustable for W & E	8″
GB International Haenel 303-8 Super	Barrel cocking, spring piston	.177	Adjustable for W & E	17.7″
GB International Haenel 312-1 Champion	Sidelever cocking, spring piston	.177	Micro Adj. for W & E	17.9″
Interarms/Walther M-CP2 Junior	CO2-powered match pistol	.177	Micro adj. for W & E	8.8″
Kendall International Air Match 600	Sidelever single-pump pneumatic	.177	Micro adj. for W & E	9″
Marathon AR 200 Rifle	Barrel cocking, spring piston	.177	Adjustable for W & E	17″
Precision Sports BSA Mercury-Super	Barrel cocking, spring piston	.177	Adjustable for W & E	19.2″
Precision Sports BSA Scorpion	Barrel cocking, spring piston	.177	Adjustable for W & E	7.8″

Velocity	Safety	Weight	Retail	Notes
940 fps	Yes, auto	8.8 lbs.	$350	Highest-velocity air rifle, 34-pound cocking effort.
720 fps	Yes, auto	7.2 lbs.	$247	Good choice for sport and target, adjustable trigger.
350 to 600 fps	Yes, manual	2.45 lbs.	$190	Highest-velocity air pistol has two power ranges.
525 fps	None	2.9 lbs.	$608	World-class recoilless (defeatable) match pistol, adj. trigger.
Up to 650 fps	Yes, manual	6.0 lbs.	$101	Lightweight plinker can be pumped up to ten times.
Up to 695 fps	Yes, manual	5.2 lbs.	$124	Powerful and loud pneumatic with Williams receiver sight.
Up to 315 fps	Yes, manual	1.9 lbs.	$82	Pump plinker iston takes .22-cal. pellets or darts.
710 fps	None	7.9 lbs.	$139	Nice sights and trigger make this a good hunter/target model.
470 fps	Yes, manual	3 lbs.	$75	Set incl: scope, silhouette ram, spare cylinder, cleaning rod, and scope mount.
590 fps	None	10.5 lbs.	$300	World-class match rifle with superb accuracy, recoilless.
480 fps	Yes, manual	5.1 lbs.	$150	Match-type sights give this little rifle good accuracy.
Up to 650 fps	Yes, manual	4 lbs.	$40	Pump pneumatic plinker rifle handles pellets and BBs.
385 fps	Yes, manual	3.1 lbs.	$200	US-produced match pistol requires two-step cocking/pumping.
460 fps	Yes, manual	1.6 lbs.	N.A.	Gravity feed repeater holds 60 BBs, plastic stock.
N.A.	Yes, manual	12 ozs.	$25	Luger copy fires .25-cal. plastic balls, ejects spent cartridges.
650 fps	None	10.7 lbs.	$600	World-class match rifle with excellent sights and adj. trigger.
900 fps	Yes, auto	7.7 lbs.	$210	Super-accurate hunter/target rifle with magnum power.
580 fps	Yes, auto	6 lbs.	$150	Excellent value in a hunting and plinking air rifle.
410 fps	None	3 lbs.	$195	Good sights and light trigger make this a possible match gun.
420 fps	None	2.4 lbs.	$500	Excellent stock, adjustable trigger and sights for match use.
750 fps	Yes, manual	7.5 lbs.	$249	Hooded match-type receiver sight with built-in apertures.
600 fps	None	10.4 lbs.	$449	Excellent sights and trigger, but slight recoil.
N.A.	None	2.25 lbs.	$535	Superb match pistol is much easier to operate than spring-piston types, with case, tools.
N.A.	None	2.1 lbs.	$356	Excellent value in a match pistol $30 fitted hard case comes with barrel weight and accessories.
640 fps	Yes, auto	5.7 lbs.	$75	Spanish rifle has features and accuracy worth twice the price.
825 fps	None	7.1 lbs.	$250	Very stylish and powerful rifle with walnut stock.
525 fps	Yes, manual	3.4 lbs.	$100	Large and powerful pistol with pellets, trap, and accessories.

PART SIX

BALLISTICS, AMMUNITION AND HANDLOADING

The World's Greatest Handgun Cartridge

John Lachuk

I've long since lost count of the number of people who have asked me, "What kind of pistol should I buy?" I have to answer with another question, "What do you intend to do with it?" They usually respond, "Oh, plink and target practice a little. Carry it along on hiking, fishing, and

Color Photo: To say that the .22 LR cartridge is versatile is something of an understatement. Since its introduction in 1887, it has accounted for its fair share of cans, targets, and game. Many handgun types and models have been chambered for it, including: 1) S&W 22/32 Lightweight Kit Gun, 2) Colt New Frontier, 3) S&W K22, 4) High Standard Sierra, 5) Ruger Super Single Six, 6) T/C Contender, 7) Kart .22 unit on Hoag custom frame, 8) Auto Nine, 9) High Standard M-GB, 10) Colt Match Target, 11) S&W M-41, 12) Budischowsky TP-70, 13) Colt Ace, 14) High Standard Sharpshooter, 15) Ruger Mark II. Wide variety of .22 LR ammunition has been, and currently is, available, including the newer "hot" hyper-velocity loads and more moderate target rounds.

This article first appeared in *GUNS & AMMO.*

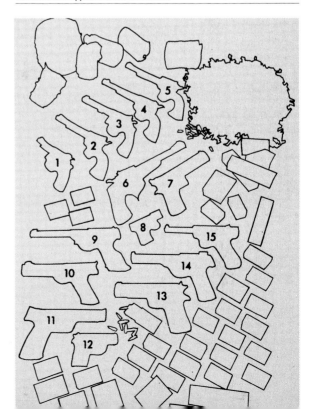

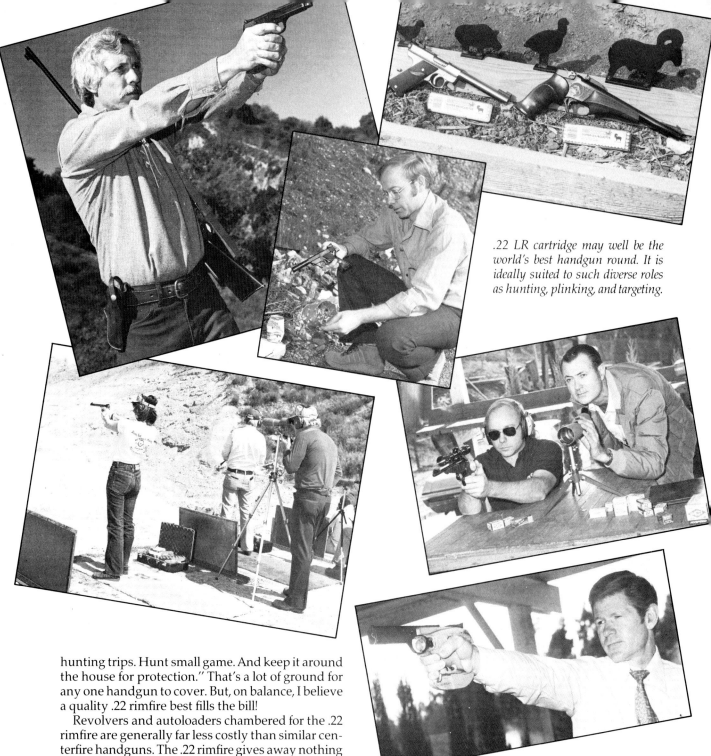

.22 LR cartridge may well be the world's best handgun round. It is ideally suited to such diverse roles as hunting, plinking, and targeting.

hunting trips. Hunt small game. And keep it around the house for protection." That's a lot of ground for any one handgun to cover. But, on balance, I believe a quality .22 rimfire best fills the bill!

Revolvers and autoloaders chambered for the .22 rimfire are generally far less costly than similar centerfire handguns. The .22 rimfire gives away nothing in terms of accuracy. And with the wide range of .22 ammunition available, from .22 CB Caps to hypervelocity .22 Long Rifles, you can just about choose any desired results at the receiving end. There are many things that a .22 Long Rifle handgun can do better than a .44 Magnum. Megaton terminal impact isn't always an asset. Caved-in eardrums and a bruised palm are often the most poignant memories of a session with a massive Magnum. Shooters unaccustomed to the brutal recoil of a .44 or .41 Magnum, or even a .357, could be better served by a mild-mannered, soft-spoken .22 rimfire for about 90 percent of their time on the firing line or in the field.

A .22 Long Rifle pistol is clearly the premier plinker. You can enjoy a protracted plinking session without mortgaging your home or spending long hours at the reloading bench. Rimfire .22 Long Rifle ammunition isn't burdensome. A couple of boxes dumped into a coat pocket can provide hours of fun. The reduced recoil and minimal muzzle blast of the .22 handgun encourages carefree plinking at random targets. Virtually any reasonably accurate handgun will do, be it single- or double-action revolver or a semiautomatic.

Targets are numbered only by safety and the limits of your own imagination. A variety of exploding objects, such as inexpensive clay pigeons, Necco candy wafers, over-ripe tomatoes, oranges, squash, etc. from the local market, make interesting targets. Small fry can stalk animal crackers as earnestly as real lions and tigers! Soft drink cans still qualify for the reclamation bin, even after you shoot them to shreds. (And the only thoughtful thing to do is to carry them out with you rather than litter the outdoors.)

Plinking at paper targets is far more entertaining if you use colorful life-sized images of squirrels, foxes, bobcats, and even deer, made and marketed by Outers. Outers makes a practical target carrier as well, consisting of a sturdy steel verticle post, sharpened to push easily into the ground, flanked by four flat steel arms. Plastic clips are provided to stretch the targets between the arms. The arms unhinge to stow along with the center post in the handy two-foot-long plastic case provided. You can gain a better appreciation for the popular game of pistol silhouette shooting by plinking at Outers' new ⅕-scale black silhouettes of chickens, javelina, turkeys, and rams, printed in rows of five images each on heavyweight paper.

Actual pistol silhouette competition is little more than post-grad plinking, firing at steel effigies of wild chickens, pigs, turkeys, and sheep, set up in rows of five each, at ranges 25, 50, 75, and 100 meters, respectively. The course is fired twice, for a total of 40 rounds. Each of the steel cutouts must be knocked from its perch — in exact order — to count as a hit. Some target ranges have a maximum distance of 100 yards (over 91 meters). International Handgun Metallic Silhouette Association (IHMSA) and NRA rules both provide for registered competition at reduced ranges — with small-scale targets. Target Masters, 9847 Glenoaks Blvd., Sun Valley, CA 91352, markets ⅜-scale silhouettes which can be fired in official matches at 25, 50, 75, and 100 yards, instead of meters.

Successfully mastering silhouette calls for more sophisticated equipment than does mere plinking. Rules preclude the use of a .22 WMR handgun, or the use of hotloaded .22 Long Rifle cartridges, such as CCI Stingers, Federal Spitfires, Remington Yellow Jackets and Vipers, or Winchester's new Super Max ammunition. Most competitors opt for standard velocity ammunition in any case, because it has ample energy to send the steel cutouts cartwheeling, and is usually more accurate. Utmost accuracy is the prime requirement of any handgun chosen for silhouette shooting. Almost as important are target-adjustable sights, free from backlash, because the elevation adjustment is changed as each successive range is fired.

A mainstay of .22 rimfire handgun silhouette shooting is the tip-up, single-shot Thompson/

.22 LR is an inherently accurate round and is well suited to targeting, as exemplified by these 25-yard groups shot by author. Clockwise from top left: Ruger Mk II, High Standard Victor, H&R M-959 Sportsman, and Ruger New Model Single Six. These guns include autoloaders, double-action revolver, and single-action revolver.

Center Contender pistol, available with a tack-driving, button-rifled, 10-inch bull barrel, which qualifies under IHMSA rules as a cataloged "production" gun, competing on even terms with other out-of-the-box pistols. Equipped with the interchangeable .22 Long Rifle 14-inch bull barrel, the T/C Contender becomes an "unlimited" pistol, successfully competing on equal terms with costly custom guns.

In response to the demands of silhouette shooters, Thompson/Center has immensely improved the Contender in the past several years, dividing the locking bolt into independently locking halves, and beefing up the coil spring for a more secure lockup, greatly improving accuracy. They revised the leverage of the squeeze-to-open trigger guard for a softer release, and made the already-crisp trigger even more brittle and easy to adjust for zero takeup and backlash. Also silhouette-inspired was the new undercut Patridge front blade and finely adjustable deep-notched rear blade. The visible-hammer, manual-cocking pistol had built-in safeties in abundance, but even so, they added a manual safety button to the hammer for good measure.

The T/C Contender can switch barrels in a matter of minutes. Coupled with dual frame-mounted firing pins, that ability allows it to handle a multitude of barrels, chambered for cartridges ranging from the .22 WMR to .30/30 Winchester.

Another single-shot, tip-up pistol that shares this rare asset is the Merrill Sportsman, manufactured by Jim Rock of Rock Pistol Manufacturing, Fullerton, California. A production-line, semi-custom gun, the Merrill features crisp adjustable trigger, target sights, ambidextrous thumb shelf, and "dead man's" safety that locks when pressure is released. Jim is well acquainted with the needs of pistol silhouette shooters, being an inveterate competitor himself. His lovely daughter, Dana, is herself a perennial champion.

Ruger rimfire revolvers are also often encountered on the silhouette firing lines. Bill Ruger tailored his 9½-inch-barreled New Model Single Six to the requirements of silhouette shooters, with Patridge blade front sight, backed by micrometer-adjustable square-notch rear.

Created in the image of the pioneer days Peacemaker, the Ruger Single Six revived the single-

Revolvers chambered .22 LR make ideal trail companions and serve well in hunting situations for delivering the coup de grace, if needed.

action revolver after it was declared dead and buried after World War II. Introduced in 1973, the revised New Model Single Six utilizes a transfer bar

The 5½" bull-barreled version of Ruger Mark I (R) auto is short enough for field use, but has sufficient muzzle weight for serious targeting.

Two of the guns upon which Ruger built its fine reputation (below); Single Six revolver and Mark I auto pistol. Both guns are chambered for .22 LR and have become classics.

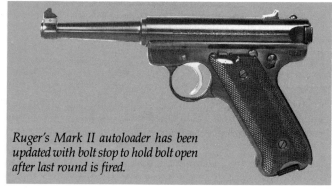

Ruger's Mark II autoloader has been updated with bolt stop to hold bolt open after last round is fired.

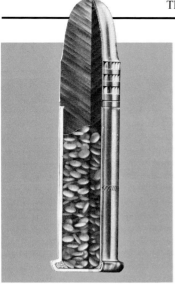

Though modern .22 LRs (shown) use smokeless propellants, when introduced in 1887 load was 5gr. of blackpowder.

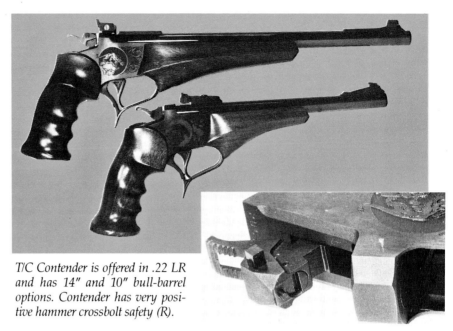

T/C Contender is offered in .22 LR and has 14" and 10" bull-barrel options. Contender has very positive hammer crossbolt safety (R).

to carry the impact of the hammer to the frame-mounted firing pin, allowing you to carry six live rounds in the cylinder without fear of accidental discharge should the gun be dropped on a hard surface, hammer down.

The Ruger Single Six is also available with 4⅝-, 5½-, and 6½-inch barrels. The 6½-inch length makes a viable silhouette gun, sacrificing little velocity or aiming precision, and doubles as a fine field companion, as well! With the alternate .22 WMR cylinder included with every gun, it becomes a formidable hunting handgun.

Autoloader fans may prefer a full-bore target pistol, such as the Smith & Wesson Model 41, to afford the high degree of accuracy required to become a serious competitor in silhouette. It also boasts a crisp, fully adjustable target trigger and checkered walnut stocks with ambidextrous thumb shelves. With a seven-inch heavy barrel, it affords the muzzle heft to dampen those inevitable tremors that make 100-meter rams so elusive. The sharply defined undercut Patridge post front sight and micrometer-click adjustable rear complete the picture.

Smith & Wesson recently made the Model 41 immensely more versatile by offering an interchangeable Field Barrel, with red-insert sloping-ramp front sight and rugged field-style adjustable rear sight. The ever-popular Smith & Wesson Model 17 K-22 Masterpiece, with 8⅜-inch barrel topped by target sights, is also an excellent choice for silhouette shooting.

For many, formal NRA National Match target shooting hasn't lost its lure. With an accurate .22 Long Rifle pistol, you can stand elbow-to-elbow with the top guns across the nation, and give a good

account of yourself — enjoying the cameraderie. If you don't wish to, you need never enter the center-fire phases at all.

A budget-priced pistol that can hold its own on any firing line is the autoloading Ruger Mark II Target Model, with 6⅞-inch button-rifled tapered barrel, topped with target adjustable sights. Optional barrel lengths include a 5½-inch bull barrel which doubles well as a field pistol, and a 10-inch slightly tapered barrel aimed at silhouette competition. Ruger recently revised the auto, with a new 10-round magazine in place of the old nine-shot version and a bolt stop.

A somewhat larger investment can net you a High Standard Victor autoloading pistol, among the top-ranking target guns made in the United States today,

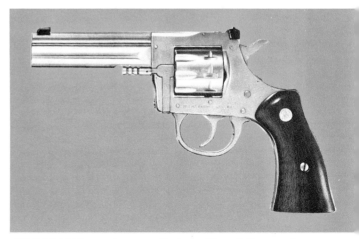

H&R M-905 has swing-out cylinder and barrel rib grooved for tip-off pistol scope mounts.

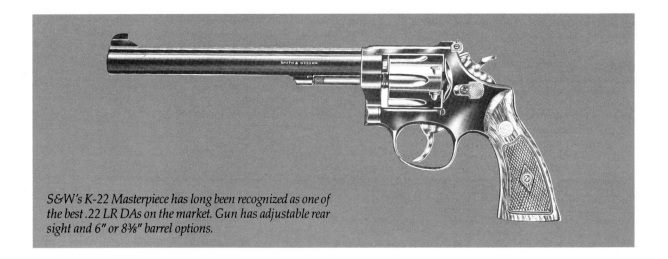

S&W's K-22 Masterpiece has long been recognized as one of the best .22 LR DAs on the market. Gun has adjustable rear sight and 6" or 8⅜" barrel options.

with 5½-inch heavy barrel, topped by a full-length ventilated rib, holding some of the finest O.E.M. target sights made. A detachable muzzle weight is included. The wide, serrated target trigger is fully adjustable and crisp. Checkered walnut grips are available with thumb shelf for either right or left hand. A .22 Short conversion kit is available, including barrel complete with rib and sights, slide, and two magazines, for use in International Rapid Fire competition.

For those of you who prefer to shoot from a carpet of pine needles rather than a concrete slab, there is a wide array of .22 rimfire handguns, any one of which can become your best friend on the trail. The above-mentioned Ruger New Model Single Six is available in corrosion-resistant stainless steel, making it virtually impervious to the ravages of weather.

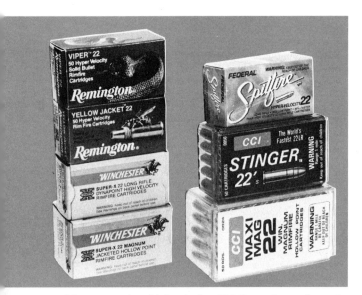

Many new ultra-high velocity .22 LRs on the market make excellent loads for small predators.

The stainless Single Six can be had in all four barrel lengths, but bearing in mind that it will be holstered at the hip for many arduous hours for every one spent in actual use, it pays to compromise on a 5½-inch barrel.

The importance of a comfortable, secure holster can hardly be over-stressed. An excellent choice for frontier-styled revolvers is the Safariland Model 43, lined with elk suede, featuring the exclusive Safariland "Sight Track," which resists the assaults of even knife-edged undercut front sight blades that can cut an ordinary holster in half. The Safariland Model 73 Cartridge Pouch easily holds several boxes of .22 ammunition and swivels to dump cartridges smoothly into the palm of the hand, as they are required.

Whether touring the wilderness on horseback, by four-wheel drive, or just shank's mare, your .22 rimfire holster-handy handgun can afford entertainment by way of casually potting pine cones, augmenting your limited larder with rabbits, squirrels, etc., and preventing pack rats, porcupines, and assorted other vermin from raiding the rest. Should you somehow take a wrong turn and end up temporarily misplaced, a .22 rimfire handgun can comfort and sustain you — even provide a reasonable level of protection in the event that you encounter marauding wild animals.

I long ago gave up lugging a .44 Magnum revolver along on big-game hunts. The rationale is apparent on the face of it. If I can't bag my game with a centerfire rifle, what chance have I of bringing it down with a big-bore handgun? A big-bore handgun isn't even a good instrument for delivering a *coup de grace*. Fired into the head, it may well ruin your mount. Fired into the body, it's often inadequate. On the other hand, a .22 Long Rifle High velocity solid point delivered behind the ear usually ends all activity with no harm to the cape.

Because I'm usually overburdened with camera gear when hunting, I resent even more any added

Sighted-in at 50 yds., .22 LR handgun shoots almost dead on to 66 yds. A scope, like the Leupold 2X, helps greatly to define target.

bulk or weight. For that reason, one of my favorite backup handguns is the time-proven Smith & Wesson .22/32 Kit Gun — one of the first produced following World War II, with Baughman sloping front sight and fully adjustable rear blade. Addition of Pachmayr neoprene Presentation Compac grips made the gun far more controllable without adding greatly to its size. In recent years, Smith & Wesson sagely began producing the Kit Gun in stainless steel, making it even more an ideal trail companion.

Other fine double-action revolvers in the kit gun category are the Charter Arms Pathfinder with three-inch barrel, available in blued steel or stainless, and the four-inch-barreled High Standard Sentinel, with round butt, checkered walnut grips, and .22 WMR fitted spare cylinder. Both boast micrometer adjustable sights and ample accuracy to make the best use of them.

It's a short step from packing a pistol on the trail to consciously hunting with it. In general, you can hunt any small game with a .22 pistol that you can hunt with assurance using a rimfire rifle, except perhaps at somewhat closer range. The range limitation is imposed by the greater difficulty of hitting with a handgun, plus an inevitable loss in velocity resulting from the shorter barrel, and the pressure loss between the cylinder and barrel gap when using a revolver.

You should shoot at no animal beyond the distance at which you can reliably place your bullet well within its vital zone, ahead of the diaphram, in the head or chest. Shots below the belt usually result in a lingering, painful death — something to be avoided at all costs! A valid rule of thumb would reduce rifle range by ⅓ when using a pistol. Thus such animals as rabbits, squirrels, and woodchucks, that are generally taken with a rifle at a maximum range of 100 yards, would be fair game for a skilled pistol shot at 66 yards. Medium-sized predators, such as foxes and bobcats, should be attempted no farther away than 50 yards. And the tough, tenacious coyote is stretching it even at a sure-fire distance of no more than 35 yards.

Whatever the distance, choose your aiming point as carefully on such animals as a ground squirrel or chuck as you would on a mule deer or whitetail. Resist the temptation to just blaze away at the whole animal. This inclination is most compelling with an autoloading pistol, because quick follow-up shots come so fast and easily. For the sake of humane kills, just pretend that you're shooting a single-shot.

Hunters should always test the grouping ability of themselves and their guns on the target range before going afield. Fire from the same positions you expect to use in the field — offhand, sitting, and

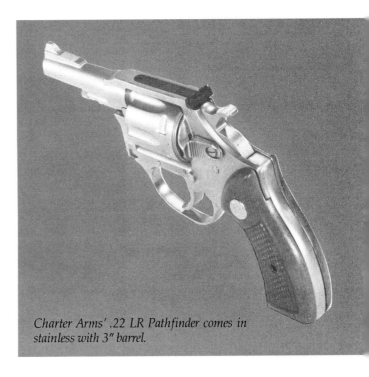

Charter Arms' .22 LR Pathfinder comes in stainless with 3" barrel.

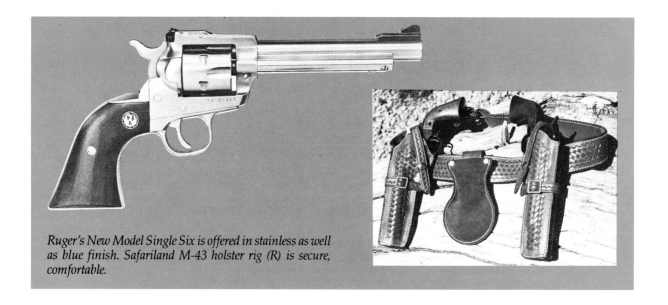

Ruger's New Model Single Six is offered in stainless as well as blue finish. Safariland M-43 holster rig (R) is secure, comfortable.

kneeling, plus two-handed across sandbags — to simulate those rare occasions when nature provides a downed tree, rock, or other natural rest. Realistically, you shouldn't shoot at animals any farther away than you can reliably direct a three-inch cone of fire. You may discover that you're a better shot than you thought. However, remember that the excitement of hunting may cause some extra wobbles.

If you're to supply a stew pot with squirrels, don't feed your pistol anything more destructive than .22 Long Rifle Winchester Super-X Dynapoints which, according to my highly reliable Oehler Model 33 Chronotach, exit the slick, button-rifled bore of my 6½-inch bull-barreled AMT Lightning autoloading

pistol at a respectable 1,153 fps. A rifle only gets about 10 fps more. In a Ruger revolver, that speed only slips slightly, to 1,128 fps. Dimple-pointed 40-grain Dynapoint bullets have the happy facility of expanding to dime diameter without blowing the tiny beasts to smithereens. Through the shoulders, they'll anchor any medium-sized rabbit without ruining it for eating.

For anything from our sinewy Western jack rabbits on up to hard-to-stop coyotes, I recommend using one of the ultra-high velocity .22 Long Rifle cartridges such as Federal's Spitfires, Remington's hollow-point Yellow Jackets and solid-point Vipers, or Winchester's Super Max. CCI Stingers started it all, and they remain the fastest and certainly among the most accurate. From the AMT Lightning, they tached a formidable 1,326 fps! The far more expensive .22 Winchester Magnum Rimfire (WMR) ammunition only gets 1,480 fps from a handgun. In fairness, it should be mentioned that the .22 WMR packs a greater contrast in foot-pounds, because it delivers a 40-grain hollow-point, rather than the 33-grain Penta-Point of the Stinger. However, the explosiveness of the Penta-Point just about offsets the advantage.

A handy distance to sight-in at is 50 yards. For all practical purposes, you can hold dead-on from the muzzle to the theoretical maximum range of 66 yards. With the ramped ⅛-inch Patridge post and Micro target adjustable rear sights zeroed at 50 yards, the Lightning groups about ¾-inch high at 25 yards, and approximately an inch low at 66.

The AMT Lightning is an excellent field pistol, as well as being accurate enough to hold its own on the firing line. The tubular stainless steel receiver is milled to accept tip-off-scope mounts, making it a good candidate for adding a scope sight. The Lightning features a 10-shot magazine, a bolt stop to

Range work helps tone the handgun hunter. Shoot at animals no further than you can hold 3" group.

hold the slide back after the last shot, thumb safety button left/rear on the stainless steel frame, a wide, serrated target trigger with Allen-head screw for backlash adjustment, a smooth, creepless release, a lip jutting out from the bottom of the trigger guard to facilitate two-hand holding, and finally, Pachmayr checkered black neoprene grips with handy ambidextrous thumb rests.

A durable, precision-fit hip holster for the AMT Lightning is Uncle Mike's padded black Nylon #6, with stout webbing belt loop and snap-down safety strap. A more elegant leather holster is the Bianchi Model 89L ".22 Protector," lined with soft silicone-suede, featuring Bianchi's exclusive metal-reinforced "Sight Channel." A matching deep-molded double magazine pouch is also available.

Many autoloading pistol fans share an emotional attachment for the fine old Luger pistol of World War I fame. It has the same appeal for them that a single-action revolver does for us old Roy Rogers fans! Even as Bill Ruger rescued the single-action revolver, so did Stoeger Industries keep the Luger alive, in the form of a new all-steel .22 LR recreation of the famed toggle-action self-loader, with the same incomparable grip shape and angle. It is currently available in a beautifully fitted and finished cased commemorative "American Eagle" edition, that makes a comely and competent field sidearm.

One of my all-time favorite field guns, the Harrington & Richardson top-break Model 999 is also now offered in an engraved "Presentation Grade," cased with a bronze medallion. This fine gun was originally designed by a handgun engineering pioneer, the famed Walter Roper. New from H&R is their swing-out-cylinder, heavy-barreled 600 and 900 series, with full-length ribs, grooved to accept tip-off mounted scopes, such as their own 3X20mm M-435.

For personal defense, .22 rimfire handguns have just one thing going for them. There are more of them out there than just about anything else. And the first requirement of a defense handgun is simply that it be there when needed! If you already have a .22 Long Rifle revolver or autoloading pistol, and can't be inspired to buy something more potent, it's you that I'm talking to.

One of author's favorite .22 LRs is S&W 22/32 Kit Gun which he carries in early Bianchi hip holster.

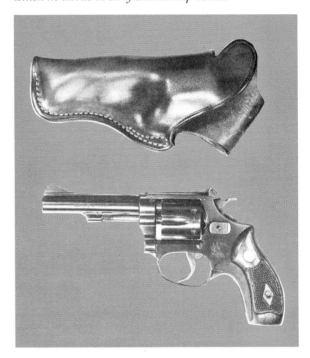

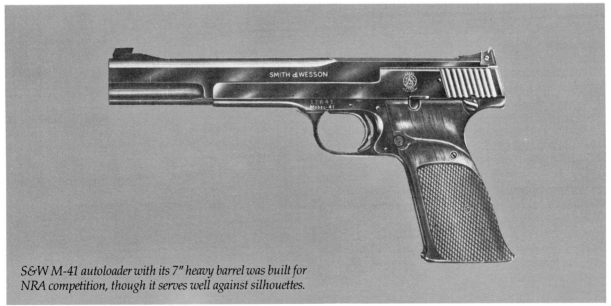

S&W M-41 autoloader with its 7" heavy barrel was built for NRA competition, though it serves well against silhouettes.

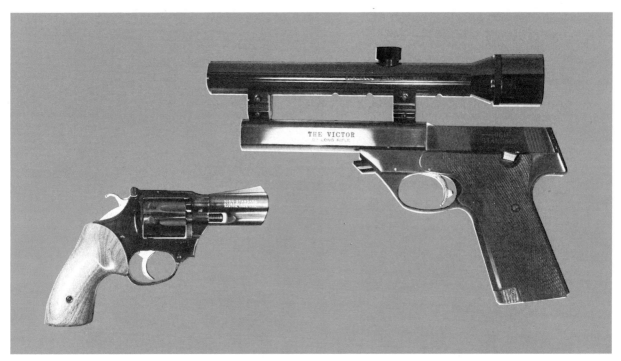

High Standard has wide line of .22 LRs, including Victor auto and Sentinel DA swing-out revolver.

Anytime you speak of defense, it implies that you're under attack, presumably in your own home, or perhaps near your RV — where it's legal for you to have a gun. It's highly probable that your attacker(s) will be unarmed, or merely carrying a knife or blunt instrument, in which case your small-bore handgun should act as a deterrent. Failing that, it should be adequate to stop your assailant before he can harm you or your family — if you act fast enough! Before you can be justified in using brute force your opponent must pose a direct threat to you or your family's life. He must indicate with words or actions that he intends to do just that. And he must be close enough to carry out his threat. That gives you a lot to think about before you squeeze the trigger!

A surprising number of small handguns are apparently designed for defense. Among the most practical is Charter Arms' eight-shot, double-action, stainless-steel autoloading Model 40 .22 Long Rifle, with open sights, burr hammer, and thumb safety on the slide. The gun is large enough to offer accuracy and easy controllability, yet small enough at 2½ ounces, with a 3.3-inch barrel, for easy concealment.

Even granting that a .22 rimfire pistol or revolver isn't the ideal answer of every purpose, properly selected with a bias toward the greatest need, it is by every measure the most versatile and satisfying handgun going!

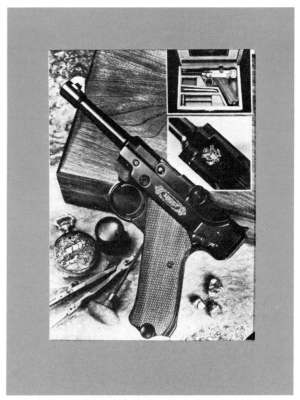

For those enamored of P-08 pistol, Stoeger offers .22 LR Luger. This modified toggle-top is available in cased commemorative "American Eagle" version.

The Grand Ballistic Illusion

Jim Carmichel

It looks like we made something of a mistake. When I say "we" I mean just about every outdoor magazine and shooting journal and all the firearms books and catalogs that have been published over the past 100 years or so.

Actually, the mistake wasn't really an error of fact. It was a failure to fully explain what we were talking about. It caused many, if not most, readers to have a faulty understanding of a bullet's flight. The printed word — or picture — seldom fails more miserably.

The error crashed down on me again awhile back when I was drying my boots over a tent stove somewhere along the Turnagain River in northern British Columbia. One of my fellow hunters was a pleasant fellow from Germany who, like most of his tribe, loves guns and will tell hunting yarns until the last drop of schnapps is wrung from the bottle. He was well versed on rifles, ammunition, and related equipment, and quoted from memory the velocities and energy figures of a wide range of cartridges. That's why I was surprised when he insisted that when a bullet exits the muzzle of a rifle, it climbs above the bore line. According to his understanding of a bullet's flight, it is as though a bullet had wings and could rise upward during the first part of its flight.

When I explained that this is impossible, he grinned in triumph.

"Ah, Mr. Carmichel, I will now show you where you are mistaken," he told me.

After digging through his expensive leather duffle, he came up with a German shooting catalog and eagerly flipped the pages to a section on ballistics and presented me with the irrefutable evidence.

"And now what do you say?" he asked.

And there it was — as plain as bear sign on flat rock. It wasn't proof of his argument; rather, that diagram and others like it cause the endless calls and letters I receive that usually begin: "My hunting pal and me have a bet we want you to settle. He says a bullet climbs when it leaves the barrel. I say it goes flat…"

The drawing in the German catalog seemed clear at first sight and was almost identical to hundreds of other such illustrations that we've all seen in hundreds of shooting publications. The drawing showed a hunter aiming his rifle at a moose that was said to be 300 meters distant. Two dotted lines issued from the rifle. One, identified as the line of sight (sometimes the line of bore was used), went straight to the animal's shoulder. The other, identified as the bullet's path, angled upward from a level bore and then curved downward so that it intersected the line of sight at point of impact on the moose's shoulder.

Obviously, anyone who takes this diagram, and

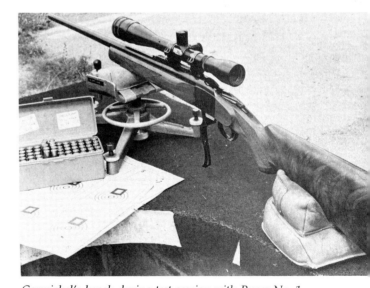

Carmichel's bench during test session with Ruger No. 1. After decades of reporting such tests and explaining the workings of firearms, he feels he and other gun writers have failed to correct basic misunderstandings about trajectory. Many shooters still believe bullet rises above bore line. Here, in text and diagrams, he clears away cobwebs.

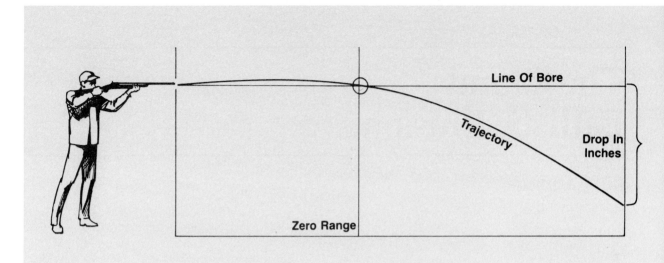

One form of erroneous trajectory drawing that often appears in shooting publications. Rifle's bore is horizontal, yet the bullet's flight rises above line of bore before curving back down to hit target. This is impossible because gravity affects bullet on exit from

those like it, at face value — without reading the fine print — immediately concludes that a bullet begins climbing as soon as it spins out of rifle or handgun barrel. No wonder my companion and thousands upon thousands of other shooters are willing to bet the farm that bullets rise like skyrockets. As I said, the blame rests with guys like me and with ballistic diagrams that don't tell the whole story. We apologize.

Now let's set things right. We'll start with the classic example of a rifle that is held so that the bore is perfectly level and horizontal to the earth's surface when the bullet exits the muzzle. What happens? Old Man Gravity takes charge and immediately begins pulling the bullet downward. This is caused by one of the earth's favorite, and oldest, laws, and there's no way we can avoid gravity, except by cheating.

If you're interested in *seeing* how fast gravity makes a bullet fall, just hold one in your hand and drop it. The same gravity that makes a bullet fall immediately when dropped from your hand makes a high-speed bullet come to earth. The classic demonstration is a level rifle held at a given height above level ground and a bullet held in your hand at the same height. If you drop your bullet at the same instant that an identical bullet leaves the muzzle of the rifle, they will hit the ground at *almost* the same instant, even though the bullet from the rifle will also have traveled several hundred yards. (The reason I say *almost* at the same instant is that some funny things happen to a speeding bullet but, for all practical purposes, they hit at the same time.)

Why do all those pictures make it look like a rifle bullet angles upward? The reason is that we try to cheat gravity by tilting the rifle's bore slightly so that it is inclined upward by a fraction of a degree in respect to the line of sight. In other words, we actually launch the bullet at a slight upward angle. It doesn't rise by itself. That's the part that isn't made clear in most trajectory diagrams.

The reason we launch the bullet at a slightly upward angle is to increase the range at which we can hit a target. Remember back when you played Little League center field and tried to pick off runners at home plate? You didn't throw the ball in a level straight line because, if you had, it would have fallen far short of the target. To increase your range, you threw the ball at an upward angle and it came back down to reach the catcher at the right height. It's the same with rifles. In fact, a bullet fired on the level falls surprisingly fast. For example, a streamlined 180-grain bullet fired from a .30/06 drops about 2½ inches below the bore line by the time it goes 100 yards. At 200 yards, the bullet has fallen nearly a foot and, at 300 yards, it has dropped more than two feet. Obviously, this would make it pretty hard to hit a deer at long range. Therefore, we cheat gravity just a little bit.

CHEATING GRAVITY

We do this by inclining the bore in relation to line of sight so that the bullet hits, say, two inches above where we aim at 100 yards. We don't really cheat gravity this way. Actually, we get it to cooperate with our ploy. Gravity takes hold of our bullet and pulls it back earthward in a beautifully curved line called a trajectory. Thus, by angling the .30/06 barrel

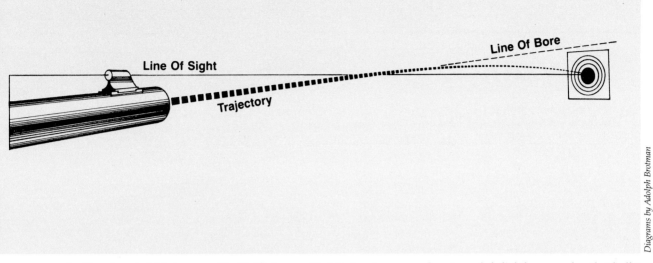

muzzle. Drawing at right shows reality. If rifle is zeroed to hit at a given range, bore is angled slightly upward so that bullet crosses line of sight at about 25 yds. and then comes back down to hit target. Note that bullet does not rise above line of bore.

upward so that the bullet is two inches above point of aim at 100 yards, we can count on Old Man Gravity to bend the trajectory downward so that the bullet hits right where we aim at 200 yards and is less than a foot below where we aim at 300 yards. This gives us a much better chance of hitting a distant target. This is what those confusing trajectory diagrams were trying to make clear.

Do you know that a bullet's trajectory doesn't always follow a curved path? The curvature is most pronounced when we hold the rifle level — meaning parallel with the ground. As we elevate or lower the muzzle from the horizontal, the curve straightens out gradually. If we shot straight up or straight down, the bullet's path would be perfectly straight. This is why we tend to overshoot our target when shooting uphill or downhill. The trajectory simply doesn't have as much downward curve as it does when we shoot over level ground.

If you were to aim your rifle straight up with the bore perpendicular to level ground, the bullet would travel upward in a straight line, come to a stop, and then fall straight back down along its original path. It's unsafe to try this yourself, but rest assured that the bullet would seldom fall back into the gun barrel. First of all, it's almost impossible to aim a rifle perfectly straight up and, even if you could, some atmospheric turbulence would almost always blow it off course.

OTHER PUZZLES

And that brings up another topic of campfire debate. If you fire a bullet straight up, will it fall with the same speed and energy with which it went up? The answer is both yes and no. If you tried this trick in a vacuum, the falling bullet would indeed be traveling at the same speed with which it went up. For example, if the bullet was launched at 2,000 fps, it would be traveling at that speed when it came to earth. But when we try the trick in our normal atmosphere, the bullet doesn't come down nearly as fast as it went up. This is because of air resistance. The falling bullet reaches a terminal velocity that is a "sort-of" balance between the pull of gravity and atmospheric drag. Anyone who has been hit on the head by falling shotgun pellets in a dove field or duck blind knows that this is a mighty good thing because the shot merely tickles. The shot would hit at muzzle velocity if it had been fired straight up in a vacuum.

The question that begs to be answered when a rifle bullet is fired straight up is: Will it still be spinning when it falls to earth and, if so, will it fall point first or base first?

As it happens, a bullet retains its rotational speed more efficiently than its velocity. When the bullet reaches the apex of its straight upward climb, it is still spinning rapidly and retains much of its gyroscopic stability. Thus, it falls base first. But, if the bullet isn't fired straight up — say, for instance, that it's fired at about an 85-degree angle or less — it performs a gyroscopic progression that causes it to have a point-forward attitude throughout its flight.

Gravity does some ugly things. It makes it harder for us to hit a distant target. It causes our wrinkles to sag and our bellies to hang over our belts. But look at the bright side. If it weren't for gravity, we'd fall off this beautiful earth.

Analyzing Accuracy Data

William C. Davis, Jr.

We shooters spend a lot of time shooting groups to compare the accuracy of different loads, bullets, or guns. How successful we are depends on how well we have designed the test and whether we take the time and have the capability to draw sound conclusions from our test results.

When we want to compare two different loads, or bullets, or guns, we usually shoot a few groups with one, then a few groups with the other. We compute the average extreme spreads, and we find that the average with one is smaller than the average with the other. Can we then conclude that the one load, or bullet, or gun, is really more accurate than the other? Not necessarily.

Suppose we fired three groups with one particular load and gun, and then fired three more groups with the same load and gun, under the same conditions.

We know that the average of the first three groups would probably be either a little larger or a little smaller than the average of the second three groups, all fired with the *same* load and gun. That is the manifestation of chance. So how do we know whether the averages we obtain with two *different* loads or guns really indicate that one is more accurate than the other?

What we usually do is think about whether the difference in averages is great or small, how many groups we have fired, and how many shots per group. We then make an intuitive judgment, which is another term for our best educated guess. But there are better ways.

Statisticians tell us that we should determine whether the results of a test show a *significant* difference between one sample and another. So we need a statistician. Then we might ask, "How do we know whether the difference is significant?" That depends on the factors that we recognized intuitively in the first place: "How large is the difference? How many groups did we fire? How many shots per group?"

If we give that information to the statistician, he might ask what *level of significance* we require. By that he means, "How sure do you want to be that the difference is real, and not due to chance?" When called upon to decide that question, we might say that we would like to be 99 percent certain that the difference is real. Given that information, the statistician can do his analysis and tell us either that the difference is significant or it is not.

If it is not, does that mean we have wasted our time and learned nothing more than we knew before we shot the test? Intuitively, we think we know better than that, but then what can we do? The statistician says that perhaps if we had more data, then he could help us. But how much more data do we need to make a decision, and is it worth the effort?

Perhaps we can afford to take the risk of being wrong, but what is that risk, on the basis of what we already know? If we knew that the results we already have indicate with 98 percent confidence that the difference is real, then that might be good enough for our purposes. Remember that we told the statistician we wanted 99 percent confidence, and he tested only for that.

This article first appeared in THE AMERICAN RIFLEMAN.

On the other hand, if our present results give us only a little more than 50 percent confidence that one load is better than the other, then we have accomplished very little. We could have tossed a coin, knowing nothing at all about the two loads or guns, and our probability of picking the accurate one of the two would be 50 percent.

The computer program listed here should help us to make some sense out of all these statistics. Statisticians will find it unconventional, but perhaps it makes more sense than the conventional approach to us non-statisticians.

What it will give us, after we have input our accuracy data, is the best possible estimate of the *probability* that one of the loads we tested is truly more accurate than the other. A statistician would call it a "point estimate" of that probability.

Most of us understand what is meant by "probability." If the weatherman announces that the probability of rain tomorrow is 90 percent, we understand that a prediction of rain would have nine chances in 10 of being right, and one chance in 10 of being wrong. So it is with decisions about accuracy, based on this program.

Suppose we want to compare the accuracy of two different loads. What we will need is a record of the extreme spreads of some groups obtained with each load. To simplify the program, it has been designed for comparing the data on the basis of the same number of groups with each load, and the same number of shots per group. We do not need to compute the average extreme spreads beforehand, because the program will do that for us. Let us try an example.

Suppose we are testing two different handgun loads at 50 yards. We have fired five five-shot groups with each load. We load the program into the computer, and enter RUN. The video displays a short description of the program, and the instructions:

```
NUMBER OF GROUPS WITH EACH SAMPLE MUST BE THE
SAME.
NUMBER OF SHOTS PER GROUP MUST BE THE SAME.
NUMBER OF SHOTS PER GROUP?
```

To which we enter: "5." The video now asks:

```
NUMBER OF GROUPS IN EACH SAMPLE?
```

To which we enter "5." The video now asks us to enter the extreme spreads of each group in the first sample, and we enter them as follows:

```
ENTER THE GROUPS FOR THE FIRST SAMPLE.
NUMBER 1? 2.90
NUMBER 2? 2.74
NUMBER 3? 3.57
NUMBER 4? 3.86
NUMBER 5? 5.00
```

And for the second sample:

```
NUMBER 1? 5.25
NUMBER 2? 4.13
NUMBER 3? 5.69
```

```
NUMBER 4? 2.75
NUMBER 5? 3.25
```

The computer now prints out our results:

```
THE GROUPS IN SAMPLE ''A'':
2.90 2.74 3.57 3.86 5.00
THE AVERAGE EXTREME SPREAD FOR SAMPLE ''A'' IS:
3.614
THE GROUP IN SAMPLE ''B'':
5.25 4.13 5.69 2.75 3.25
THE AVERAGE EXTREME SPREAD FOR SAMPLE ''B'' IS:
4.214
THE STATISTIC ''T'' FOR THESE SAMPLES: .887
THE PROBABILITY THAT ''A'' IS MORE ACCURATE
THAN ''B'' (PCT): 80
```

Now we can decide whether the test was sufficient for our purposes. If we are satisfied with an 80 percent probability that the load giving the smaller average extreme spread is truly the more accurate load, then our test was sufficient. If we want more assurance before we decide which load to adopt, then we must shoot more groups, and run the program again, using the additional data.

It should be noted that the program will always assign the designation "Sample A" to the load (or bullet, or gun) which produced the smaller average extreme spread, and "Sample B" to the other load (or bullet, or gun). We cannot do that beforehand. The STATISTIC "T" mentioned in the printout is a number that has meaning to statisticians, who might want to give it some consideration. If you are not a statistician, you need not be concerned with its meaning.

You should keep in mind that a probability of 50 percent was where you started. Knowing nothing at all about the performance of the two loads, you could have picked one arbitrarily as the more accurate, with a 50 percent probability of being right. If the probability you compute from your data is not much better than that, then you know virtually nothing about which load is the more accurate. If the two loads give nearly the same performance, you may never get a number much above 50 percent, but then you have proved that it doesn't matter which load you choose on the basis of accuracy.

If you want to save time and computer memory in copying the program from the listing, you can omit from any line the colon that precedes the letters "REM", and everything that follows in that program line. Those are "REMarks," for the benefit of users who are interested in the logic and mathematical basis for the calculations; they have no effect on the program itself.

If you are not interested in statistics, you can well afford to skip this paragraph and go to the next one. For those who are interested, it should be said that this program is based on the fact that the shots fired at a target perpendicular to the trajectory will typically form a circular normal distribution.

It has been well established that, in a circular

normal distribution, the coefficient of variation of the extreme spread for individual groups is a function of the number of shots fired per group. That function is well approximated by the equation in line 130 of the program.

The "probabilities," or "confidence levels," for significant differences between the average extreme spreads of the respective samples are inferred from a one-tailed analysis based on the cumulative "T" distribution, which is adequately represented by the polynomials in lines 1000 to 1110. For those interested in the more esoteric details of the analysis of dispersion data on targets, readers are referred to the article "Determining Rifle Accuracy," in the NRA book titled "HANDLOADING," and to the

excellent booklet titled STATISTICAL MEASURES OF ACCURACY FOR RIFLEMEN AND MISSILE ENGINEERS, by Frank E. Grubbs, Ph.D., available from the author at 4109 Webster Road, Havre De Grace, MD 21078. Tables of the cumulative "T" distribution can be found in many standard texts and handbooks on statistics.

Readers are permitted to copy this program from the listing for their own personal use. Other uses, without specific permission, are prohibited because the program is copyrighted. For readers who choose not to copy the listing for themselves, this program, together with some other statistical programs for shooters, is available on a cassette or disk from PABsoft, Box 15397, Ft. Wayne, IN 46885.

```
10 PRINT" *** FINDING ESTIMATED CONFIDENCE THAT AMMUNITION SAMPLE 'A' IS MORE ACCURATE THAN SAMP
LE 'B' FROM EXTREME SPREADS OF N TARGETS OF P SHOTS EACH - FILENAME 'TGSTAT1/CMD' REV  07/05/85
***":PRINT ""
20 PRINT" *** COPYRIGHT 1983 BY WM. C. DAVIS,JR. ***":PRINT""
60 PRINT"   1. NUMBER OF GROUPS WITH EACH SAMPLE MUST BE THE SAME."
70 PRINT"   2. NUMBER OF SHOTS PER GROUP MUST BE THE SAME.":PRINT" "
100 INPUT"NUMBER OF SHOTS PER GROUP";P
110 INPUT"NUMBER OF GROUPS IN EACH SAMPLE";N
120 GOSUB 3000:REM FIND AVG EXTREME SPREAD
130 CV=.11+.812/P:REM COEFFICIENT OF VARIATION FOR P-SHOT GROUPS
140 GOSUB 2000:REM FIND STATISTIC'T'
150 GOSUB 1000:REM FIND PROBABILITY FROM CUM'T'-DISTRIBUTION
160 PP=INT(100*PR+.5)
170 IF PR<.51 THEN PP=50
180 IF PR>.99 THEN PP=99
190 PRINT"THE STATISTIC 'T' FOR THESE SAMPLES:";TAB(41);INT(1000*T+.5)/1000:PRINT" "
200 PRINT"PROBABILITY THAT  'A' IS MORE ACCURATE THAN  'B' (PCT): ";PP;
210 IF PR>.99 THEN PRINT"+"
220 PRINT" "
230 INPUT"COPY THIS? (1=YES 2=NO)";QQ
240 IF QQ<>1 THEN GOTO 430
250 LPRINT"NUMBER OF GROUPS PER SAMPLE:"TAB(41);N
260 LPRINT"NUMBER OF SHOTS PER GROUP:";TAB(41);P:LPRINT" "
270 LPRINT"THE GROUPS IN SAMPLE 'A':"
280 FOR K=1 TO N
290 IF M1=>M2 THEN LPRINT R(K); ELSE LPRINT L(K);
300 NEXT K
310 LPRINT" "
320 LPRINT"AVERAGE EXTREME SPREAD FOR SAMPLE 'A':";TAB(51);INT(1000*MA+.5)/1000:LPRINT" "
330 LPRINT"THE GROUPS IN SAMPLE 'B':"
340 FOR K=1 TO N
350 IF M1<M2 THEN LPRINT R(K); ELSE LPRINT L(K);
360 NEXT K
370 LPRINT" "
380 LPRINT"AVERAGE EXTREME SPREAD FOR SAMPLE 'B':";TAB(51);INT(1000*MB+.5)/1000:LPRINT" "
390 LPRINT"THE STATISTIC 'T' FOR THESE SAMPLES:";TAB(51);INT(1000*T+.5)/1000:LPRINT" "
400 LPRINT"PROBABILITY THAT 'A' IS MORE ACCURATE THAN 'B' (PCT):";TAB(60);PP;
410 IF PR>.99 THEN LPRINT"+"
420 LPRINT" ":LPRINT" "
430 INPUT"WHAT NEXT?
   1=SAME NUMBER OF GROUPS, SAME NUMBER OF SHOTS/GROUP
   2=DIFFERENT NUMBER OF GROUPS, SAME NUMBER OF SHOTS PER GROUP
   3=DIFFERENT NUMBER OF GROUPS, DIFFERENT NUMBER OF SHOTS/GROUP";QP
440 IF QP=1 THEN CLS:GOTO 120
450 IF QP=2 THEN CLS:GOTO 110
460 CLS:GOTO 100
470 END
```

```
1000 REM *** ROUTINE TO PRODUCE CUMULATIVE T-DISTRIBUTION **
1010 IF N=2 THEN PR=.511964+.355102*T-.0946985*T^2+8.56527E-03*T 3:RETURN
1020 IF N=3 THEN PR=.50647+.399187*T-.109986*T^2+.0100306*T^3:RETURN
1030 IF N=4 THEN PR=.49464+.441559*T-.131424*T^2+.0130471*T^3:RETURN
1040 IF N=5 THEN PR=.488626+.465505*T-.144708*T^2+.0151012*T^3:RETURN
1050 IF N=6 THEN PR=.487085+.472943*T-.147892*T^2+.0154715*T^3:RETURN
1060 IF N=7 THEN PR=.481362+.490886*T-.159558*T^2+.0175902*T^3:RETURN
1070 IF N=8 THEN PR=.484707+.484639*T-.155319*T^2+.0167787*T^3:RETURN
1080 IF N=9 OR N=10 THEN PR=.482459+.493074*T-.15917*T^2+.0172593*T^3:RETURN
1090 IF N=11 OR N=12 THEN PR=.482693+.491112*T-.156921*T^2+.0166946*T^3:RETURN
1100 IF N>12 AND N=<16 THEN PR=.480631+.503436*T-.163799*T^2+.0177646*T^3:RETURN
1110 IF N>16 THEN PR=.47942+.50981*T-.166233*T^2+.0179374*T^3:RETURN
2000 REM *** ROUTINE TO FIND T ***
2010 SA=CV*MA:REM STD DEV OF GROUPS IN SAMPLE A
2020 EA=SA/SQR(N):REM STD ERROR OF MEAN MA
2030 SB=CV*MB:REM STD DEV OF GROUPS IN SAMPLE B
2040 EB=SB/SQR(N):REM STD ERROR OF MEAN MB
2050 ED=SQR(EA^2+EB^2):REM STD ERROR OF DIFF (MA-MB)
2060 T=(MA-MB)/ED:T=ABS(T)
2070 RETURN
3000 REM *** ROUTINE TO FIND AVERAGE EXTREME SPREADS ***
3010 PRINT"ENTER THE GROUPS FOR THE FIRST SAMPLE."
3020 FOR K=1 TO N
3030 PRINT"NUMBER ";K;
3040 INPUT S
3050 GOSUB 3510
3060 SS=SS+S
3070 NEXT K
3080 M1=SS/N:S=0:SS=0:PRINT" "
3090 PRINT"ENTER THE GROUPS FOR THE SECOND SAMPLE"
3100 FOR K=1 TO N
3110 PRINT"NUMBER ";K;
3120 INPUT S
3130 GOSUB 3520
3140 SS=SS+S
3150 NEXT K
3160 M2=SS/N:S=0:SS=0:PRINT" "
3170 IF M1=>M2 THEN MA=M2:MB=M1
3180 IF M1<M2 THEN MA=M1:MB=M2:PRINT" "
3190 PRINT"THE GROUPS IN SAMPLE 'A':"
3200 FOR K=1 TO N
3210 IF M1=>M2 THEN PRINT R(K); ELSE PRINT L(K);
3220 NEXT K
3230 PRINT" "
3240 PRINT"THE AVERAGE EXTREME SPREAD FOR SAMPLE 'A' IS:";TAB(41);INT(1000*MA+.5)/1000:PRINT" "
3250 PRINT"THE GROUPS IN SAMPLE 'B':"
3260 FOR K=1 TO N
3270 IF M1<M2 THEN PRINT R(K); ELSE PRINT L(K);
3280 NEXT K
3290 PRINT" "
3300 PRINT"THE AVERAGE EXTREME SPREAD FOR SAMPLE 'B' IS:";TAB(41);INT(1000*MB+.5)/1000
3310 PRINT" "
3320 RETURN
3500 REM *** ACCUMULATOR FOR INDIVIDUAL GROUPS ***
3510 L(K)=S:RETURN
3520 R(K)=S:RETURN
```

```
    NUMBER OF GROUPS PER SAMPLE:              5
    NUMBER OF SHOTS PER GROUP:                5

    THE GROUPS IN SAMPLE 'A':
     2.9  2.74  3.57  3.86  5
    AVERAGE EXTREME SPREAD FOR SAMPLE 'A':            3.614

    THE GROUPS IN SAMPLE 'B':
     5.25  4.13  5.69  2.75  3.25
    AVERAGE EXTREME SPREAD FOR SAMPLE 'B':            4.214

    THE STATISTIC 'T' FOR THESE SAMPLES:             .887

    PROBABILITY THAT 'A' IS MORE ACCURATE THAN 'B' (PCT):        80
```

A Study in Stopping Power

John F. Thilenius
and William R. Meehan

Forest Service regulations require that at least one member of each work party carry a rifle in Kodiak bear country. In the past, most Forest Service personnel in southeast Alaska were accustomed to firearms. Today, the Service employs people who not only know little or nothing about firearms, but in many cases have a strong aversion to them. Before they can be sent afield they must be trained to use rifles for their own protection. That has created problems.

Up to now most arms training has centered around rifles favored by experienced Service personnel: short-barreled, bolt-action .375 Holland & Holland Magnums. Many trainees have discovered that shooting one of those healthy kickers was an experience they'd rather not repeat. Some became more afraid of the rifles they had to carry than the bears they might meet.

Life, and training, would have been much simpler if less powerful rifles could be used. The question was: which to choose? Which would offer adequate close-range protection against a charging Brown?

The effectiveness of sporting rounds — and especially their bullets — is normally judged at the ranges at which big game is taken. What about performance up close — at say, 15 to 20 yards? How

This article first appeared in *RIFLE.*

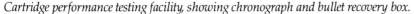

Cartridge performance testing facility, showing chronograph and bullet recovery box.

would the different calibers stack up as stopping rounds?

To find the answers to those questions, the Forest Service launched a test program a few years ago. The article that follows is a condensation of the experimenters' report.

METHODS

Most testing was done with rifles, but we also evaluated handguns and the 12-gauge shotgun. Handguns are often worn by people when their work requires the use of both hands. The short-barreled 12-gauge shotgun also has a reputation as a good weapon at close range. Both slugs and buckshot were tested in the shotgun. In some instances, weapons firing a given cartridge were available with different barrel lengths. We tested as many as possible to evaluate the effects of barrel length on bullet performance.

We used ammunition manufactured by several companies, and made no attempt to compare similar loads of different manufacturers. We fired three shots with each combination of cartridge, bullet weight (or type), and barrel length. To limit bias in the data, we fired in random order.

To determine penetration depth and to recover fired bullets, we used the testing medium recommended by Bob Hagel (1978), who found that recovered bullets shot into a moistened mixture of 50 percent fine silt and 50 percent fine sawdust (by volume) were similar to bullets removed from various big-game animals, including bear.

We built an open-ended wooden box 12x12x24 inches to hold the silt/sawdust mixture, covering the ends with scrap pieces of carpet to prevent spillage through the bullet holes. To facilitate locating bullets, we placed the mixture in 4x10x12 inch cardboard file wallets. Six tightly filled wallets fit snugly into the box.

We evaluated each cartridge/bullet and barrel length combination in four ballistic categories: striking energy, penetration, retained bullet weight, and bullet expansion. All shots were fired through the photoelectric screens of a Ballistocraft chronograph to determine bullet velocity.

Recovered bullets and bullet fragments were washed in hot water and detergent, then rinsed, dried, and weighed to the nearest grain. To determine expansion, we measured the maximum diameter of the bullet (or of the largest fragment) to the nearest tenth of an inch and again at a point 90 degrees from the maximum diameter. Both retained bullet weight and expansion were expressed as a percentage of the weight and cross-sectional area of an unfired bullet pulled from a cartridge identical to that fired in the tests.

Our first step in evaluating overall ballistic performance was to calculate the average value in each

category for the three shots fired from each test combination. We then divided each average by the maximum average value in its category to convert it to a relative proportion of the maximum value encountered during the tests. The quotient was rounded to two significant decimal places and multiplied by 100 to eliminate decimals. This transformation also eliminated the different category units and allowed all four to be arithmetically combined into a single performance score. We calculated this overall score by multiplying the four relative scores of each test combination. To eliminate the use of unwieldy eight-digit numbers as scores, we divided

Bullet recovery box. The six file wallets inside were filled with a silt/sawdust mixture recommended by Bob Hagel.

Hole made by 510-grain .458 Mag. File wallet was fourth in the box!

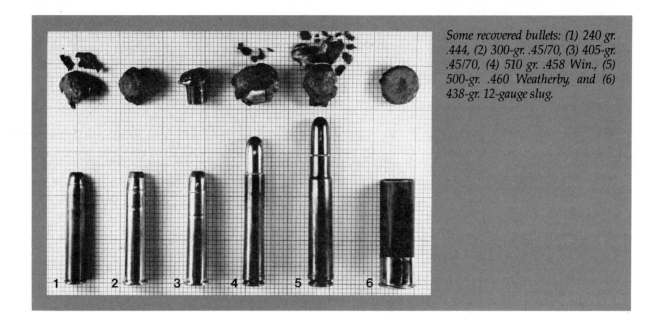

Some recovered bullets: (1) 240 gr. .444, (2) 300-gr. .45/70, (3) 405-gr. .45/70, (4) 510 gr. .458 Win., (5) 500-gr. .460 Weatherby, and (6) 438-gr. 12-gauge slug.

the product by 100,000 and rounded the quotient to the nearest whole number. This provided a two- or three-digit score for each test combination, which we ranked in highest to lowest order.

HOW THEY RANKED — AND WHY

.458 Winchester Magnum. Overall, the .458 ranked first. Bullet penetration was deepest of all the cartridges tested — average depth: 19 inches. Striking energy was 79 percent of the .460 Weatherby. The bullet expanded well (4.6 times) and retained 82 percent of its unfired weight. The 510-grain Winchester factory bullets did not fragment, but the 500-grain bullets of the .460 Weatherby did — the major reason for their second-place ranking.

Recoil in the 9.4-pound rifle was 54.7 foot-pounds or about 71 percent of that of the .460. Less recoil, a lighter rifle, and better bullet performance make the .458 Winchester preferable to the .460 Weatherby. A short-barreled, bolt-action .458 would be an excellent choice for an experienced rifleman. Shortening the barrel to 22 or even 20 inches should not reduce ballistic performance much. Any weight reduction, however, would increase recoil.

.460 Weatherby Magnum. This cartridge was ranked second overall. The large-caliber, heavy bullet at relatively high velocity had good penetration, but not the deepest. Although the chronographed velocity did not approach advertised velocity, the bullet energy exceeded that of the .458

Winchester by over 1,300 foot-pounds. Average retained bullet weight was 65 percent. The bullets had a tendency to fragment. Cross-sectional area expansion was adequate and overall bullet performance good, but not the best.

The high overall performance of the .460 Weatherby was obtained in a heavy-recoiling, 10.7-pound rifle with a 26-inch barrel. We used a Weatherby Mark V rifle equipped with a receiver sight. It was difficult to use this sight because of the stock's high comb. This, plus the heavy recoil, made it very uncomfortable to shoot. The stock shape, heavy weight, and long barrel detract from the utility of the rifle in the heavy bush of coastal Alaska. This could be ameliorated if the rifle were remodeled, but shortening the barrel to 20 inches would lower velocity and energy. This might be beneficial if it also reduced the tendency of the bullet to fragment.

A short-barreled .460 would have tremendous muzzle blast, and the recoil of a .460 Weatherby weighing less than 10 pounds would be severe. It would be difficult to recover from the recoil and operate the bolt to chamber a second cartridge rapidly. For these reasons, the .460 Weatherby rifle is generally a poor choice for bear protection in coastal Alaska.

.375 Holland & Holland Magnum. The .375 Holland & Holland Magnum was one of the cartridges tested with different bullet weights and in rifles with different barrel lengths. With the 300-grain bullet in a rifle with a 24-inch barrel, it ranked third. With the 270-grain bullet in the same barrel it ranked fifth. Performance rankings for the rifle with a 20.5-inch barrel were tenth for the 300-grain bullet and sixteenth for the 270-grain bullet. Energy exceeded 4,200 foot-pounds in the longer-barreled rifle for both bullets and 3,700 foot-pounds for the shorter-barreled rifle. Bullets of both weights fired in the longer-barreled rifle penetrated about two inches deeper, but there were only minor differences in retained bullet weight and relative bullet expansion. Velocity losses in the shorter barrel were 160 fps for 270-grain bullets and 137 fps for 300-grain bullets. Chronographed velocities were close to those advertised for the rifle with a 24-inch barrel.

Recoil in the 8.6-pound rifle with a 24-inch barrel ranged from 37 to 43 foot-pounds. The 7.2-pound rifle with the shorter barrel had heavier recoil — 39 and 44 foot-pounds for the 270- and 300-grain bullets, respectively. The heaviest recoil value was 57 percent of the recoil value of the .460 Weatherby and 81 percent of the .458 Winchester.

The similarity in overall ballistic performance and not too severe recoil make the lighter rifle with the shorter barrel preferable, although some ballistic performance is lost. The 300-grain bullet is preferable to the 270-grain bullet. This type of .375 rifle is commonly carried in Coastal Alaska. The rifle must be rated at a capacity of three cartridges (magazine capacity) since it is unsafe to have a cartridge loaded in the chamber and depend on a mechanical safety to prevent discharge. This applies to bolt-action rifles with the possible exception of those made on military actions, such as the Mauser or Springfield with their 180-degree safety levers. Few .375 caliber rifles have such safeties. Regardless, the .375 Holland & Holland Magnum is an excellent cartridge for protection from bears at close range. Our tests merely reinforced its already excellent reputation.

.338 Winchester Magnum. The .338 Winchester was tested with three bullet weights (200, 250, and 300 grains) and in rifles with two barrel lengths, 24 and 20 inches. The 225-grain bullet was not available when we made the tests. The shorter-barreled rifle gave slightly better overall ballistic performance. With the 300-grain bullet it was ranked fourth and was close to the 300-grain .375 Holland & Holland with a four-inch longer barrel, although the .375 Holland & Holland had 740 foot-pounds more striking energy with a 300-grain bullet. The 300-grain .338 Winchester bullet had only .6 inch less penetration, retained slightly more bullet weight, and had slightly greater expansion. The 300-grain .338 bullet is no longer manufactured, which is unfortunate because the 250-grain bullet gave much poorer overall performance than either the 300- or the 200-grain bullet. The 250-grain .338 bullet is no longer available, either. The overall per-

formance of the .338 with the 200-grain bullet was one of the surprises in our tests. It was ranked sixth and eighth, the rifle with the shorter barrel giving the better performance. The 200-grain .338 bullet averaged 15 inches of penetration compared with 12.2 inches for the 250-grain bullet.

The 250-grain bullet had a tendency to shatter in the test medium. The 200-grain bullet should be selected if the 300-grain is not available. In the 7.2-pound .338 rifle with a 20-inch barrel, recoil was 35.6 foot-pounds with the heaviest bullet. This was somewhat less than in the .375 with the same weight of bullet in both light and heavy rifles. The load featuring the 200-grain bullet generated 28.9 and 26.0 foot-pounds of recoil respectively in the 20- and 24-inch barrels, and was not uncomfortable to shoot. Shortening the barrel had only a slight effect on velocity for the 300- and 250-grain bullets. With the 200-grain bullet, a greater reduction in velocity occurred. Chronographed velocities were similar to advertised velocities.

The reasonable recoil in a light, short-barreled rifle with impressive overall ballistic performance makes the .338 Winchester cartridge a good choice for bear protection.

.358 Norma Magnum. The .358 Norma Magnum ranked twentieth in our tests — mainly due to poor retained bullet weight and relative expansion. The 250-grain Norma factory bullets did not hold together well in the test medium. Retained bullet weight was low since this factor is based on the largest recovered bullet fragment. Although the bullets fragmented, penetration of the largest fragments was relatively deep.

Recoil of the .358 Norma Magnum was similar to recoil in the .338 and .375 rifles with 250- and 270-grain bullets. Other disadvantages are the cost and difficulty of obtaining the ammunition. Because of these considerations, the .358 Norma Magnum is not recommended.

7mm Remington Magnum. The 7mm Remington Magnum was the highest ranked (fifteenth) of the small-caliber cartridges. Bullet penetration was only moderately deep, and the bullets fragmented to some extent. Average retained weight was only 44 percent. Bullet expansion was the highest of all the bullets tested and that attribute gave the 7mm Remington its relatively high overall rank. Most other small-caliber Magnum cartridges had relatively poor expansion values.

The exception was the 8mm Remington Magnum 185-grain bullet which had high expansion but also had substantial weight loss and poor penetration.

The striking velocity of the 7mm Remington 175-grain bullet was barely 2,700 fps at 15 yards, well below what would be expected from published bal-

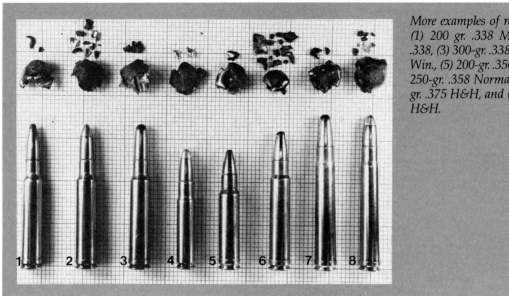

More examples of recovered bullets: (1) 200 gr. .338 Mag., (2) 250-gr. .338, (3) 300-gr. .338, (4) 200 gr. .358 Win., (5) 200-gr. .350 Rem. Mag., (6) 250-gr. .358 Norma Mag., (7) 270-gr. .375 H&H, and (8) 300-gr. .375 H&H.

listic data. Nevertheless, it appears the design limits of the bullet were exceeded.

Recoil was calculated at 18.5 foot-pounds in the 9.1-pound rifle tested. There does not appear to be any special reason for selecting the 7mm Remington for short-range protection. Its overall ballistic performance is marginal for this purpose.

.300 Weatherby, .300 Winchester, and 8mm Remington Magnums.   These three cartridges are considered together. All are loaded with moderate-weight bullets (180 to 185 grains) at velocities between 2,850 and 3,050 fps, and heavier bullets (200 to 220 grains) between 2,700 and 2,800 fps. These high velocities with moderately heavy bullets resulted in striking energies that exceed the design level of the bullets, especially the heavier ones. Fragmentation was prevalent among all of them and weight losses were 60 percent or more. The average weight of the largest fragment of the 8mm Remington 220-grain bullet was only 28 percent of the unfired bullet weight. The 185-grain bullet in the 8mm Remington was the best of the lighter-weight bullets in these three cartridges, ranking twenty-first in overall performance. Penetration was poor, however, and fragmentation excessive.

The 180-grain bullet in the .300 Winchester also had poor penetration and substantial weight loss, as well as relatively poor expansion, all of which contributed to its ranking in last place.

The ranking of the .300 Weatherby with the 180-grain bullet was somewhat of a surprise. Factory 180-grain cartridges are loaded with Nosler partition bullets which have an excellent reputation. In our test, the 180-grain bullets in the .300 Weatherby penetrated well, but lost over 50 percent of the unfired bullet weight and did not have particularly good expansion. The 180-grain bullet was much better in overall performance than the 220-grain bullet which fragmented badly. This was also true for the 200-grain bullet in the .300 Winchester.

None of the small-caliber Magnum cartridges can be considered as good selections because of excessive fragmentation of bullets.

.45/70 U.S.   We tested the .45/70 in two bullet weights (300 and 402 grains) and in rifles with two barrel lengths (20 and 22 inches). Both rifles were Marlin 1895 lever actions. In both, the 300-grain bullet ranked much higher than the 405-grain, primarily because of the poor expansion of the latter. At 1,200 to 1,300 fps striking velocity, some of the 405-grain bullets acted as solids and penetrated as much as 24 inches. This was the greatest penetration recorded in the tests.

The 300-grain bullets, with 300 to 400 fps more velocity, did not penetrate deeply but held together, expanding well and uniformly. Low velocities resulted in low striking energy. Shortening the barrel by two inches had no effect on the performance of the bullet. In fact, the rifle with the 20-inch barrel performed better with the 300-grain bullet than did the longer-barreled rifle.

Recoil in the Marlin 1895, which weighed less than 8 pounds, was much less severe than that of the large-caliber Magnums.

The poor action of the 405-grain bullets may limit their use for protection against bears. The 300-grain bullets in the commercial ammunition we used are designed for animals the size of deer and may expand too rapidly and lack sufficient penetration for use on bears. In our test they did not fragment too badly. The absence of a proper bullet is unfortunate. The .45/70 can be obtained in a compact, moderate-weight, lever-action rifle that may be easier and faster to operate for some people, particularly those who are left-handed.

Perhaps the current reinterest in .45/70 rifles will cause the manufacturers to produce a more suitable bullet. We do not consider factory .45/70 ammunition particularly suitable for a rifle for protection against bears, especially with the 405-grain bullet.

.444 Marlin. In overall performance, the .444 Marlin cartridge ranked thirteenth. Although penetration was not especially deep, the bullet held together and expanded well. Striking velocity exceeded 2,200 fps in the rifle with the 22-inch barrel. Consequently, striking energy was over 2,650 foot-pounds.

The flat-nose, soft-point bullet loaded in the .444 Marlin appears similar to that of the .44 Remington Magnum revolver cartridge. Although the .444 cartridge ranked relatively high, we still have reservations about shooting at a brown bear with a bullet designed for a handgun cartridge. If a well-constructed bullet of about 300 grains was available in factory ammunition, the .444 could become an adequate cartridge for protection from bears. We were unable to obtain the recently introduced factory cartridges loaded with 265-grain bullets.

.358 Winchester and .350 Remington Magnum. These were included to fill out the full range of cartridge possibilities. The .358 Winchester ranked higher (fourteenth) than the .350 Remington (twenty-fourth). Better retained bullet weight and greater bullet expansion accounted for the higher rank of the .358 Winchester. These two cartridges illustrate the poor relation between penetration and striking energy. The .350 Remington had 443 foot-pounds more striking energy than the .358 Winchester, but only .2 inch more penetration. In our tests there was relatively little difference between the .358 Winchester and some much larger, more powerful cartridges. Unfortunately, we were unable to obtain 250-grain bullets for either cartridge. The 200-grain bullet in the .358 Winchester, however, seems to be a well-balanced load. The relatively low striking energy was the factor that reduced the ranking of the .358 Winchester and, to some extent, the .350 Remington. In addition, the average retained bullet weight for the .350 Remington was 52 percent compared with 71 percent for the .358 Winchester.

Recoil was moderate and similar in both rifles. The .350 Remington rifle weighed a pound less than the .358 Winchester rifle. Both cartridges can be considered minimal for protection from bears at close range.

.30/06 U.S. With the 220-grain bullet the .30/06 ranked eleventh, and with the 180-grain bullet it ranked twelfth in overall ballistic performance. The 220-grain bullet penetrated 17.7 inches. This was 4.5 inches deeper than the 180-grain bullet, but the striking energy of the two bullets was similar. The 220-grain bullet had only 87 foot-pounds more energy at 15 yards. The 180-grain bullet retained slightly more weight than the 220, and also expanded slightly more relative to the initial cross-sectional area. The 180-grain bullet also had less tendency to fragment than did the 220.

Recoil for both bullet weights was mild compared with large and medium-bore Magnums. Chronographed velocities were much lower than advertised. The 220-grain bullet averaged 2,261 fps for three shots, whereas the 180-grain bullet averaged only 2,456 fps at 15 yards.

The light recoil potential and the good overall ballistic performance make the .30/06 a reasonable cartridge for bear protection. Because of the deeper penetration of the 220-grain bullet, it is better than the 180. For inexperienced persons or those of small stature, the .30/06 with 220-grain bullets may be a better choice than one of the large- or medium-bore Magnums. A seven- to 7.5-pound .30/06 with a 20-inch barrel would be a handy, portable rifle for protection from bears. A .30/06 has a major advantage over rifles using Magnum cartridges — magazine capacity is five rounds. Another advantage is the availability of left-handed bolt-action rifles in this caliber. The .30/06 is also available in slide-action and semiautomatic rifles.

.308 Winchester and 7X57mm Mauser. These two cartridges were included in the tests to represent the minimal cartridges that might be used. They are also often used by deer hunters. The ranges of the brown bear and the Sitka black-tailed deer (*Odocoileus hemionus sitkensis*) overlap through much of coastal Alaska, and deer hunters need protection from bears similar to that of working professionals.

Of the two cartridges, the .308 Winchester ranked higher (eighteenth) than the 7X57mm Mauser (twenty-fifth). The greatest difference was in retained bullet weight. The 7X57mm Mauser bullets lost almost half their weight, whereas the .308 Winchester bullets shed less than 25 percent of their original weight. The 7X57mm bullets had about one inch deeper penetration, but the range in penetration varied less in the .308 Winchester. Penetration of the 175-grain bullet in the 7X57mm Mauser was greater than that of the 175-grain bullet in the 7mm Remington Magnum, although striking energy was almost 600 foot-pounds less in the 7X57mm.

Recoil was mild for both cartridges. However,

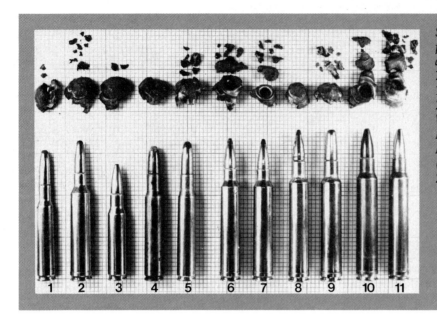

Some of these rounds' performance proved disappointing while others did unexpectedly well: (1) 175-gr. 7x57, (2) 175-gr. 7mm Mag., (3) 180-gr. .308, (4) 180-gr. .30/06, (5) 220-gr. .30/06, (6) 180-gr. .300 Win. Mag., (7) 200-gr. .300 Win. Mag., (8) 180-gr. .300 Weatherby Mag., (9) 220-gr. .300 Weatherby, (10) 185-gr. 8mm Mag., and (11) 220-gr. 8mm Mag.

both rifles used weighed more than 8 pounds. We do not recommend either of these calibers for protection from bears.

.44 Remington Magnum. The .44 Remington Magnum load fired from a handgun ranked thirty-second compared with loads fired from rifles and the 12-gauge shotgun, but ranked first compared with other handgun cartridges. It was included with the rifle cartridges for comparison purposes only and was ranked by the rifle and shotgun attributes.

In overall performance it was similar to the 8mm Remington Magnum 220-grain bullet and the .300 Winchester Magnum 180-grain bullet. The 240-grain lead gas-check bullet held together extremely well, had over 11 inches of penetration, and expanded moderately. Only the low energy value reduced its ranking level in the rifle and shotgun category.

The .44 Remington Magnum was by far the best handgun cartridge. Two bullets (240 lead gas check; 240 jacketed soft-point) were tested in revolvers with five-, 6.5-, and 7.5-inch barrels. No substantial difference was observed between the velocities of the two bullets in the same length of barrel, but the lead gas-check bullet ranked higher overall in ballistic performance than did the jacketed soft-point. The lead gas check ranked first, second, and fourth. Generally, the lead gas-check bullet expanded well and retained almost all its original weight. The jacketed soft-point had somewhat greater average penetration, but also much greater variation in penetration than the lead gas check. It also had slightly greater striking energy.

As would be expected, recoil was greater in the .44 Magnum revolvers than in any other handgun tested. It ranged from 16.4 foot-pounds in the 6.5-inch-barreled revolver with the jacketed soft-point load to 12.4 foot-pounds in the 7.5-inch barrel with the same load. The superiority of the .44 Remington Magnum makes it the cartridge choice for a *backup* weapon. We do not think a revolver using this cartridge should be considered a primary weapon for protection from bears.

The slight difference in overall ballistic performance between long and short barrels makes a revolver with a short barrel just as effective as one with a longer barrel. A short-barreled revolver is light, easier to carry, and may be drawn from a holster more quickly. Carried in a cross-draw or shoulder holster, a short-barreled .44 Magnum revolver is at hand at all times. When work requires both hands, a rifle is often put aside. A rifle a few feet away is useless for protection from bears, but a handgun could be a lifesaver.

.357 Smith & Wesson Magnum, .41 Remington Magnum, .44 Smith & Wesson Special, .45 Auto, and .45 Colt. The overall ballistic performance of these handgun cartridges was much poorer than that of the .44 Remington Magnum. They were included in the test because they are commonly owned by many persons working in coastal Alaska and might be carried in the field. With one possible exception, we do not recommend them, even for *backup* protection.

The possible exception is the .41 Remington Magnum. We were unable to obtain the high-velocity, jacketed 210-grain-bullet factory load for our tests. This loading may be suitable for *backup* use because its ballistics are closer to those of the .44 Remington Magnum than are any of the other cartridges.

12 Gauge X 2¾-Inch. The variety, rapid-fire potential, and reasonable prices of 12-gauge repeating shotguns with short barrels and the impressive appearance of the one-ounce (438-grain) rifled slug have made this combination popular as a weapon against bears. In our tests the 12-gauge 2¾-inch rifled slug did not have a high overall rank, because of the relatively low striking energy and the lack of bullet expansion. The lack of bullet expansion is somewhat misleading. The unfired rifled slug is .672-inch in diameter. The 1.7X expansion ratio increases this to a cross-sectional area of .62 square inch, which is only slightly smaller than that of the expanded bullets of the .458 Winchester and .460 Weatherby Magnum rifle cartridges. The penetration of the rifled slug was good (15.3 inches) and

SHORT-RANGE BALLISTIC PERFORMANCE

	Ranking			Bullet		Ballistic Performance						Firearm	
Cartridge	Score	Rank	Weight (grains)	Type 1	Brand 2	Velocity 15-yd. (fps)	Energy 15-yd. (ft/lb)	Penetration (inches)	Retained Weight (percent)	Expansion Ratio	Recoil (ft/lb)	Weight (pounds)	Barrel Length (inches)
.458 Win. Mag.	538	1	510	RSP	W-W	2,074	4,871	19.0	82	4.6	54.8	9.4	24
.460 Wby. Mag.	487	2	500	RSP	WBY	2,364	6,204	17.2	65	3.8	76.8	10.7	26
.375 H&H Mag.	301	3	300	SSP	W-W	2,541	4,303	16.8	67	4.0	41.1	8.6	24
.338 Win. Mag.	260	4	300	RSP	W-W	2,314	3,568	16.2	61	4.8	35.6	7.4	20
.375 H&H Mag.	239	5	270	RSP	R-P	2,659	4,241	14.2	64	4.0	37.2	8.6	24
.338 Win. Mag.	213	6	200	PSP	W-W	2,699	3,235	15.0	69	4.2	28.9	7.4	20
.338 Win. Mag.	197	7	250	SSP	W-W	2,507	3,491	12.2	57	5.3	33.4	7.4	20
.338 Win. Mag.	191	8	200	PSP	W-W	2,834	3,563	12.3	60	4.7	26.0	8.6	24
.338 Win. Mag.	186	9	300	RSP	W-W	2,360	3,710	16.8	57	3.4	31.2	8.6	24
.375 H&H Mag.	185	10	300	SSP	W-W	2,401	3,843	13.8	63	3.6	44.1	8.8	20.5
.30/06 U.S.	157	11	220	RSP	R-P	2,261	2,498	17.7	65	3.6	15.3	8.8	22
.30/06 U.S.	153	12	180	RSP	R-P	2,456	2,411	13.2	71	4.4	14.8	8.8	22
.444 Marlin	146	13	240	FSP	R-P	2,237	2,668	11.0	72	4.5	27.6	7.3	22
.358 Win.	142	14	200	SSP	W-W	2,366	2,488	12.0	71	4.4	33.4	7.4	22
7mm Rem. Mag.	141	15	175	PSP	W-W	2,709	2,853	13.0	44	5.6	18.5	7.2	24
.375 H&H Mag.	137	16	270	RSP	R-P	2,456	3,735	12.3	50	3.9	39.4	7.2	20.5
.45/70 U.S.	133	17	300	HSP	FED	1,573	1,649	13.0	84	4.8	15.6	7.1	20
.308 Win.	128	18	180	RSP	FED	2,430	2,360	12.7	73	3.9	13.6	8.4	22
.45/70 U.S.	124	19	300	HSP	FED	1,666	1,849	11.0	96	4.1	18.6	7.8	22
.358 Norma Mag.	115	20	250	PSP	NOR	2,730	4,139	15.2	41	2.9	25.0	8.4	24
8mm Rem. Mag.	107	21	185	PSP	R-P	2,991	3,676	10.7	32	5.5	29.1	9.4	24
.300 Wby. Mag.	104	22	180	PSP	WBY	3,033	3,678	15.2	46	2.6	28.0	9.6	24
.338 Win. Mag.	100	23	250	SSP	W-W	2,594	3,735	14.7	45	2.6	30.0	8.6	24
.350 Rem. Mag.	93	24	200	SSP	R-P	2,568	2,931	12.2	52	3.2	34.5	6.4	18.5
7X57mm Mauser	87	25	175	RSP	FED	2,419	2,274	13.8	52	3.6	12.7	8.9	24
12-ga. X 2¾"	74	26	438	LRN	FED	1,398	1,902	15.3	96	1.7	26.1	7.1	20
.45/70 U.S.	65	27	405	RSP	R-P	1,322	1,572	15.8	93	2.1	17.7	7.8	22
.300 Win. Mag.	60	28	200	PSP	FED	2,699	3,237	15.2	36	2.2	25.9	7.8	22
.300 Wby. Mag.	59	29	220	RSP	WBY	2,798	3,826	15.2	34	2.0	30.8	9.6	24
.45/70 U.S.	50	30	405	RSP	R-P	1,211	1,319	17.8	98	1.4	13.6	7.1	20
8mm Rem. Mag.	49	31	220	PSP	R-P	2,779	3,773	12.8	28	2.5	18.9	9.4	24
.44 Rem. Mag.	47	32	240	LGC	R-P	1,401	1,046	11.5	97	2.6	13.9	2.9	7.5
.300 Win. Mag.	44	33	180	PSP	FED	2,959	3,268	10.3	30	2.8	26.3	7.8	24

[1] RSP = roundnose softpoint: SSP = semipointed softpoint: PSP = pointed softpoint: FSP = flatnose softpoint: HSP = hollow softpoint: LRN = lead roundnose: LGC = lead gas check.

[2] W-W = Winchester-Western: R-P = Remington-Peters: FED = Federal: WBY = Weatherby: NOR = Norma.

only four percent of the unfired weight was lost. No fragmentation occurred. Low energy was due to the low velocity of the slug.

We also tested the penetration of 00 buckshot. The first round was fired at the box from 15 yards. At this range, the nine pellets had a spread of about 12 x 12 inches and a penetration of only two to three inches. We then shortened the range to 15 feet. From this distance, the spread was two inches in diameter, and the maximum penetration of a single shot was seven inches. At the shorter range, the nine pellets appear to act as a single projectile and the 00 buckshot load might be relatively effective. This is not true at 15 yards.

The slide-action shotgun with a short barrel is relatively light and compact and has good pointing characteristics. Recoil was similar to that of weapons firing small-caliber Magnum rifle cartridges. It also has a large magazine capacity and can be fired rapidly. From our tests it would appear the slug is much superior to buckshot for protection against bears. Whether buckshot could kill a bear at ranges beyond five yards is doubtful. A mixed magazine load of slugs and buckshot can be used, but there appears to be little advantage to this.

To be effective, the 12-gauge slugs must be thought of as similar to the bullets in a rifle. Hitting vital areas is the important thing. Hitting a brown bear with a load of buckshot at ranges beyond five yards may mean a non-lethal wound and a very angry bear.

Because bullet velocity is an inherent component of bullet energy, it was not one of the factors we used to rank ballistic performance. We did, however, look at its relation to bullet penetration because velocity is the most common single factor that others have used to rank ballistic performance. We found, in general, that bullet penetration decreased as striking velocity increased. Notable examples of this were the high-velocity and small-bore Magnum cartridges, such as the .300 Winchester and .300 Weatherby Magnums with lighter-weight bullets. The inverse relationship between striking velocity and bullet penetration should be viewed only as a tendency; our data demonstrated considerable variability.

When penetration is compared with striking energy, the relationship is direct — that is, in general, penetration increases with an increase in energy. Again, the predictive ability of this relationship is poor and should also be considered as a tendency. For both striking velocity and energy, the confounding factors appear to be design of the bullet and strength of the bullet materials. A discussion of these factors is beyond the scope of our work.

There is no well-defined distinction between combinations of weapon and ammunition that are adequate or inadequate for protection against bears. The final decision on adequacy must be made by each individual, and should include consideration of weapon size and weight, recoil, and the person's experience with firearms. Our data can, however, be used as a general guide to the effectiveness of the weapons and ammunition tested. A rifle in .375 Holland & Holland Magnum caliber in the hands of a person who can comfortably tolerate the recoil is a much better choice than a .30/06 of comparable caliber. A .30/06 with 220-grain bullets, however, might be a better choice for a person sensitive to recoil, who may shoot the lighter-caliber weapon with more confidence and accuracy.

For a shooter who can handle the recoil, a bolt-action rifle in .458 Winchester Magnum with 510-grain soft-points is the surest weapon available.

Our tests of bullet performance at short range were conducted by shooting into a uniform test medium, not into brown bears. The medium did not have a heavy, wet coat of hair; thick, resilient skin; dense muscle tissue or massive bones. It wasn't angry and excited, either. Consequently, the validity of equating the test results with a real situation involving a brown bear may be questioned.

Nevertheless, we believe the tests provide a good relative evaluation of bullets shot at short range and may be used for comparisons between different cartridges and bullets. Two major points can be inferred from our tests: 1) none of the many different types of bullets tested was completely adequate, and 2) high striking velocities may not be particularly beneficial at short ranges. The best results were from bullets that were relatively heavy for their caliber and were fired at relatively moderate velocity. Many experienced people have noted this, and we have merely verified their observations under relatively controlled conditions.

Hunting Rifle Accuracy: Full-Length Versus Neck Sizing

Dave Scovill

In spite of the volumes of information available to reloaders, I don't ever recall reading a report that compared the accuracy of full-length sized cases to neck-sized cases fired from an average, off-the-shelf sporting rifle. I've pretty much gone along with the idea that neck-sizing should produce the best accuracy. The basis for that belief stems from the fact that serious target shooters rely on neck-sized cases to shoot those elusive one-hole groups. The implication seems clear enough. If target shooters rely on neck-sizing to provide the best accuracy, it should do the same for the rest of us — assuming the rifle in question is accurate in the first place.

The basic difference between the two approaches is that neck-sizing reduces the diameter of the neck only, leaving the case body untouched. Full-length resizing reduces the diameter of both neck and case body by .002- to .004-inch, depending on the interior dimensions of chamber and sizing die.

Full-length resizing is generally recommended for hunting ammunition which must feed flawlessly and allow the bolt to close with ease. That is especially true for pumps, lever-actions, and semi-autos, which lack the powerful camming action of a bolt. Full-length resizing is also advisable if more than one rifle is chambered for the same cartridge. Chambers of individual rifles vary slightly, even those from the same manufacturer. Full-length resizing ensures that handloads will function properly in any rifle chambered for them.

On the other hand, neck-sizing lets the case body form an almost perfect fit with the chamber it was fired in. Even if the fit between case and chamber is a bit snug, a bolt-action generally provides enough power to push the round into battery effortlessly. Resistance sometimes met as a case shoulder butts into a chamber wall must be distinguished from that caused by a stretched case when the edge of the mouth is forced against the end of the chamber. Cases must be trimmed from time to time to ensure they don't exceed maximum allowable length. This is true for all bottlenecked cases, whether they headspace on rim, shoulder, or belt.

Most handloaders who neck-size, also size cases full-length periodically to prevent excessive expansion which might prevent stress-free chambering.

This article first appeared in *HANDLOADER.*

Test rifles were representative, untuned sporters. In back, Savage Model 110D in .243 Winchester. In foreground, Ruger Model 77 in 7X57.

At the same time, cases should be trimmed to minimum specifications. Some bench shooters use such mild loads that full-length resizing and trimming are seldom, if ever, required. Pressures created by hunting ammunition, on the other hand, often make full-length sizing and trimming unavoidable.

Another method employed by those seeking improved accuracy is partial sizing. A case is allowed to enter the sizing die just far enough to squeeze part of the neck down leaving a slight secondary shoulder on the neck itself. The degree of partial sizing can vary and depends on the amount of pull required to hold the bullet firmly in the case. This method also prevents the die body from contacting the case shoulder and ensures the case will headspace perfectly in the chamber it was previously fired in.

There are advantages and disadvantages associated with all sizing methods. When neck-sizing, there is a chance the neck will be canted out of alignment with the central axis of the case body, enough to degrade accuracy. At the same time, neck-sizing subjects a case to minimal stress and extends case life. In Speer's *RELOADING MANUAL NUMBER NINE,* Neal Knox explained in detail how to prevent neck misalignment. As the winner of the 1974 NBRSA Heavy Varmint Class National Matches, his advice is well worth heeding. Then again, he used techniques which require some specialized equipment and a rifle capable of shooting those one-hole groups. For the average hunter/handloader, such measures may be impractical.

The greatest disadvantage of full-length resizing is that it works the case repeatedly, forcing brass to flow forward into the neck area. That not only increases neck-wall thickness, but will ultimately lead to thinning the case wall about half an inch above the rim. Brass flow also occurs in neck-sized cases, although to a lesser degree. Suffice to say, cases should be inspected carefully after each firing.

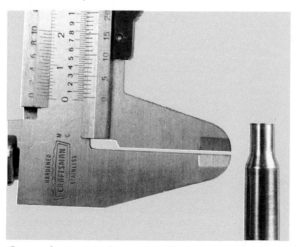

Case necks were sized to a point .035-inch from junction of neck and shoulder to avoid setting shoulders back.

A few months ago, with the coyotes howling up a storm on the ridge just north of the house, I thought it appropriate to work up a few varmint loads for my 7X57 Ruger Model 77. Using cases sized in an RCBS full-length die and charged with 52 grains of H-414 over CCI's 200 primers, the best I could manage with either Sierra's 120-grain spitzer or Hornady's 120-grain hollow-point was 1½ to two inches (three-shot groups). That was fine for relatively close-range shooting, but something better was needed to punch the football-sized vitals of a coyote at 250 to 350 yards.

In an attempt to squeeze groups down a bit with both bullets, I sized a few Federal cases in an RCBS .284 Winchester die which left the 7X57 case body untouched. Necks were sized to within .035-inch of the shoulder.

Using the same powder charge and primers as before, 10 cases were loaded with each bullet to an overall length of 3.1 inches. Previous experience with those relatively short bullets had taught me that seating depth provided optimum accuracy in this particular rifle. The throat of my early Model 77 mikes .470-inch, allowing light bullets to be seated out that far if I handle them carefully. I've been advised by Len Pardee of Sturm, Ruger that later Model 77 rifles chambered for the old 7X57 have throats measuring .297-inch. That last is SAAMI standard for the cartridge.

Back in the early 1970s, Ruger cut the longer throats to accommodate 175-grain European bullets but has since discontinued the practice. Exactly when, they can't say. Other manufacturers have also used different throat lengths, so it's a good idea to check the throat in any 7X57 before reloading for it. Whenever possible, it's recommended that bullets be seated about ¹⁄₁₆-inch short of touching the rifling for best accuracy. If bullets are seated out too far and allowed to contact the rifling before firing, excessive pressure may result, so take care when selecting seating depth.

Repairing to the range, I fired three, three-shot groups at 100 yards with my newly designed varmint rounds. The average for the Sierra 120-grain spitzer was 1.95 inches, while the patterns fired with Hornady's 120-grain hollow-point defied measurement. One out of three bullets missed the target board completely.

Unable to understand why the groups fired from the neck-sized cases were larger than those fired from full-length-sized cases, I decided a little more testing was in order. Reviewing the 77's range log revealed the Ruger had recorded much tighter groups with several other bullets using a variety of powders, primers, cases, and seating depths. There were even a few three-shot groups which measured less than ¾-inch with 175-grain factory loads from Federal, Winchester, and Remington. All, with the exception of the factory loads, had been fired from cases sized in a standard RCBS 7X57 die.

The next move was to shoot three, three-shot groups with Sierra's 140-grain spitzers, Speer's 145-grain spitzers, and Hornady's 139- and 154-grain Spire Points, using full-length-sized cases. Then the tests would be repeated, shooting the same loads in neck-sized cases. To eliminate as many variables as possible, the same cases were fired with the same bullets in both series of experiments. The data for each load is listed in the accompanying table. The idea was to compare accuracy only, so I limited the test to H-414 and IMR-4350 powders with CCI 200 and 250 primers respectively. Those powder, primer, and bullet combinations had delivered acceptable accuracy in the past. It would be interesting to see how they'd perform in neck-sized versus completely resized hulls.

In reviewing the load-data tables, bear in mind that I have used all the loads listed extensively without seeing any evidence of excessive pressures in my rifle. As mentioned, this Ruger 77 has an unusually long throat and those loads represent *a safe maximum in this rifle only!* Using a shorter over-all loaded length in a short-throated rifle may result in excessive pressure as case capacity is reduced.

The only load fired from neck-sized cases which provided an improvement in accuracy over the same load fired from full-length-sized cases used Hornady's 154-grain Spire Point over 49.5 grains of IMR-4350. The difference between the averages obtained using Sierra's 140-grain spitzer was so slight, it could be ignored. Not that three, three-shot groups represent clear-cut proof of what might happen in another rifle, but the results weren't quite what I expected.

As an afterthought, I decided to load the 139-grain Hornady bullet in the same cases used with the Sierra bullet. There was no denying that the 140-grain Sierra shot rings around the others using neck-sized cases and it occurred to me that the cases might have been the cause. As a double check, I also loaded my last 10 Speer 130-grain spitzers over 51 grains of H-414 in full-length-sized cases. That would be the control load in the Ruger. If there was something amiss with my shooting technique, the rifle bedding or the rest, that load would reveal it. In previous accuracy tests, it punched three-shot groups averaging an inch or less, consistently.

As an added control measure, although I may not have needed it, I borrowed a Savage 110 chambered for the .243 Winchester. I'd sold it six years before in spite of the fact that it was the most accurate out-of-the-box rifle I ever owned. Going back in my records for that rifle's loading history, I selected a load using Sierra's 100-grain spitzer over 40 grains of IMR-4350 and CCI's 200 primer. Cases were sized in a standard RCBS full-length die adjusted to squeeze the neck to within .025-inch of the shoulder. That duplicated the load I had used to take 17 coyotes at ranges from 100 to just over 400 yards.

Firing the 130-grain control load first, the average

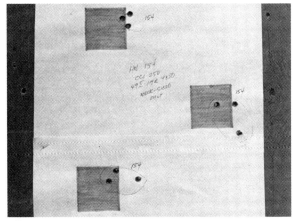

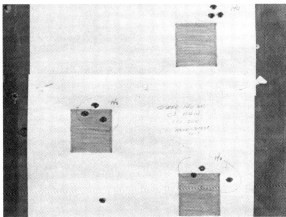

Target at top shows groups with Hornady's 154-grain Spire Point over 49.5 grains of IMR-4350, which averaged 1.22 inches from neck-sized cases. (Bottom) Sierra's 140-grain spitzer backed by 51 grains of H-414 averaged 1.03 inches, also using neck-sized cases. When same load was fired from full-length-sized brass, average group size dropped to .92-inch.

for three groups was 1.08 inches. No disappointment there. Next came the 139-grain Hornady bullets loaded in the same cases used previously with the 140-grain Sierra spitzers. The average was a somewhat saddening 2.15 inches — almost a half-inch over the same load fired in the other cases. Last to go was the .243 Winchester control load. The first shot was fired as a sighter, the next four went into .45-inch. From the results, I concluded that the increase in group size using neck-sized cases was real and not the result of poor shooting or a bum rest.

I am unable to explain the results. There are just too many variables to pinpoint the cause of comparative inaccuracy using neck-sized cases. After the shooting was over, I met with Donald R. (Doc) Thomas, a well-known experimenter from Klamath Falls, Oregon, who has done considerable work developing wildcat cartridges. I told Doc about the results of my tests and he just chuckled. We both seemed to agree, there appears to be no clear-cut

Excessive neck sizing can cause case shoulders to buckle.

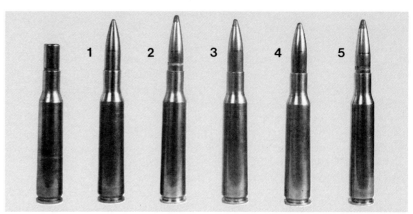

Dummy 7X57 round (far left) features Hornady 154-grain Spire Point seated upside down to show long throat of Ruger's chamber. Compare its length with test bullets which are marked at bore diameter (.276) on their ogives: (1) 120-grain Sierra, (2) 139-grain Hornady, (3) 140-grain Sierra, (4) 145-grain Speer, and (5) 154-grain Hornady.

advantage to neck-sizing cases for a run-of-the-mill hunting rifle. Had I used a standard 7X57 neck-sizing die, the results might have changed somewhat.

Checking the cases that were neck-sized, I found no perceptible signs of neck misalignment when the loaded round was rolled over a mirror. Besides, there are always the 140-grain Sierra results to show

that the .284 Winchester F-L die worked reasonably well. It didn't do badly with the 154-grain Hornady either. At this point, I can only say that I fired almost 130 rounds and may have proved absolutely nothing, except that my Ruger 77 doesn't care much for neck-sized cases. Worst of all, I still haven't gone coyote hunting.

Case-sizing Test
Load Summary: Ruger Model 77-7X57mm

Bullet (grains)	Powder	Charge (grains)	Case	Length Overall (inches)	Velocity (fps)	Average Group (inches)	
						F-L sized	Neck sized
120 Sierra	H-414	52.0	Fed	3.1	3,018	1.4	1.95
120 Hornady	H-414	52.0	Fed	3.1	2,988	1.8	—
139 Hornady	H-414	51.0	Fed	3.2	2,824	1.08	1.7
140 Sierra	H-414	51.0	R-P	3.125	2,832	.92	1.08
145 Speer	IMR-4350	50.0	Fed	3.075	2,756	1.2	1.6
154 Hornady	IMR-4350	49.5	Fed	3.135	2,745	1.73	1.22
					Average:	1.35	1.50

Control Loads
Ruger Model 77-7X57mm

Bullet (grains)	Powder	Charge (grains)	Case	Length Overall (inches)	Velocity (fps)	Average Group (inches)	
						F-L sized	Neck sized
130 Speer	H-414	51.0	Fed	3.1	2,924	1.08	—
139 Hornady	H-414	51.0	R-P	3.2	2,826	—	2.15

Savage 110 D-243 Winchester

| 100 Sierra | IMR-4350 | 40.0 | Fed | 2.71 | 2,845 | .45 | — |

NOTE: Above loads are not recommended, but listed to show test results. None of the listed 7mm loads should be fired in early Mauser or Remington rifles chambered for the 7X57mm Mauser cartridge.

Now You Can Get the Lead Out!

Jim Carmichel

Whenever two or more shooters get together, we tend to muzzle-blast each other with our own special brand of goofiness. I'm talking, of course, about steel shot. No other topic known to shooting sportsmen has created more controversy, confusion, ill will, and intentional misrepresentation than steel shot. If you're confused by all the bickering about the pros and cons of steel shot for waterfowl hunting, you're not alone. The whole affair began innocently enough but, come to think of it, so did the Thirty Year War.

The problem is that duck and goose hunters scatter tons and tons of lead shot over waterfowl habitat. Some waterfowl gobble up the lead pellets and give themselves an acute case of lead poisoning. This unhappy condition can be fatal either as a consequence of the lead itself or in indirect ways such as lowering the birds' resistance to disease. A chain reaction is also set in motion that can have widespread ecological effects. For example, eagles that feed on the carcasses of lead-tainted ducks may also become innocent victims.

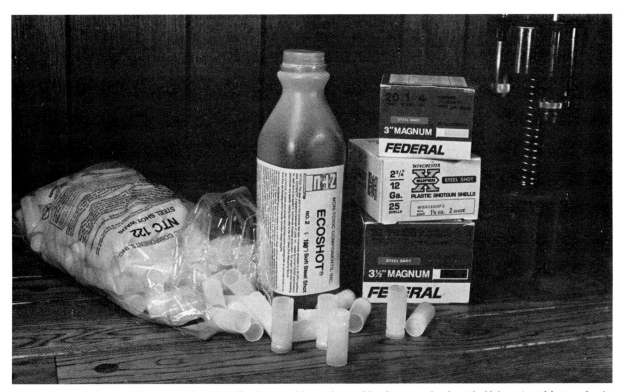

Non-toxic steel shot is at last available to handloaders, and home-brewed loads cost only about half the price of factory loads. Thick-walled cup wads prevent scratching of gun barrels. (However, it is still not wise to use steel-shot loads in fine old guns.)

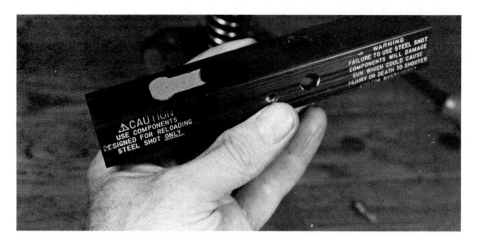

Charging of cases is made easier by special charge bar, designed for use with steel shot only.

Several years ago, when the consequences of lead ingestion by waterfowl became apparent, the U.S. Fish and Wildlife Service and the firearms industry began a program of research for a lead-shot substitute. All sorts of materials and coatings were tried — far too many to list here. The one substitute that best met the list of criteria was steel, and thus was launched the development of today's steel-shot shotshells.

DISADVANTAGES

The two biggest disadvantages of steel, as compared to lead, are that it is harder and lighter. Being lighter, it is ballistically inferior to lead and its hardness can or could damage a shotgun's barrel. If a soft lead pellet passes through a shotgun barrel, it simply flattens itself against the bore and, at worst, gently polishes the surface. With steel shot, we have steel against steel and the result can be a scratched barrel. Moreover, when the hard clump of steel shot encounters the choke, serious and permanent damage can result.

The ballistic problems with steel shot are stated in Isaac Newton's physics. If lead and steel shot of equal diameter are launched at the same muzzle velocity, the steel shot, being lighter, loses velocity and energy at a faster rate than the lead shot. In practical hunting terms, this means that a load of steel shot does not have as great a killing range as a charge of lead shot containing the same number and size of pellets.

Steel or iron shot is not new; it dates at least back to World War II. Lead was critical to the war effort, so iron shot was loaded in the shotshells used in gunnery practice. Winchester later loaded iron shot in the Super Ferro shells that they sold at their franchised gun clubs. The rough iron shot scratched shotgun bores all to hell, so it was used only in club-owned guns.

These known traits of ferrous shot, and the reduced performance as compared with lead shot, didn't paint a very pretty picture for steel shot's future. I'm sure ammunition makers who had experience with iron shot would have been happy to forget the whole thing, but Big Brother stepped in and made steel shot a part of every waterfowler's future. Beginning at various dates throughout the 1970s, the use of steel shot became mandatory in many waterfowl-hunting areas. The fuss was worse than the time Morris Baxter's glass eye fell out at Aunt Martha's tea party and was swallowed by her bulldog.

Seeing the writing on the wall, some ammunition makers got busy in their research labs in an effort to develop the best possible steel-shot loads. If the law of the land required steel shot, they intended to offer hunters the best possible loads. Other manufacturers and organizations took the negative approach and employed all sorts of poorly advised obstructionist tactics. The head flack artist of one big company, to give one example, devoted his days to telling everyone that duck hunting was doomed if we used steel shot. Of course, that got lots of hunters in a fighting mood and a bad situation became worse. Fortunately, the flack jockey was eventually canned and is no longer paid to annoy sportsmen. Another time, a spokesman for an ammunition maker stood before a group of gun writers and tried to tell us that it was impossible to load more than one ounce of steel shot in a 12-gauge shotshell. Come to think of it, I haven't seen him around for a while either.

THE NEW LOAD

These things came to pass about 10 years ago. Since then, we've learned a lot about steel shot. Ammunition makers now load standard-length 2¾-inch 12-gauge shells with 1¼ ounces of steel shot, and three-inch Magnums with 1⅜ ounces. The big 10-gauge load holds 1⅝ ounces, and 20-gauge shooters can launch a full ounce of steel payload. Considering the density of steel, that's a lot of shot. By way of comparison, a one-ounce load of steel has as many pellets in it as 1½ ounces of lead pellets of the same size.

Ammunition makers also learned how to protect your shotgun's barrel from steel shot by using shot cups with extra-thick walls. If you use a modern shotgun, you don't need to worry about steel shot ruining the barrel. Don't shoot steel-shot loads in your prized Parker or L.C. Smith double, though, because some choke damage can occur. And don't shoot Magnum loads of *lead* shot either. They, too, can damage the chokes of old, soft-steel barrels.

The best thing we've learned about steel shot is that it kills ducks and geese very nicely. Some folks still say steel shot is no good, but I've noticed that the guys who complain the loudest can't hit ducks with lead shot, either. Over the past dozen years, I've fired hundreds of steel-shot loads at ducks and geese and I've watched thousands more being fired by other hunters. Theoretically, steel shot shouldn't kill as far as lead, but in actual hunting circumstances they perform about equally well. This is because at ranges of 60 yards and beyond, where lead has the advantage, nine out of 10 hunters can't make consistent hits with any kind of shot.

We've also found that we can double-cross Isaac Newton by simply using a larger size of steel shot than we normally would with lead shot. This improves ballistics somewhat and still yields good pattern density because of the high shot count of the steel-shot loads. This high shot count, by the way, not only makes it possible, but actually advisable, to use less choke than we do with lead loads. I've been using a modified choke with steel shot, which gives me a bigger pattern and improves my hit percentage. If you have ever tested steel-shot loads on a pattern board, you know that they pat-

Large-capacity NTC wad cups protect shotgun bore, as they are thicker than cups intended for lead shot. Before loading, each cup must be slit into four petals, as shown here, so that shot will fly free shortly after leaving gun's muzzle. New tool does slitting job neatly and easily.

tern beautifully. This is because steel pellets are rounder than lead shot and therefore fly straighter.

HANDLOADS

When steel-shot ammunition first hit the market, its price caused quite a fuss. Steel-shot loads cost about half again as much as lead-shot loads. Here of late, the prices of steel loads are about the same as top-quality lead-shot shells, which is still plenty expensive.

For several years, shotgunners have tried to reload steel shot with uniformly poor results. The problem was the lack of suitable reloading components. Good steel shot has not been available to handloaders, and suitable wads and shot cups have been unobtainable. Some handloaders tried to put together steel-shot loads using air-gun BB shot and ordinary wads, but that scratched barrels and may have ruined chokes. Proper steel shot is considerably softer than BB air-gun shot or ball bearings. It has a DPH (Diamond Pyramid Hardness) rating of 90 or less. I understand that the only source of soft steel shot is Lydall, Inc., and that until recently they sold their trademarked ECOSHOT only to ammunition manufacturers. Now ECOSHOT is available to handloaders through Non-Toxic Components, Box 4202, Portland, OR 97208 (503-226-7110). NTC also sells special plastic wads with the necessary wall thickness and capacity to cushion and protect a shotgun's bore from steel shot.

The problem with the wads intended for use with lead shot is that they are so thin that the steel shot sometimes cuts through the cup and causes bore scratching. The molded-in slits in lead-shot cups also permit the steel pellets to squeeze through and cause scratching. And it's also true that no lead-shot cup has enough capacity to contain a full charge of steel shot. If the steel pellets spill over the top of the cup, some barrel scratching is bound to happen. The thick NTC cups are of extra-large capacity and have no slits in their sides. Before use, however, the cup must be slit into four petals so it will open and allow the shot to fly free shortly after exiting the muzzle. With the ECOSHOT reloading kits, NTC includes a comprehensive steel-shot reloading manual that tells reloaders how to prepare their shot cups for best performance. The manual also contains loading data. To make reloading steel shot even easier and more foolproof, some reloading-tool makers, such as Mayville Engineering Company (MEC), 715 South St., Mayville, WI 53050 (414-387-4500), are offering special replacement parts for their tools that are designed specifically for steel-shot loading.

At last, steel-shot reloading is a wholly workable proposition and produces shells at about half the cost of factory loads.

PART SEVEN

ALTERATIONS, IMPROVEMENTS AND GUNSMITHING

Glass Bedding Remington Rifles

R.L. Jamison

Rifles with tubular receivers, such as the Remington series that began with the Models 721 and 722, and continues today with the Model 700, are particularly suited to improvement through the judicious use of glass bedding. Done properly, glass bedding installed in one of these rifles not only defies detection but also resists the tendency of the receiver to roll in its mortise and yields a more durable and weather-resistant — if not more accurate — firearm.

To check the existing bedding on round-receiver rifles, remove the middle action screw (if there is one) and check the existing inletting for high or low spots and interference of the mechanism with any part of the stock. In many instances safety mechanisms interfere with proper metal-to-wood fit or screws bear unevenly on the stock. The inletting fit is checked by applying a thin coat of Prussian blue spotting tint or Jerrow's Inletting Black to the metal parts that contact the stock. Prussian blue is available at most automotive and machine shops. Jerrow's is sold by gunsmith suppliers. Oil tinting color can also be used. Oil tint has no dryers in it and can be wiped off when you are finished. Do not use paint.

Disassemble the rifle and apply tint to the areas of the barreled action that contact the wood. Reassemble the rifle. I do this at the range and shoot five to 10 shots before again disassembling the rifle. This gives the stock and barreled action a good chance to settle in.

After taking the rifle apart, examine the stock and the barreled action for areas of uneven contact. These areas must be relieved before any bedding compound is used. Most factory stocks are fairly close, and a small amount of scraping or sanding in the necessary spots on the stock will correct any problem areas.

Another way to check the bedding is by alternately tightening and backing off the action screws and observing the effect on metal-to-wood fit along the inletting line or bore line of the barrel and action. Remove the receiver tang screw completely. Alternately loosen and tighten the recoil-lug screw. Observe the movement, if any, of barrel and action at that point. Next, loosen the recoil-lug screw and loosen the metal-to-wood relationships.

This article first appeared in *THE AMERICAN RIFLEMAN*.

ANALYSIS OF YOUR FINDINGS

1. Movement of tang and/or barrel with tang screw loosened indicates a "high" area near the recoil lug or chamber of the barrel. If only the tang springs up and down, the tang area is "low" in the stock.

2. If, when the recoil-lug screw is backed off, this portion appears to rise out of the stock, the wood in the lug area is low.

After they have been located, relieve any high areas within the stock with even pressure at all points. Check this with the magazine box removed, as it may prevent the action from bottoming completely. Once the barreled action indicates even positioning in the stock, replace the magazine box assembly in the stock and check for possible metal-to-metal interference. I use Prussian blue on the magazine box, recoil lug, and magazine counterbore in the receiver. Also, check the length of the action screws to be certain they are not bottoming out in the action threads.

After the factory inletting has been evened up, it may be prepared to receive glass bedding. This is done by relieving selected areas in the action mortise and barrel channel, using either chisels and gouges or a hand grinder such as the Dremel Moto-Tool.

PREPARATION OF THE STOCK

Begin preparation of the stock by working on the barrel and barrel channel. If you choose to free-float the barrel, tape it from about 1¼ inches ahead of the receiver to a point clear of the stock fore-end. Two-inch-wide freezer tape is a good choice. Now relieve the bedding in the barrel channel until the taped section will enter the channel and the barreled action can be fully seated in the stock.

Remove the barreled action from the stock and relieve the area under the untaped portion of the barrel to a depth of $^3/_{32}$- to $^1/_8$-inch. This relief cut and succeeding ones can either be cut to an even depth — in which case a bead of glass will show around the bedded barrel and action — or undercut to provide full clearance beneath the stock yet preserve the appearance of the original wood-to-metal fit. The former method is easier and cleans up gaps

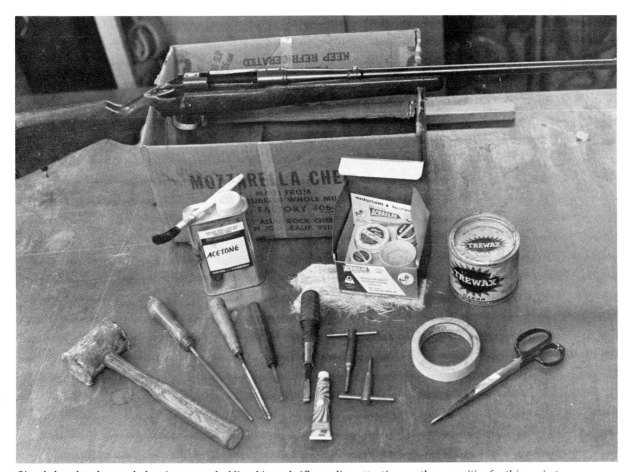

Simple hand tools, wood-cleaning agent, bedding kit, and rifle needing attention are the necessities for this project.

in the inletting. The latter technique looks nicer, provided wood-to-metal fit was good at the outset.

Continue the relief cut for the full length of the barrel channel, using whichever technique has been chosen to provide clearance for the taped portion of the barrel. Now it's time to work on the action inletting.

Start on the action mortise by cutting $3/16$- to $1/2$-inch of wood from behind the recoil lug. Cut a similar relief, but $1/32$- to $1/16$-inch wide, on the sides and in front of the recoil lug. Lower the bottom of the recoil-lug mortise (and the relief cuts) about $1/16$-inch. On many round-receiver rifles there is considerable clearance between the front of the magazine box and the magazine mortise in the inletting. If this is the case, all well and good. If not, cut a $1/32$- to $1/16$-inch clearance between them. (Note: Do not use this technique when bedding a rifle with a detachable box magazine, such as Remington's Model 788.)

When the areas around the recoil lug and magazine box are completed, remove from $1/16$- to $3/32$-inch from the area where the front receiver ring bears.

The area around the rear tang must also be relieved. Cut out $3/32$- to $1/8$-inch of wood from underneath the tang. Take slightly less from the sides of the action mortise. Again, these reliefs may be either even depth or undercut. Finally, if the trigger mechanism permits, cut a $1/8$-inch relief behind the magazine box to add some stiffness at that point. (Note: Do not do this on rifles with detachable box magazines.)

Two final relief cuts are needed, under the trigger guard at the front and rear, and around the action screws. These cuts, when filled with glass, will provide pads that prevent crushing of the wood under pressure from the action screws.

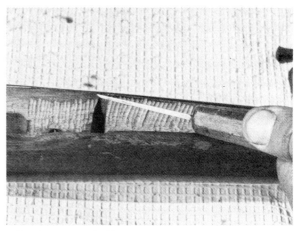

After deciding rebedding is necessary, author uses small gouge to relieve stock areas to receive glass-bedding material. Undercutting wood along the top of stock makes neater job.

If you are working with an old stock, it should now be cleaned to remove any oil from the wood. With a newly inletted stock, let it sit for a couple of weeks so the wood can normalize.

Now apply a heavy coat of paste floor wax to the exposed finished wood surfaces to make removal of the inevitable runover of bedding compound easier. Masking tape is now applied to the edges of the inletting to protect the outside of the stock from excess bedding compound.

PREPARATION OF THE METAL

Begin preparing the barreled action by disassembling it. Remove the trigger, bolt release, magazine stud — in a 788 — and anything else that may be bolted on the receiver's exterior. Use thin tape to cover those portions of the receiver to be free-floated and cover large openings like the magazine cut. Use paraffin or modeling clay to fill small cuts, such as the alignment notches for the recoil lug that are found on the front of Remington Model 788 receivers.

Carefully tape — again freezer tape works well —the front and sides of the recoil lug. Use a razor knife, or blade, to trim the tape so that the bedding will fully contact the back (toward the tang) and bottom of the lug. Later, when the tape is removed, this leaves a small clearance between the bedding and the front and sides of the lug.

The next step is to give the entire exterior surface of the barrel and receiver two coats of release agent to minimize the chance of gluing the metal and wood together. Brownell's release agent, which comes with Acraglas kits, is about the easiest to work with and can be purchased separately. Floor wax — liquid or paste — and carnauba auto waxes also work well. So does petroleum jelly. Use two

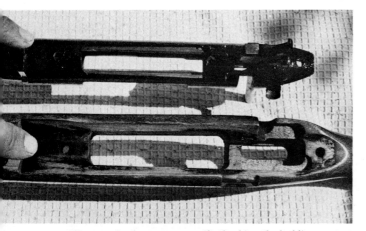

First step in the process entails checking the bedding contact with Prussian blue or Inletting Black.

Author opted to glass bed this M-721's tang, front ring, short section of barrel, and rear of recoil lug. Masking tape on those areas is for clarity; it is removed before bedding. Some may choose to bed entire receiver and barrel.

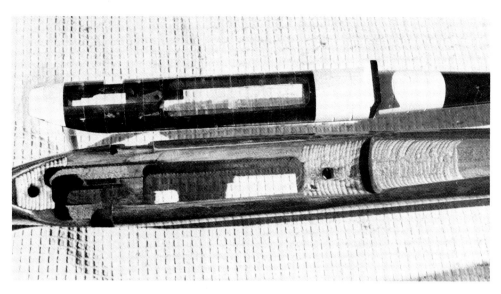

coats, and coat everything, including the magazine box, trigger guard, action screws, and the inside of the action-screw holes in the receiver.

Selection of the brand of glass bedding compound is up to the individual doing the work. Each type has its own advantages and disadvantages. Acraglas is used here because it is flexible in terms of usefulness and readily available. Whatever is used — Acraglas, Micro-Bed, Bisonite — read the instructions and digest them before proceeding.

Go through the motions a time or two to get an idea of the sequence of events. Once the bedding compound has been mixed, there will be very little time to stop and figure out what to do next.

THE BEDDING PROCEDURE

When the bedding compound is prepared, begin by applying it to the barrel channel. Then do the action mortise. Pour, if the consistency permits, or use a wooden tongue depressor to spread the compound. Acraglas works best when made up to about the same consistency as cold honey. With other brands of glass bedding, there may not be a choice of consistency. Whatever is used, apply it liberally.

When the bedding compound is in place, set the barreled action gently in the stock. The more gradually the action is set in place, the less likelihood of forming air pockets in the bedding.

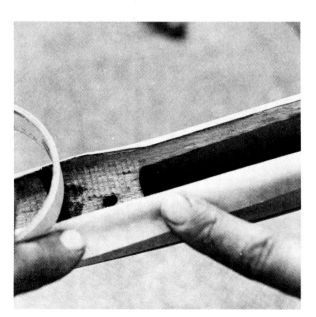

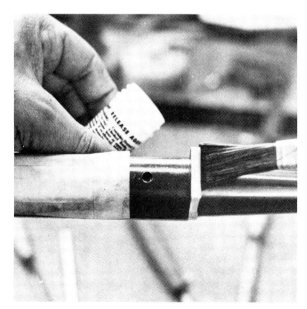

Waxing and masking stock finish (L) help make cleanup easier once bedding material has set. Author then (R) masks non-contact metal surfaces and brushes on release agent.

After a dry run of procedures, bedding materials are mixed according to manufacturer's exact instructions and daubed into stock inletting.

I use a cardboard box for a cradle to hold the stock while doing this and discard it when done. Thus a vise is not needed. It is best to begin by inverting the stock, apply bedding, and insert the trigger guard and magazine box. Then turn the stock upright, apply bedding, and ease the barreled action into the stock. I squeeze the barreled action into the stock until most of the barreled action is at proper depth. Then I insert the front action screw and use slow and even pressure to pull the action to its final depth. As I tighten the recoil-lug screw, I lightly and rapidly tap the action and barrel (much like a concrete vibrator) to settle these parts in evenly *without any forcing* of tang or barrel.

Do this final settling of the barreled action slowly, for you can distort the barrel or action with trapped bedding compound in the same way as improper wood fit if the compound doesn't have a chance to flow away from tight spots. I use minimal tang-screw pressure, not enough to visibly move the tang, and this movement can be observed by the action of the bedding compound adjacent to the tang as the screw is drawn down.

Once you are satisfied things are settled in okay, wipe off as much compound as you can. I use throwaway gloves when doing this, so I can clean up pretty quickly. I generally bed a stock early in the morning for two reasons. First, it is cooler in the morning, so the bedding sets up slower, and I have some extra working time. Second, I have time to monitor the left-over resin to see how fast it's hardening in the stock. When it's starting to get tough, nearly hard, I rotate the stock screws a little. This is to make sure they will turn when the bedding has hardened fully.

Once the compound has hardened, I let it set for between four and six hours. I then pop the barreled action loose to make sure all is well and immediately return it to the stock by aligning the screws with witness marks made prior to removal. Some may argue that this disturbs the bedding job but I've never had any problems, and I always get my jobs apart with ease later on.

Once the bedding compound has set undisturbed for at least 24 hours, disassemble and clean up both the stock and the metal work. If the stock has been properly masked and protected, clean-up should be simple. If by chance some resin found its way onto the finish, it often will come off with side pressure from a hard nylon comb.

When pulling the barreled action from the stock, replace the two action screws with inletting stock screws. Back the inletting screws out from full tight position one or two turns and rap lightly with a small rawhide mallet in alternating cycles. This will prevent damaging the stock screws and gives a better surface to hammer on. Do not back out the stock screws too far at first, as the more thread contact you have the less chance of thread damage. If you do not have stockmaker's screws or guide pins, the alternative way to get the rifle out of its stock is to clamp the barrel in a padded vise, as close to the fore-end tip as the vise jaws will permit.

With action screws out, use one hand to support the receiver and to hold a hardwood block against the top of the stock just where the barrel and receiver come together (the bearing surface on the wood is thickest there). Use a soft-faced mallet to drive the block and stock downward; alternate sides.

*Now barrel and receiv-
er, with their contact
surfaces thoroughly
coated with release
agent, are lowered into
waiting stock (top) and
action screws snugged.
Later, when bedding
compound has set,
stock bedding should
be found free of voids
(bottom).*

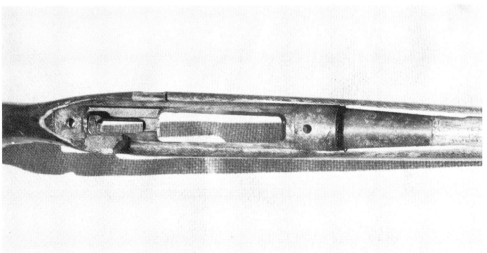

Never try to remove the barreled action by using a mallet on the barrel ahead of the stock fore-end. This will cause the action to rotate in the bedding at the recoil lug, damaging some areas of the bedding.

Check the bedding for air pockets. If there are some, and they are match head size or smaller, I wouldn't worry about them. If you did get a big void in the area of the recoil lug, this area must be ground out and rebedded. Rebedding can cause problems, as it is easy to get high spots in the total bedding job, and you may have to start all over again. This is why you should do everything right the first time.

Once the barreled action has been removed from the stock and the clean-up of stock and metal parts is completed, reassemble the rifle. Oil all of the parts well prior to assembly so that rusting will not occur. The metal parts will "sweat" and rust if not oiled inside of the stock. I tighten the recoil-lug screw the most and only snug the tang screw.

The pictures illustrate the taping of various parts of the action and barrel. These areas are taped so that once the barreled action is assembled into the stock with the tape removed, these surfaces will have clearance from the stock. To assure yourself that this is happening, use spotting blue on the metal and check for contact areas, removing any glass resin where it is not wanted. The rifle is now ready for test firing.

Glass bedding round-receivered actions is relatively easy once you think it through and take the precautions outlined here. Experience shows that these rifle actions are relatively stiff, and once properly bedded shoot extremely well. In doing your own glass bedding you have improved your rifle's accuracy and have saved yourself some money.

Gun Lubricants & Preservatives

Roy Dunlap

Lubrication is the action of introducing a material between surfaces otherwise contacting each other, to reduce or eliminate friction, wear, and heat. Lubed surfaces do not really contact; they slide on a film of molecules or flakes of the lubricant. When the lubricant breaks down, is contaminated, runs off, or is eliminated by any means, increased friction results.

Nearly all of our present-day lubricants have been in existence only a short time. From the dawn of history until the 1860s, all oils and greases came from animal fats, except for a few vegetable oils such as olive oil.

From King Solomon's 3,400 war chariots to the countless wagons of the Civil War, axles — and weapons — were greased with fat and tallow from practically all large animals. The fine lubricating oil for watches and gun locks came from the sperm whale. No, not the rendered whale oil used for lamps until 1870, but the sperm oil from the narwhal — a cavity in the whale's head which contains gallons of oil, ready to use.

Sperm oil was the specified small-arms oil of the U.S. Army up to and during World War I. However, the principal oil used by colonial Americans was bear oil. Black bears were killed by the tens of thousands for lard and oil up into the 1830s, east of the Mississippi.

Just 126 years ago, in 1859, a Colonel Drake brought in the first petroleum oil well in western Pennsylvania, and five years later doctors were using petrolatum to seal burns and wounds of soldiers. We have the same thing today; we call it Vaseline®, or petroleum jelly. Crude oil was refined into many products in a very few years.

In 1865 the E.F. Houghton Co. came into being, to find uses for "rock oil" (crude oil). One of the company owners, a Dr. Lyon, refined the jellies, made salves and cosmetics and hair pomade, and registered the name Cosmoline. By 1869 he was selling it to the government as a rust preventative and preservative.

This article first appeared in *THE AMERICAN RIFLEMAN.*

In 1874 Dr. Lyon won a medal from the Franklin Institute for developing Cosmolubric — a mineral lubricating oil. The citation said it was a "good substitute for natural sperm [oil]." So we have had our regular lubricating oils only 111 years.

Refinement of and experimentation with petroleum products goes on, now alongside chemical products that make oil from other sources and from combinations. Further, we have the dry lubricants such as graphite, molybdenum disulphide (called moly from now on), motor mica, Teflon®, and probably others I do not know about.

DuPont has a spray can with "fluorocarbon telamer," called Slip Spray, sold in auto supply stores. DuPont Teflon® lubes are available in sprays, both wet and dry. The wet type stays wet; the dry dries to a powder. Hoppe's puts out a Teflon which dries to powder in seconds. These dry lubricants, particularly in spray application, are good for getting into receivers of pump and autoloading rifles and shotguns exposed to low temperatures and all extremely dusty environments. Dri-Slide is a moly-lube dry powder.

In the lubricating oils for use inside actions where well-fitted moving parts function, we have many good choices. The original, Houghton's Cosmolubric, numbered 270A, is now a light synthetic. It is made primarily for instruments and has some rust preventative in it. Cosmoline 1116, a general-purpose water-displacing lubricating oil, is good to -70°F.

Many of the light gun oils are polarized to give some preservative quality. RIG 2 Universal Oil Lubricant comes in a spray can and is a polarized light oil compound to penetrate and displace surface moisture and leave a film for lubrication. It contains a solvent which evaporates out. The base is sulphur-free oil and can be used as a moisture-remover on any metal surface.

Just recently, the DuPont people who created Teflon®, and incidentally own Remington Arms Co., have come along with a product called Rem Oil that contains Teflon® and is credited with lubricating, cleaning, and rust-preventive and moisture-displacement qualities.

Hoppe's MDL Rust Inhibitor Lubricant is a somewhat similar product. Outers Gun Oil comes in a spray-can and bottle, while Hoppe's puts out a nice little plastic bottle of lubricating oil with a long (one inch plus) steel applicator tube, a good feature.

It also offers powdered Teflon® in the same container, as well as "fluid grease" lubricant, which is a synthetic that applies as oil but is actually a grease. Its temperature range is from -65° to 250°F. Birchwood Casey makes two gun-lubricating products. Synthetic Gun Oil has a range of -55° to 300°F, which also makes it good for small bearings that get hot.

MoS2 Super Lube is moly in solvent and spray-can application. The solvent dries in a second, leaving a coat of dry moly particles to lubricate. It's good for all dry-lube requirements. Moly is a strange material, not really mixing with any carrier, but best in good greases.

The best I have ever found was Plastilube with moly, No.1 consistency. An industrial product, it comes in large quantities and is made by Warren Refining & Chemical Co. of Cleveland, Ohio. I used the plain Plastilube for Garand rifles 25 years ago and found it to be by far the best lubricant for auto arms. I got the company to put some up in one-pound cans for me and sold it at Camp Perry for a few years. The No.1 is about Vaseline®-consistency, does not change with temperatures, does not pick up foreign matter, thicken in use, or deteriorate. Lube all friction areas and forget it for the season. The company once told me that in spite of the name, Plastilube has a petroleum base.

Additional grease or paste lubricants include the old familiar Gunslick by Outers, which is graphite. RIG's +P Stainless Steel Lube is claimed to be ideal for auto and pump arms and has a moisture-removing action useful on all types, especially for lubing slides and rails of stainless pistols.

CS Lubricant is a blue paste designed for use on stainless surfaces. It's good for any surface requiring an extreme pressure lubricant, which means it has good anti-gall quality. Galling is when two metal surfaces bind and even tear into each other, a common problem with aluminum alloys and stainless steels. Incidentally, petroleum-base lubricants and oils do not do well with brass, copper, or aluminum: for these, soaps or animal-fat lubes, such as lanolin, are better, though some waxes can be used for emergency action.

Moly has the ability to penetrate or merge with the surface of steel and keep it slick. In earlier years, handloaders were cautioned not to use moly in case lubricants, as sized cases would carry the moly into rifle chambers, impregnate surfaces, and injure the chamber wall's ability to hold the case as it is fired, increasing back, or bolt-thrust. In a straight-taper or long-taper case this could happen, but in fact, the idea remains more theory than fact. Moly really makes a poor case lube — I've tried it!

The penetrating ability of moly is used somewhat by Lubri Bond Gun Lubricant as a multi-purpose permanent lubricant. The firearm is well cleaned with degreaser, then the moly liquid (they say a paint-binder is used) is sprayed and allowed to dry for 24 hours, leaving a coating of .0002- to .0005-inch. Arms should be disassembled first, parts coated, and then assembled again after drying.

So, decide on what types of lubricants suit your types of firearms. Revolver parts usually need a light oil, though a moly grease can often do wonders for a stiff action and heavy trigger pull. Firing pins in all arms need a standard light gun oil.

Autoloaders — rifle, pistol, and shotgun — need

heavy-duty lubes like moly grease for general service. The regular gun oils serve well for lever and pump types with normal applications to wear and friction areas. Accralube Precision Oil is good on set triggers, patent trigger mechanisms, locks on quality double shotguns, and other applications where close fitting needs a light lube that resists cold.

Keep guns in boxes or cabinets if possible, to keep dust off. Use gun cases to carry arms, not to store them. Contact with surfaces can remove the oil film on a gun's exterior.

Preservation, of course, is maintaining the quality of the item involved. With a firearm, it means protecting by coating the surfaces with a substance to prevent air, moisture, gases, dust or other foreign matter from contacting wood, metal, or plastic.

Practically all oil-content lubricants have some preservative value, and wiping the barrel and action areas with an oiled or prepared wiping cloth will protect a gun for a week or so. But if a gun is to be stored for any length of time, particularly in coastal or other damp environments, the products made specifically for arms preservation are far superior.

"No Rust For The Wary" — this punning but very sensible slogan shows on one of the E.F. Houghton letterheads. I have mentioned the origin of petroleum jelly and the name "Cosmoline" used by Houghton for more than 100 years and familiar to practically every U.S. veteran.

There have been many variations in types made, but we mostly remember the brown-to-black GI Cosmoline, sometimes as hard as paint and as difficult to remove. As a soldier in 1942, I cleaned up BARs stored in 1919 in hot-dip Cosmoline. They came out looking new, which they were. And I can remember during the 1930s seeing three Sharps rifles made before 1880 and stored with the old Cosmoline in barrels; they cleaned up perfectly. That's long-term storage!

Short-term preservation is what concerns the average gun user most, protection lasting a few weeks. It's best to seal the surface of a cleaned bore with oil or light grease coating and wipe the exterior with a greased pad or wiper made for such a job, like the Birchwood-Casey Anti-Rust Gun Cloth. It is really paper, impregnated with their Sheath protector; little ones come in a plastic envelope, very handy to carry on hunts.

For even greater protection, you can spray the firearm exterior with one of the oil- or wax-base spray-can products. Practically all of the firms in the gun-cleaning-product field put out some sort of spray with preservative power. Birchwood-Casey Sheath, a polarized oil, should protect up to two years if not disturbed or rubbed off metal, its maker claims. It clings to parts at up to 250°F, so it won't run off on a hot day.

Some of the other products in the field include Beeman's MP-5, RIG 2 Universal Oil Lubricant, Pachmayr Rust Preventative, and G-96 Gun Treatment. Houghton's new Cosmoline spray is penetrating and water-displacing. It leaves a film .0001-inch thick and comes in a can with an adjustable spray nozzle to give fan or pinpoint application.

Many people have excessively salty or acidic perspiration and can produce rusty fingerprints on gun barrels without even trying. These unlucky ones should use both the wipers and sprays!

The wiper pad of shearling (close-clipped sheepskin) impregnated with RIG showed up about 50 years ago and is now furnished as the RIG Rag. Wipe the gun every time you finish handling it, and it will look new as long as you own it.

For non-greasy or oily surfaces, allowing some handling of the arms, the wax-residue protectors are possible. The spray RustGuardit has proven quite good. These spray on wax and, held in quick-drying solution, leave a coating adhering to the gun to protect against fingerprints and rust.

For long term storage of months or years you need RIG or an equally effective grease or very heavy oil, like TDP Accragard Bore & Metal Protector or Cosmoline Rust Veto for medium film, Cosmoline Weathershed for thick film. These two come in spray-cans, not so suited for applying to bores, but great for outsides.

I have long recommended that for layaway storage, a gun should be thoroughly cleaned, then given a coat of RIG in the bore and on the outside, then wrapped in wax paper and stored in a box or cabinet. Kept in a normal environment, neither humid nor dry, arms should be okay for several years. At least half a dozen rifles and handguns, plus tools, went about five years during World War II and survived in great shape.

Airtight containers exclude moisture, but they may have some in the air inside to begin with and temperature change could condense it to vapor. The size of the container is important because of the volume of air. A couple of pistols oiled up inside a small ammunition box are not bad, but in a large chest, not good.

The assorted gun-safes sold for theft-protection are good storage spots for wax-paper-wrapped arms. I have my doubts about the efficiency of the assorted heat sources advertised to combat humidity, as it requires a lot of heat to bring down really high humidity. The dessicants, which absorb moisture from air, that you can stick in the kitchen oven every few days to dry out are better. Keep guns out of plastic bags, gun cases, etc. Some of the linings, paddings, and plastics used may be corrosive.

I once used some "foam rubber" to pad notches in a wooden gun carrying case I made. In two days it had rusted and pitted the barrels wherever it touched, and it came from a commercial gun box. Foam rubber is not good, though it is okay with wax paper between it and the steel. Never pad a notch in rack or case with cloth; eventually it will absorb the protective film on the barrel.

Wood can be a problem in long storage as, aside from oil finishes, surfaces can discolor, check, and perhaps change from chemicals in the preservative sprays. Even linseed oil is not perfect. I think perhaps safflower seed oil, just as used for cooking, is a good rub for the wood. Like linseed oil, it oxidizes — hardens — in time, but does not darken. I have tried it off and on for a dozen years without complaint. A cloth patch dampened with it and wiped on wood should protect its finish regardless of type, epoxy, varnish, plastic, or oil.

What wood and plastic both need is protection against light and excessive heat. I do not know how some of the plastic/epoxy finishes would stand up if subjected to weeks of freezing.

Never mind what you read in the ads about how they tested everything in their factory laboratory for 999 hours at -40°C to 280°F. Remember, at least 50 percent of our modern arms equipment and cleaning, lubricating, and preserving agents have not been in existence long enough to tell much about long-time performance. I have read ads saying a product is good for 10 years when I know it was only created five years ago!

Unfortunately, I can't test everything and then write this article. Waiting for results would take 15 years, and I just can't put this off until 2000 A.D. So go with what we know and believe from tests we do know about. Keep light, dust, and pressure off stored, preserved arms, and you need not worry.

You only wanted to know how to take care of your gun? Well, clean the barrel with a bore cleaner like Marksman's Choice or Break Free CLP if it is a centerfire using jacketed bullets, dry and oil it, or grease it, whatever your need calls for (whether days or months between shootings). If it is a gas-operated semi-auto, clean the gas piston and port with solvents, and before you shoot next time, put a few drops of lubricant down the gas cylinder.

With revolvers the main problem is the owner who often loads ammunition too hot for his lead or jacked bullets and gets a lot of cone and barrel metal fouling. The Lewis cleaners employing brass cloth patches for clearing cones with the tools furnished can get excessive lead out of cones in a hurry. Keep some 4/0 steel wool on hand; it can be bought at the good hardware or artist's supply stores. It's good for getting lead out of barrels and for wiping fouling from cylinder-fronts and removing any rust you may pick up. Wet a pad with bore cleaner and another with oil, keep separate, in plastic bags, or better, in glass jars, the same with oiled or greased wiping pads.

Keep your firearms in good condition, keep them shooting, but above all, keep them.

The Sanded-In Finish

David Simpson

A good craftsman has a vested interest in keeping tension and frustration to a minimum. He is always on the lookout for ways to make life easier, like a drowning ship's rat paddling after a chunk of floating bulkhead. That's not laziness — just self-defense.

With that in mind, let me describe a method of stock finishing, using commonly available materials, that saves about half the effort expended in the usual process; that is, building up layers of finish and cutting them back to the wood with sandpaper

to fill the pores. The method I use is based on the discoveries of two gunmakers, Phil Pilkington and John Smyrl, who seem to have arrived at the process independently.

It's odd that no one stumbled on this technique before. Bob Brownell did say something about "sanding-in" in his book GUNSMITH KINKS, but only used it on the first coat or two of finish. What Pilkington and Smyrl do is wet-sand a stock to fill,

This article first appeared in *RIFLE.*

Sanded-in finishing technique works well with most oil-modified varnishes, including those shown here. (R) Express Oil Sealer is polyurethane; other three products are tung/phenolic/linseed oil mixtures. Watco Danish Oil Finish (L) can be mixed with tung oil or linseed-based finishes and employed as a darkener.

finish, and polish all at the same time, never letting a coat of finish dry *on the surface.*

That last is critical, because modern finishes dry to extremely tough films which are designed to resist the sort of abrasion we apply with sandpaper. Letting a spar varnish polymerize, then trying to cut it back to the wood is not only frustrating, but just plain *dumb.* We have done it that way because tradition said that to fill wood pores in gunstocks, one must build up a layer of oil, then sand back. Well, that works great with boiled linseed oil but hardly at all with contemporary tough oil-modified varnishes.

We also want to keep sanding to a minimum because we want all those carefully wrought details in the stock to stay that way. We just work to higher standards of detail than stockmakers did even 20 years ago.

Don Allen, a stockmaker of some repute, has often said that more stocks are ruined during the finishing process than at any other time. I must admit that all this sanding does sound like a paradox: How can what seems like more abrasion help preserve details? The difference lies in creating a sludge that fills pores instead of trying to cut through a layer of polymerized hell! The secret of the sanded-in finish is *that you never have to sand through a tough coat of finish designed to resist the very thing you are attempting.*

In choosing a finish, it helps to remember why stockmakers have used self-filling varnishes and why they even bother to fill all pores well with the oil-based varnishes we prefer for looks and ease of repair. The main reason we fill pores level with the surface is for moisture resistance, but this also gives a more elegant look and feel. It is safe to say that the best oil-based varnish finishes created now are better than the greatest efforts of the golden age of gunmaking, say, from the time of Boutet through the beginning of World War II. If you take a close look at some older examples, particularly German and English, you will notice that many of the old geezers depended upon partially filled finishes to protect the wood. There are exceptions, of course, and it is also possible that many applications of renewing and preserving oil applied after manufacture could fill pores completely.

The old linseed oil finish, raw or boiled, is a goner. What are commonly called oils, like Linspeed and Tru-Oil, are simply oil-modified varnishes. What we use today to produce an oil finish is one of the many varnishes, interior or exterior.

One of the best things about the sanding-in technique is that it can be used with almost any varnish thinned to the correct consistency. For maximum moisture resistance, it would be pretty hard to beat a tung/phenolic/linseed spar varnish. It could well be that Monty Kennedy was right, 30 years ago, when he said that a spar or bar-top varnish was the

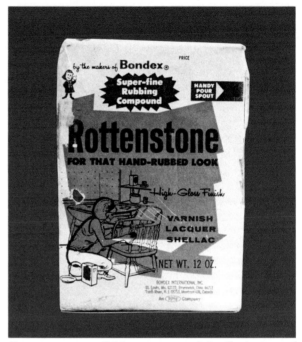

Rottenstone, a polishing agent used in final stage of sanding-in process. It buffs an extra-fine finish on stock.

best finish to use on stocks.

I also recommend John Bivins' Express Oil Sealer for this technique. If you favor the characteristics of polyurethane in your work, this is probably the best available. It can be ordered from Lowell Manley Shooting Supplies, 3684 Pine St., Deckerville, MI 48427. While the Bivins finish is carefully made in small batches, making it of very high quality, you could probably get by with one of the other common urethanes, such as that manufactured by Flecto, sold under the familiar Varathane label.

My own favorites for the best combination of looks and protection are the thinner tung/phenolic/linseed varnishes such as DuPont's 704c or Carver Tripp's Tung Oil Base-Danish Oil Finish. I get Tripp's at a local home center but you may have to call the factory in San Diego to get the name of your nearest retailer. What I like most about Tripp's Danish oil is that it is exactly the right percentage of solids for the sanded-in method (about 25 percent). Unlike other Danish oils on the market, it also dries quickly.

Gunmaker Phil Pilkington is also marketing a finishing system especially formulated for use with the sanded-in technique. He calls it Classic Gunstock Finish and sells it with a polishing and renewing formula he calls Classic Linseed Stock Rubbing Oil and a very detailed set of instructions. Pilkington, who was trained as a chemist, has included something in his finish which delays drying and allows excess sludge to be removed easily, yet leaves the pores packed with finish and sanding particles. His basic formulation is very much like a spar varnish, but whatever the mixture, it is excellent. It can be ordered directly from the Pilkington Gun Co., PO Box 1296, Muskogee, OK 74401.

While on the subject of materials, I must caution you about two other familiar finishes that cause some problems when used with the sanded-in technique. They are Flecto's Natural Oil Finish No.66 and Watco Danish Oil. While each is a penetrating finish with the right amount of solids for sanding-in, both dry too slowly. All the finishes I have mentioned dry by oxidation from the outside in. Once the outer surfaces are dry, the underlying finish still has a way to go. With Watco or Flecto's No.66 this drying process takes longer, and if the sandings are applied before the finish is completely dry, the pores will fill very slowly or not at all.

Watco, which comes in several colors, can be used as an oil stain and warming toner when mixed with a hot finish like DuPont 704c, which dries quickly. This gives a stockmaker the option of adding a bit of color to his finish, as in the old alkenet or bloodroot formulas. Watco's ability to penetrate is amazing and I use it to feed an existing finish. It will actually penetrate a fully oxidized coat of varnish. For sanding-in, mix your choice of Watco colors with 704c in a two parts to three parts ratio. Then thin that with enough mineral spirits to give a water-thin penetrating consistency. Adding Watco to the 704c gives a finish that dries much faster than plain Watco. Use the same mixture all the way through the sanding-in process. Adding Watco to something like spar varnish will cause it to be less water resistant due to the higher percentage of linseed oil. If moisture is liable to be a problem, better stick to a pure spar or polyurethane.

The sanded-in finish is fairly easy to apply, and what sounds like a bunch of work goes rather quickly. Do your final sanding (prior to the application of the finish) with No.220 grit wet-or-dry paper (used dry) and inspect carefully to make sure you have removed all sanding marks. Dampen the stock once to raise the grain, drying over the stove burner or with a hair dryer.

To prepare the finish for application, it must be thinned to about 25 percent solids. Mineral spirits are appropriate for thinning most varnishes but check the instructions on the can to be sure. *Mix only as much thinned finish as you need for a day's work.* Most of these finishes are made to be used unthinned. The addition of mineral spirits will unbalance them and cause them to set up in the container.

Do not cut off the raised grain whiskers with steel wool or the like — you will just be making extra work. Instead, the first application of finish will freeze them in place and the first wet sanding will cut them off. Using a brush, soak the diluted finish into the stock, applying repeatedly until the stock will soak up no more. Don't build up a coat on the surface of the wood, but make sure that the wood will not take any more varnish. Wipe out any finish remaining on the surface of inletted areas.

Allow the finish to dry for *two days.* That is longer than necessary in most climates, but make absolutely sure the finish is dry all the way through.

Now you are ready for pore filling. Cut a sheet of No.320 grit wet-or-dry paper into two-inch squares. Tearing only wastes paper and causes poor results with the finer papers which you will use later. Use rubber erasers of appropriate shapes to back the paper. The softer the backing the faster the paper will cut. Remember, on some details you don't want anything so soft that the sharp edges may be rounded off.

Dilute enough finish for the day's work and begin by *wet sanding,* with the grain, all the detailing: under the comb flutes, around mouldings, cheekpieces, and the like. I find this much less frustrating than doing each detail as I come to it. While I am still fresh, I'm more likely to take the care needed not to round anything off. Use very light pressure and let the paper do the work. You may have to abandon the eraser and use paper folded into various shapes to fit whatever contour you are attacking. You will notice you can feel the cutting action of the paper and you'll see a sludge of sanding dust and finish accumulating. Stop sanding an area when you can see the sludge is covering the pores and when you can no longer feel the paper cutting the frozen whiskers. Proceed to the other details and complete all of them before sanding any of the large areas of the stock.

Now, go on to those areas, working a small portion at a time, cutting the whiskers and building sludge. *Do not spare the sandpaper.* When the paper no longer cuts with light pressure, change to a fresh piece. Add finish to the work area whenever the sludge becomes too dry to work easily. The sludge has to be fairly thick to fill the pores, though. After doing a couple of areas, you will get the hang of it. Continue until the entire stock is sanded out and covered with sludge.

Now you have a stock covered entirely with a layer of crud that is saving you a lot of labor. The next step is to re-wet the entire stock with fresh finish, moving your fingers in a circular motion to work this new finish into the existing sludge, mixing well. Continue until the entire stock is wet and gleaming. At this point rub another coat into the inletting, but be sure to wipe it out completely before putting the stock up to dry.

Set the stock aside until the finish becomes syrupy and resists being pushed with a finger about five to 10 minutes. Now remove the mixture from the surface, leaving as much finish *in* the pores as possible. That is done with non-absorbent paper napkins, the kind found at fast food restaurants. Don't use household paper towels. Because of their high absorbency, they tend to suck finish out of the pores. Wipe the sludge off the stock in a circular motion, working gently, just hard enough to remove most of the sanding debris. You may have to work a bit harder at the end when the finish has stiffened.

If you don't move fast enough and an area becomes too tacky to wipe off, re-wet it, wait a bit, then hit it again. Don't wipe too vigorously. If you leave a bit of the sludge on the surface, it will be easy to remove during the next sanding.

Set the stock aside and allow it to dry another *two days*. Repeat the above wet sanding step with No.320 grit wet-or-dry. On French or English walnut you will probably begin to notice the pores filling nicely.

Allow the stock to dry *two more days* then repeat the No.320 grit sanding for the third time, proceeding exactly as before. That should fill the pores completely on all but the coarsest walnuts, which may need a fourth wet sanding. What you should have at this point is a stock with all the pores completely filled, with a dull finish and maybe a bit of sludge remaining on the surface.

After another two days' drying time, wet sand as before but this time use No.400 grit wet-or-dry paper. As before, let the paper do the work, changing it often, floating it over the surface of the wood, working all the details first, then proceeding to the

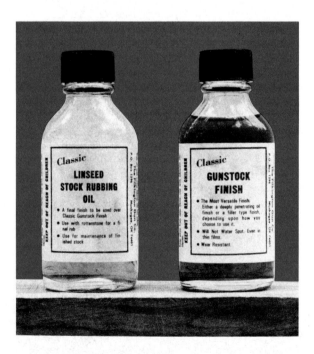

Pilkington Gun Co. markets a pair of finishing products especially designed for the sanded-in technique. One bottle contains finish; the other is final rubbing oil.

large areas. Again, wipe off the residue with paper napkins just hard enough to remove about 99 percent of the mixture.

Allow another two days' drying time. You will now have a quality finish that has all the pores filled and that is completely within the wood. You are now ready for the two polishing steps that will add a soft luster to your handiwork. The first is to repeat, as before, your wet sanding but this time you will use No.600 wet-or-dry, a polishing paper. Let the paper do the work and change it as often as it dulls. I even like to add a couple of layers of soft cloth between paper and eraser to give a better polishing and floating effect. When you finish, wipe *all* the sanding sludge off the stock with either cotton flannel or T-shirt material. Make sure that whatever you use is 100 percent cotton, because common synthetic blends are not absorbent enough for the purpose.

Instead of using a circular motion for your wiping, work with the grain of the wood, cleaning just hard enough to remove all the sanding residue. *Do not* polish the stock by rubbing hard with the cotton. The finish is still too wet and delicate to stand this.

After a couple of days' more drying time, you will have a very high-quality, though quite dull finish. You may stop here and checker if you wish. I like a bit more warm sheen on my own stocks and carry the polishing one step further.

For this step, make up a rubbing pad of several layers of flannel covering a rubber eraser. Dip it into a shallow bowl containing diluted finish. Watco is also an excellent compound for this purpose. Then apply rottenstone to the pad, either by dipping the wet flannel into a container of the polishing agent or sprinkling it on from a salt shaker. Rub this mixture over the stock, polishing the finish, working with the grain of the wood, never in a circular motion. Use very little pressure. Add more finish and rottenstone to the pad as necessary. The entire step should take from 10 to 15 minutes. When you have finished polishing, put the stock aside for about 30 minutes; then come back and gently remove all the sludge from the surface of the wood, using a fresh piece of flannel.

Add fresh finish to the pad, if necessary, to remove any partially dried residue. Now rub on a thin coat of straight finish with your fingers. Next, wipe off just hard enough to leave a very thin coat of finish, a molecule thick, on the wood. Put the stock aside for a couple more days before checkering or handling. By that time the finish has fully polymerized and seems to take on a bit more sheen when rubbed out.

After the last rubbing, the sanded-in finish is complete. What you have is an elegant, smooth surface that shows wood color and figure to its best advantage. All pores are completely filled, yet all the

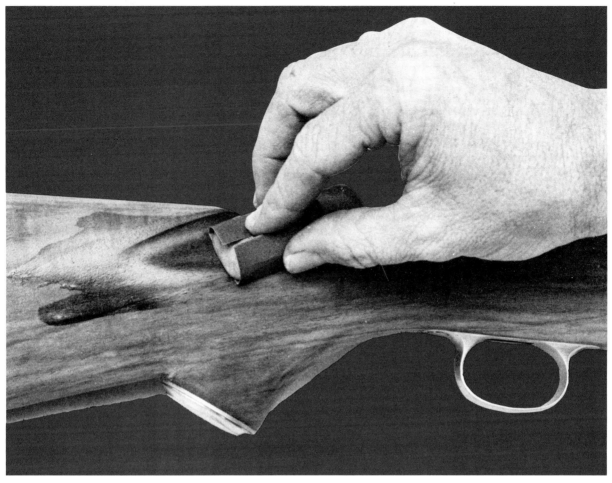

All detailing should be wet-sanded before larger, flat or round areas of the stock are tackled. That helps preserve sharp edges which might be inadvertently rounded off.

finish is *in the wood*. It is what is now known as a classic finish and is suitable for guns to be used as well as those destined for exhibition only.

I find very little reason for a built-up finish in my own work, but some people prefer it. Such finishes are a bit more water resistant, but are also harder to repair. It is easy to go on to a built-up finish from the sanding-in technique, but a switch in materials is necessary for the built-up stages. The *only* finish I have had any real luck in using for this is Dem-Bart's Checkering Oil. It is just the right consistency for wiping on very thin coats and seems to dry quickly enough to be practical.

You can wipe on coats by hand after you have reached the No.400 grit stage in your sanding-in, letting each coat dry a couple of days. I cut back the gloss slightly after every third coat with 4-ought steel wool. You may also apply this oil with a poupee like that used in French polishing. I make mine with a ball of flannel wrapped in a section of sheer nylon hose. Support Hose material doesn't work as well. Rub on a pretty generous coat of Dem-

Bart oil (which can be ordered from Brownell's), let it set up about 30 minutes, then wipe off all but the thinnest possible coat of finish. If you are using the stocking method, it helps to wet the flannel with oil, wring it out, wrap in with a single layer of stocking and wipe. About four coats, two days apart, should do it and you may not need the steel wool step. Just don't use Dem-Bart oil over any of the polyurethanes because all those formulae cross-link so tightly while drying that later coats of other materials will not form a chemical bond with them.

If you find your built-up surface is too shiny, you may cut back a bit with the rottenstone rub described above, but be sure not to cut through the built-up layers. Wait several weeks before that step to ensure the built-up layers are fully oxidized.

It occurs to me, in closing, that I have cranked out a great pile of instructions here for something that is very simple. Despite this, I urge you to try the method as described. It's guaranteed to help keep the wolf of lunacy from the door.

Accurizing the M1 Rifle

J.B. Roberts, Jr.

When the glass-bedding job on my DCM-M1 was completed, the rifle, which had sprayed hits all over the SR bullseye, shot well within acceptance criteria for the National Match M1 rifle. Those limits were not tough: 3½-inch average extreme spread for three 10-shot groups at 100 yards; no single group over a five-inch extreme spread. That, according to the 1961 NATIONAL MATCH RIFLE BULLETIN, was all it took, though in all fairness, most rifles did better.

Those criteria were also geared to the accuracy requirements of the old five-point targets, a 12-inch five-ring for 200 and 300 yards, a 20-inch five-ring for 600 yards, and 36 inches at 1,000 yards. They won't really get the job done on the current 10-point series of targets; nor will they suffice for real competition on the 600-yard stage of the 200-yard reduced course where the 10-ring is just larger than 3¾ inches in diameter. My rifle, for example, after it had been glass bedded, would group 50 consecutive shots in the seven-inch-diameter 10-ring of the SR target, good for scores in the 80s on the 600-yard reduced target. Fortunately, where my M1 was concerned, there was something more that could be done.

The U.S. Navy, in the late 1960s, did a considerable amount of pre-planned tinkering with M1 rifles, both .30 caliber and converted to 7.62mm NATO, for match use. They turned up a number of kinks having to do with the wood- and metal-to-metal fit — not the bedding — of the M1 that resulted in a more precise-shooting rifle. That is to say the Navy's M1s would shoot rounder groups that were smaller by virtue of having fewer fliers. These procedures have been published, but there is no harm in recapping them and revising the techniques so that the hobby gunsmith can make the modifications.

Begin by disassembling the rifle, removing all metal and wooden parts from the barrel. Set the stock group and trigger-housing group aside. They won't be needed until it's nearly time to reassemble the rifle.

Inspect the operating rod to insure that it is *straight*. Looked at from the side, there are two bends in the rod. They are intentional, providing clearance so the operating rod will not strike the breech portion of the barrel. The section of rod between the bends and the two end sections must be straight, and the front (on which the gas piston is fitted) and rear portions (the operating-rod handle) must be parallel. Checking the rod from above, it must be like an arrow. There are gauges to check rod straightness, but the hobbyist will have to depend on a "calibrated eyeball." Don't fret. If the operating rod is bent badly enough to need replacement, the bends can be seen.

Next, measure the diameter of the bright steel gas piston attached to the front of the operating rod. It must be at least .525-inch. If the rod is bent, or if the diameter of the piston is less than .525-inch, replace the operating rod.

This article first appeared in THE AMERICAN RIFLEMAN.

Liner in M1's front handguard is not needed in target rifle. Its removal helps grouping, but renders handguard itself useless as protection for the barrel.

You may also wish to check the inside diameter of the gas cylinder. Make the check at a point about ¼-inch below the clearance hole for the gas port. Maximum diameter is .532-inch. Above that dimension, replace the cylinder. (Note: Unlike glass bedding, reworking the metal parts of an M1 may be expensive. Parts that are unserviceable will have to be replaced, and the job calls for tools that may not be in the average tool box.)

Presuming that the operating rod and gas cylinder are serviceable, let's shift our attention to the lower band and handguards.

Start actual work with the rear handguard and trim 1/16- or 3/32-inch from its back end. Shortening the rear guard by that amount will prevent it from contacting the receiver when the rifle is assembled.

The front handguard requires a little more work. It must be modified so that, when attached to the lower band, it does not contact either the barrel or the operating rod.

The first step in reworking the front handguard is to remove the sheet-metal liner from inside the operating-rod channel. It's easy to do. The liner is held in place by tabs at either end. Bend them straight, grab the liner with a pair of pliers, and jerk it out of there. Then throw it away.

Now, with a round-faced punch and a pair of pliers, bend the sheet metal cap on the forward end of the front handguard so that it does not contact the barrel. There will be some trial fitting involved, here, but the desired end result is that the barrel floats inside the guard. Since the operating rod must also move freely inside the guard, now is a good time to check that and, if need be, to relieve the sides of the operating-rod channel.

Once the barrel and the operating rod are free of contact with the front handguard, we are going to permanently attach the front handguard to the lower band.

The best way to do that is to drill clearance holes for two No.6 woodscrews in the portions of the lower band where the area of contact with the guard is the greatest. Turn the band over and, on the flat rear surface, countersink the holes to at least partially accommodate the screw heads. Then use two No.6 X ½-inch woodscrews to join the two parts.

It is also wise at this point to reinforce the screw attachment by gluing the handguard to the metal. Brownell's Acraglas works fine for this purpose. So does Devcon. There is a third alternative, to be discussed shortly. Whatever is used, when the adhesive has dried, use a small flat file or hand grinder to dress off the protruding screw heads.

At this point we fit the rear handguard and the assembled lower band and front handguard to the rifle. The lower band must be a driving fit on the barrel. If it is not (and it probably isn't after being

(L) Barrel should not bear inside modified front handguard. Peening the front reinforce clear of contact helps achieve this condition.

(R) Floating handguard is permanently attached to middle band using glass bedding compound. Two No.6 woodscrews add strength to the joint.

Grind the woodscrews flush with surface of middle band to provide clearance for reassembling rifle.

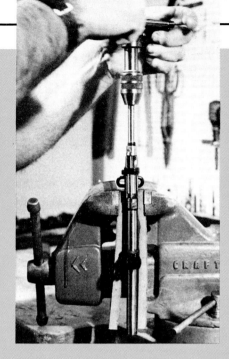

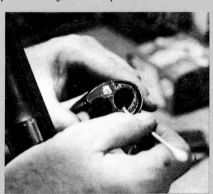

(L) Ream or bore out rear ring on gas cylinder to give about .010-inch radial clearance between rear ring and barrel.

If middle band is not tight on barrel, a high-temperature adhesive may be used to permanently bond the parts.

disassembled and reassembled for glass bedding and for trial fitting of the front handguard) it must be tightened. This is best done by peening the edges of the barrel-clearance hole on the rear of the band — and on the front too if a long drift punch is available — and then gluing the band in place on the barrel.

The adhesive used for this step must be of a type that does not deteriorate at relatively high temperatures. Fiberglass bedding and common epoxies will not do the job here, since two strings of rapid fire will generate sufficient barrel heat to begin breaking them down. I use General Electric RTV-106, a silicone-base adhesive that will hold at temperatures of up to 500°F for long periods and at 600°F for 15 or 20 minutes. RTV-106 is available from dealers in building materials and adhesives and costs about $7.00 for a 2.8-ounce tube.

If there is no chance that the handguard will ever be removed, RTV-106 may be used to bond the handguard to the band. It will, however, be a part of a permanent installation. The heat needed to break down the RTV-106 will ruin the barrel — thus limiting removal of the band to occasions upon which the barrel is to be changed — and burn the handguard to cinders. For my part, I used RTV-106 on the band, Acraglas on the handguard.

There is one thing to keep in mind from now on. Call it a handling instruction, if that seems appropriate, but remember it — never (NEVER!) pick up an accurized M1 rifle by the front handguard, ever again. 'Nuff said.

Let's turn our attention back to the gas cylinder. Just as the barrel must not contact the handguards, except where absolutely necessary, the gas cylinder must not contact the barrel, except at the front where the two join together. The gas cylinder must not contact the front handguard either.

Start modifying the cylinder by filing a 30° bevel on each side of the tongue that extends rearward from the stacking swivel and, in the unmodified rifle, protrudes about ⅜-inch into the operating-rod channel in the front handguard. That keeps the tongue from touching the handguard.

Then, remove about ¹⁄₃₂-inch from the rear end of the cylinder and the ring above the cylinder. This operation is best done on a milling machine since the back of the cylinder must be straight and square. Lacking a mill, or the convenient services of a machine shop, the job can be done with a file. When done that way it is a job requiring skill and painstaking care. When it is completed, the gas-cylinder assembly will not contact the front handguard.

The final modification to the gas-cylinder assembly is the enlargement of the inside diameter of the rear mounting ring so that it does not touch the barrel. This, too, is a job for a machine shop, although it can be done with an expandable reamer.

If the latter method is selected, a pilot will be required — and must be fabricated — to keep the reamer straight. Turn the pilot on a lathe, .520+/-.003-inch diameter and eight inches long. That diameter will slide easily through the three splines

(L) File 30° bevels on edges of guide tang on the gas cylinder and shorten cylinder by milling or by careful filing.

(R) To hold gas cylinder in place, peen over cylinder splines on barrel. Bore spud prevents damage to the lands.

that hold the gas cylinder on the barrel, and that length will provide guidance for the reamer for its entire cutting length.

Ream the rear ring from its nominal .620-inch diameter, up to .640-inch, a radial increase of .010-inch — and be careful. The web between the gas cylinder and the ring is about .050-inch thick before reaming. The .040-inch of metal left after reaming is still thick enough, but only just. Do not thin the web too much. A Critchley "C" expandable reamer with a working range between .5938-inch and .6562-inch is the tool to use.

When the gas cylinder is reassembled on the barrel, there are two criteria governing the way it fits. First, it must be tight. Second, when seated so that the gas port in the barrel is aligned in the clearance hole in the cylinder assembly, the gas-cylinder lock must not turn more than 60° past bottom dead center before stopping against the face of the cylinder. If this last condition is not met it can be corrected artificially. But there is no permanent cure short of procuring a supply of gas cylinders and cylinder locks and trial fitting them until a combination is found that will work. For economy's sake the artificial correction is the better choice.

To tighten the gas cylinder on the barrel, lightly peen the spline cuts on the barrel until the cylinder has to be driven lightly into place. Drive the gas cylinder onto the barrel until the gas port is wholly visible at the rear of the clearance hole. Reassemble the remaining parts of the barrel and receiver group. Close the bolt.

Then, using the gas-cylinder lock as a tool, swage the gas cylinder rearward until two conditions are met. The gas piston (the chromed head of the operating rod) must be completely inside the cylinder and the gas-cylinder lock must not be more than 60° past bottom dead center. When those two conditions are met, stake the rear of the splines on the barrel to keep the gas piston from moving further to the rear. When staking is completed, turn the gas-cylinder lock screw back to bottom center, insert the gas-cylinder lock screw, and put it down *tight*.

The job is almost done, but there is one more thing. The operating rod must not bind or rub against the ferrule on the stock group. To insure that it doesn't, coat the inside of the ferrule with Prussian blue or a similar spotting compound, reassemble the rifle, and cycle the action several times. Any rubbing will show up as spotting compound on the rod. If there is binding, relieve the inside of the ferrule with a round file until it ceases. Now, the job is complete.

Test shooting my M1 following these modifications resulted in a reduction of group size (a 50-shot composite group) from a 6¾X5-inch oval to a 5¾ circle at 200 yards. That's plenty good enough to hold the nine-ring on my personal nemesis, the MR 52 target.

Maybe, by experimenting with reloads, I can do better. I don't think so. I think I've reached the barrel's limit. But, I'm going to try. Meantime, I'm going to take my DCM-M1 to some rifle matches and try to make Sharpshooter.

(Photo by Stanley W. Trzoniec)

Newsworthy guns introduced this year include (From Left): Marlin autoloading M-9 Camp Carbine, chambered for 9mm Luger cartridge; Iver Johnson double-barreled (over-under) .50-cal. muzzleloading rifle; Remington 12-ga. Mag. M-1100 Special Purpose auto with non-reflecting finish for waterfowl and turkey hunting; Alpha stainless-steel bolt-action, shown with Leupold Silver Scope (Carmichel plans to use this rifle in .284 on his next sheep hunt); Mossberg Regal pump shotgun, available in 12 or 20 ga., with ACCU-Choke or fixed choke; Ultra Light Arms bolt-action with Kevlar-and-graphite camouflage stock (test rifle, in 7mm-08, weighed only 5 pounds scoped, and it proved to be accurate); and Thompson/Center break-action single-shot rifle, available with interchangeable barrels in 8 calibers. T/C shown here is set-triggered Aristocrat Model, but same gun is now available as Hunter Model (shown in cover photograph) with adjustable single-stage trigger.

APPENDIX

ANNUAL UPDATE

Gun Developments

Jim Carmichel

In American firearms history, this year is going to be recorded as a year of dramatic technological advances and as the year of the great European invasion. Not since the 1950s have so many European gun manufacturers made such efforts to please the American hunter. They remind me of hungry wolves eyeing a plump moose.

During the dozen or so years following World War II, European gunmakers catered to the American market with a host of inexpensive but beautifully built sporting arms. In those days, European firms were still struggling for their existence and were eager for American greenbacks. However, as the European economic picture improved, the American market became less attractive. Increased labor costs, for example, plus ever-spiraling inflation, eventually made European guns so expensive to produce that they could not compete with American firms on the American market. Gradually, they withdrew.

Now the sporting arms market is a new battleground, created by the high value of the U.S. dollar against other currencies. This doesn't mean that we're going to get top European hand-craftsmanship

at bargain prices the way we did back in the 1950s; it only means that the Germans, Austrians, and Belgians feel that they can once again succeed in the American marketplace. You'll be especially disappointed if you're hoping for more of those wonderful old Mausers and Mannlichers made the way they were before the 1960s. Most current European sporting arms, especially rifles, are mass-produced on computer-controlled machinery and feature no more hand fitting than do most American-made guns. In fact, the only recognizable feature left over from the great days of German and Austrian rifle building is the attitude of some makers when they seem to ask, "Why make it simple when it's so easy to make it complicated?" Some middle-European rifles still have enough buttons to push, levers to pull, and trick triggers to play with to gladden the heart of even the most jaded connoisseur.

BROWNING

One very good piece of news from Europe is the return of the old Belgian-made Browning Superposed Over-Under shotguns. They were discontinued several years ago, you'll recall, when runaway inflation and an unsettled labor force in Belgium made it impossible for Browning to market the shotguns in America. With the situation now under control, Browning is reintroducing the Superposed line as it previously existed, complete with fancy grades right up through the dazzling Midas grade. The folks at Browning tell me that the new Superposed guns are identical to the earlier models and that the engraving is done entirely by hand and, in many cases, the same hands that did it years ago.

You're also going to discover that Browning bolt-action rifles have been slimmed down to a more classic profile. This is a considerable improvement over that somewhat chubby BBR (Browning Bolt Rifle) that they introduced a few years back.

REMINGTON

The guys at Remington have coined a new phrase to describe the direction they're taking with some of their guns. "Special Purpose," they're called —"SP" for short. The idea is to equip and finish a gun for a particular type of hunting. This year's SPs include a Model 1100 autoloader and a Model 870 pump shotgun. Both come with three-inch Magnum chambers and your choice of 26- or 30-inch, full choke, chrome-lined barrels. These Special Purpose shotguns are, of course, for waterfowl and turkey hunters. To that end, the metal surfaces are coated with a non-reflecting "Parkerized" finish. Likewise, the stocks have a dull finish.

Last year, Remington introduced an economy-priced bolt-action called the Sportsman 78, which is essentially a Model 700 mechanism fitted with a plain-finished birch stock. This year, the Sportsman 78 line has been expanded to include a short-action version so that, in addition to last year's .270 and .30/06 calibers, you now can choose .243 or .308, as well. A budget-priced autoloading shotgun called the "Sportsman" is also in tune with this market strategy. Essentially, this is a no-frills Model 1100 with a birch (rather than walnut) stock, and pressed (rather than cut) checkering. However, the receiver is still machined steel, the gas-operated mechanism is the same, and the barrel is fitted with a ventilated rib. Only a 12 gauge is available for this year.

Elk hunters who have despaired of ever finding one of the few remaining rifles in .350 Remington Magnum caliber will be delighted to hear that Remington is making a special run of the Model 700 classic-style rifles in this hard-hitting caliber.

MARLIN

I wish more gunmakers could be like Marlin. They make good guns, they are proud of what they make, and they back up their products with reliable service. They don't feel the need to scramble after someone else's share of the market and seldom feel the need to change their line. That's why Marlin's

offering of a wholly new model is a matter of more than passing interest. New for this year is a semi-automatic rifle chambered for the 9mm Luger cartridge.

Called the Model 9 Camp Carbine, this new firearm is intended to serve as a light-weight companion piece for 9mm handguns. It is by no means a deer-class hunting carbine, but rather a handy sport shooting piece for plinking or pot shots at varmints. The carbine has a trim 16½ inch barrel, an overall length of 35½ inches, and weighs 6¾ pounds. The receiver is drilled and tapped for scope mounting.

USRAC-WINCHESTER

The U.S. Repeating Arms Co., makers of the traditional line of American-made Winchester rifles and shotguns, keeps pounding at the marketplace with new ideas and an ever-expanding line of equipment. Last year, for example, they introduced the first short-action version of the fabled Model 70 bolt rifle. This year, they are capitalizing on the short-action concept by using the shorter, more rigid action in short-cartridge versions of their Featherweight and Sporter Varmint rifles and a new Mini-Carbine. Calibers available in the short-action models are the .223 Remington, .22/250, .243, and .308.

The Featherweight is USRAC's best-looking rifle and is one of the world's best bolt rifles at any price. The new Mini-Carbine weighs less than six pounds, making it a true flyweight, but the Sporter Varmint is neither fish nor fowl. It is too heavy to be a hunting rifle and too light for serious varminting. It would benefit mightily from a longer and fatter barrel and a beavertail stock.

Until this year, USRAC/Winchester's big-bore, lever-action rifles have been available only in a more or less deluxe grade. This year, they're making them in ordinary, unchecked hunting grades. This means that you can get Winchester's lever-action hotshots — the .307, .356, and .375 — in down-to-earth, economical woods rifles. And all of Winchester's centerfire lever rifles now feature angular ejection.

USRAC is offering a pretty gun this year in their 9422 Classic. This is their .22 Rimfire (also available in .22 Winchester Magnum Rimfire), styled after the great Model 64 rifle. The Model 64 was one of the classiest lever-action rifles, and the 9422 Classic inherits a lot of its charm and good looks, what with the pistol-grip stock and 22½ inch barrel.

For the budget-minded, USRAC is offering new rifles and shotguns under their Ranger trade name. These include rifles that are essentially Model 70s and Model 94s made using inexpensive hardwoods to reduce the price.

Despite rumors to the contrary, USRAC is still producing the great Model 21 double shotgun. In fact, the custom line has been expanded to include different styles of 21s for the first time in years. A prospectus on the Model 21 is available for a small fee from USRAC. You can also obtain, at no charge, more information on the Model 21 and other special order guns from the USRAC/Winchester Custom Shop, 275 Winchester Ave., New Haven, CT 06511.

OLIN-WINCHESTER

There is still a bit of confusion about Winchester and the makers of Winchester guns. The simple facts of the matter are that the Olin Corporation owns the Winchester trademark. Olin continues to manufacture Winchester ammunition and is the importer of foreign-made firearms bearing the Winchester name. USRAC continues to manufacture domestic Winchester guns and uses the Winchester name by means of a license agreement with Olin.

This year, Olin is adding to their line of imported Winchesters by offering a Diamond Grade Model 101 over-under with four sets of barrels to provide the serious skeet shooter with four competition guns in one. With matched weight barrel sets in 12-, 20-, 28-, and .410-gauge, a competitive skeet shooter can shoot an entire tournament program with one gun. One advantage of interchangeable barrel sets is that the competitor has a gun that feels identical in all events. The 12- and 20-gauge barrels are muzzle vented for reduced recoil and added control.

Of course, the Diamond Grade is a pretty thing, too, with fancy wood, checkering, and rich engraving. The whole set comes in a specially fitted luggage-type travel case — a class act all the way. The price, I was surprised to learn, isn't all that steep, considering the value.

WEATHERBY

Can you believe it? This is the 40th anniversary of Weatherby Firearms. Roy Weatherby, the man who started it all, is as active as ever and is probably the best-liked guy in the gun business.

Last year, Weatherby's big announcement was the availability of lightweight fiberglass stocks on their Mark V Magnum rifles. Though fiberglass stocks have been around for years, Weatherby's move was significant because they were the first major American gun manufacturer to adopt synthetic stocks. This year, the company is taking the next logical step by offering tough, lightweight synthetic stocks on their competitively priced line of Vanguard rifles. These are called Fiberguard rifles, and weights run about 6½ pounds in standard and magnum calibers. The Fiberguard stock is finished in wrinkle-type, low-glare forest green. Each rifle is hand-bedded into the fiberglass stock and I bet they'll shoot like crazy.

RUGER

Fanciers of Ruger's over-under shotgun will grin about the new 12-gauge Red Label model with a stainless steel receiver.

Ruger's biggest news for the year is their all-new XGI gas-operated semi-automatic rifle in .308 caliber. This military or paramilitary rifle owes much of its styling and mechanical features to the M-1 Garand rifle of World War II fame and its descendant, the M-14. Ruger makes no bones about this, hence the name XGI. Get it? The weight is 8.2 pounds.

ULTRA LIGHT

You've probably never heard of a little West Virginia rifle-making company by the name of Ultra Light. Get used to that name, though, because they bode to make a big noise in the industry. They are making a centerfire, bolt-action rifle that weighs — now get this — *five pounds*, complete with Leupold 3X-9X compact scope. Without the scope, the rifle weighs *four pounds*.

The secret of today's super-light sporters is, of course, stocks made of synthetic materials. But Ultra Light goes a lot further. Their stock is made of Kelvar, the stuff used in body armor and truck tires, reinforced with graphite fibers. The UL Model 20 bolt-action, which comes in right- or left-hand configurations, is specially made for this rifle and weighs only 1¼ pounds. This is how the weight is kept at a minimum. By using super-light actions and stocks, the company is able to use 22-inch Douglas barrels and thus insure excellent accuracy. The 7mm/08 test rifle that I recently saw fired three-shot groups measuring less than an inch. Write Ultra Light Arms, Inc., Box 1270, Granville, WV 26534.

MOSSBERG

New for 1985, the well-established Mossberg company has introduced a new line of Model 500 Regal Series pump shotguns. Mossberg is well known for their reliable and very useful firearms at low prices. These guns are generally regarded as a good choice for the man who doesn't want to mortgage the farm because he wants to go hunting or take up target shooting. The new Regal shotguns take a novel tack because they are highly polished and deeply blued, and the action is highly polished, too, resulting in a smoother lockup. Other features include a gold-plated trigger, jeweling on the bolt, and a ventilated rib. The stock is real walnut and checkered. The thumb-operated safety is on the top rear of the receiver. These guns are available in 12- and 20-gauge with either ACCU-Choke or standard fixed choke.

EXEL

Last year, we mentioned the Exel company and their stylish line of imported shotguns. This year, they have about the best value you're going to find in a sweet little .410 side-by-side double. It's nicely put together, and fits beautifully. Write to Exel, 14 Main St., Gardner, MA 01440.

IVER JOHNSON

If you've been wondering what ever became of Iver Johnson, you'll be relieved to know that the old firm is alive and well and surviving in Arkansas under new ownership and, as I've been told, progressive management. Over the past several years some miserable junk was dumped on the market under the Iver Johnson name, but I'm told those days have ended. To set things right again, the new ownership is offering a well-built, over-under muzzleloading rifle. The two-shot rifle comes in .50 caliber with 26-inch barrels, and the gun is regulated so that both barrels hit within two or three inches at 50 yards. Bores are chrome-lined and the rifle features a clever breeching system for easy takedown and cleaning. Weight is about 8½ pounds, which ain't all that heavy for a two-barreled rifle. Write to Iver Johnson, 2202 Redmond Road, Jacksonville, AR 72076.

ALPHA

After a false start or two, the Texas-based firm of Alpha Arms has their act together with a really solid, high-performance hunting rifle. Their bolt-action design, already one of the best, has been further upgraded with a wing-type safety. You now have a choice of deluxe stock with fancy wood and custom checkering or a super-tough stock made of resin-impregnated laminates. It's the same stuff that fancy knife handles are made of, and it's waterproof through and through. Alpha also offers a totally stainless steel rifle that, when combined with their laminated stock, should be about the most weather-resistant rifle on the hill. I've ordered one of these in .284 Winchester caliber and plan to use it on my next sheep hunt. If anything goes wrong, it shouldn't be the rifle's fault. Write to Alpha Arms, 12923 Valley Branch, Dallas, TX 75234.

THOMPSON/CENTER

If you've been thinking about buying a Thompson/Center single-shot rifle but have been holding back because of the double set triggers, you'll be happy to learn that a single-trigger version is now available. The new, somewhat less expensive version is called the Hunter Model and features a redesigned forend as well as an adjustable single-stage trigger. Like the Aristocrat Model, which still comes with double-set triggers, the Hunter Model is available in eight calibers and features an interchangeable barrel system. (See the chapter on "Thompson/Center's One-Gun Battery".) To change calibers, all you need to do is swap barrels and you're in business for everything from woodchucks to moose.

BEEMAN

Robert Beeman is the most progressive importer of firearms that I know of. He started out in a modest way with a line of air guns. Within a few years, he has become not only the biggest name in the adult airgun field, but he also offers some top-of-the-line powder burners as well, including the West German Krico line. Bob has so much stuff that you have to see the Beeman catalog to believe it. Their most innovative offering this year is a .22 Rimfire that ignites an ordinary .22 Rimfire round with a jolt of electricity. (See "Kricotronic: Electronic Thunderbolt!".) The implications of this development are revolutionary in scope.

The P1 Magnum air pistol is also new this year from Beeman. They claim that it is the most powerful air pistol made today, with a top velocity of 600 fps, using a .177 caliber pellet. Actually, the air pistol has two power ranges, with the lower speed being about 400 fps. The P1 Magnum looks and feels like a .45 Colt auto, and has a crisp trigger and adjustable target-type sights. I've been using one of these new Beeman pistols for indoor target practice. This is not a toy. It's a high-quality air pistol capable of grouping inside the 10 ring of the 10-meter air pistol target.

FROM EUROPE

A couple of bolt-action rifles that are going to get more than passing attention from American hunters are the Sauer Model 200 and the Camex-Blaser Ultimate. Though each of these operate on a turn-bolt principle, they differ radically from the usual forms. Each has a two-piece stock design and each features rapid, do-it-yourself barrel changing. Calibers are changed in a couple of minutes simply by swapping barrels and, if necessary, bolt heads. Thus, the rifle can be a .243 one moment and a .300 magnum the next.

The Camex-Blaser has an especially notable design, in that the safety operates by actually releasing the pressure on the firing pin. With the safety on, the gun is uncocked. When you press the safety lever to fire, you manually recock the spring. Both the Camex-Blaser and the Sauer 200 are remarkable designs. For more details, write Camex-Blaser USA, 308 Leisure Lane, Victoria, TX 77904. The Sauer is available from Jeffries & Fischer, Box 919, Madison, CT 06443.

And that's about it, except for my new gun tip for the year. Conco Arms is importing an Italian-made over-under that is not only one of the best-looking shotguns you'll ever see, but also one of the best values. The shotgun equals anything I can think of at twice the price. A lot of people are going to be asking, "Why didn't I buy one when they were cheap?" Write Conco Arms, Box 159, Emmaus, PA 18049.

Scope Developments

Bob Bell

A scope has several significant advantages over the best iron sights. It presents a magnified view of the target as well as a bright, sharp image, and it can be zeroed in precisely. However, most shooters seem to consider only one of these factors — magnification — when buying a scope. If a little magnification is good, they feel, more magnification has to be better. Maybe it's the traditional American "if-it's-bigger-it's-better" philosophy.

At times high power is necessary — when the target is small and the range is long, or when the utmost in aiming precision is required. Benchrest competitors are among those who need the ultimate in accuracy, and varmint hunters and target shooters lean toward the higher powers because of the specific requirements of their sports.

But the truth is, such shooters are in the minority. Most shooters who use scoped rifles are big-game hunters. Their targets are big and are normally shot at close range. Almost always, other factors are more important to their scope choice than magnification. A big, bright field of view is needed when an animal can vanish in moments in the gloomy poletimber of the East or the dense elk cover of much of the Rockies. It isn't necessary to place a bullet within a fraction of an inch of some spot; a bull elk's lung area is as big as a bushel basket, and even a small whitetail's chest is the size of a basketball. At typical shooting range, a low-power scope with a wide field and a conspicuous reticle is far superior to a high-power model with its limited field.

Early gunwriters concluded that a 2½X was best in the woods, and that a 4X would handle the plains and mountain stuff. It's hard to argue with those conclusions even today. When a big-game animal is so far away that it can't be taken with a good 4X, there's really a question of whether anyone should be shooting at it. Chances of a clean kill decrease dramatically when the range gets much over 200 yards.

I mention all this because every scope manufacturer I've talked to in recent years has told me the same thing — the 3-9X variable is his biggest seller. The preference is understandable if a hunter must use the same rifle for both big game and varmints, as this power spread is probably the best compromise for his needs. But nowadays the vast majority of riflemen have several outfits for specific uses, the one-gun guy usually being a youngster who has to make do with a single rifle and scope.

And so I wonder why anyone wants to put up with the extra weight, bulk, and inconvenience of a 3-9X on a big-game rifle — to say nothing of the extra cost. In order to get enough light through a scope at 9X, it has to have an objective lens at least 40mm in diameter. This means it must sit high above the gun, affecting its balance as well as its weight. It also means the hunter is carrying extra weight and putting up with extra bulk *all the time,* even though he almost never needs that extra power. A 2½X scope would provide as much light through a 12mm objective (about a half-inch), and a normal one-inch tube will transmit far more light than is needed. It's a strange situation.

NIKON

Scopemakers, of course, provide what the buyers want, which doubtless explains why the newest bigtime riflescope manufacturer entered the field with a 3-9X and a straight 4X. One way or another, these two scopes will handle the needs of big-game hunters.

The new manufacturer is Nikon, a name instantly recognized in the field of optics. The company was organized in 1917, when three of the top optical firms in Japan combined to form Nippon Kogaku K.K. The name eventually changed to Nikon, following the worldwide success of their cameras of that name. They have almost seven decades of experience producing microscopes, optical equipment for the military, refraction telescopes, and related items, so it's natural for them to add riflescopes.

We had the use of both scopes last winter, though unfortunately, hunting season was over when they

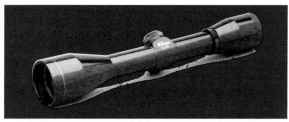

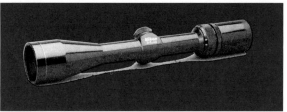

New Nikon scopes are topnotch, with fine optics and accurate adjustments.

arrived. Optically, they are high-quality items. Both have 40mm objective lenses. This is a conventional diameter on a 3-9X, on the large side for a 4X. There is one theory of light which claims that a large objective gives better resolving power than a small one, so some benefit might accrue from this. The 4X has a 28-foot field; the variable, 37-12 feet. Eye relief is 3½ inches, which means either scope can be mounted on a Magnum rifle if reasonable care is taken. I put the 3-9X on a 7mm Remington Magnum using low Redfield rings. It was a snug fit, barely clearing the barrel and bolt handle, but it worked. The 4X went on a Model 77 Ruger Ultralight .308, the slightly higher Ruger rings making things easy.

Both group shooting and checking against a collimator indicated the internal quarter-minute adjustments were accurate, and there was no discernible change in point of impact when the 3-9X was run through its complete magnification span. Lenses are multi-coated, which improved image quality over conventional single-layer magnesium fluoride coating. All in all, these are impressive scopes.

AMERICAN IMPORT

For a long time now, American Import Co. has been supplying L. M. Dickson Signature scopes. New this year are 10 rubber-armored models, along with special mounting rings to match the ridged rubber casing. Called the "Armor" models, these are made in both straight and variable powers, with conventional or wide-angle eyepieces.

ARMSON

Trijicon Riflescopes are a new line offered by Armson, Inc. Their unusual feature is a reticle that glows red when light conditions are poor, thus permitting proper aiming without impairing night vision. Three variables, a 4X, and a 6X make up this line. Armson is perhaps best known for the OEG (Occluded Eye Gunsight). With this unit, which is popular with survivalists and combat handgunners, one eye sees a red dot against a black background and the other eye sees the target area. The brain superimposes them into one image. It's a fast rig for short-range work.

ARMSPORT

In answer to the growing interest in blackpowder rifles, especially the replicas, Armsport, Inc. recently introduced an old-fashioned telescope. It's a 32-inch small-diameter 4X that looks right at home on a muzzleloader.

BEEMAN

Beeman's SS (Short Scopes) came on the market a couple of years ago, apparently designed for assault rifles. It's more than forty years since I had any interest in such rifles, but when I saw the SS-1, a 2½X that's just 5½ inches long, it looked like the answer to a problem that's intrigued me for decades — getting a scope onto a top-ejecting Model 94 Winchester. I had asked numerous manufacturers to make a short, low-power scope that could be installed right on the 94's bolt. It would move out of the way of the ejected case, then back into battery when the lever was closed. No one was interested, despite the fact that upwards of five million 94s go to the woods every fall.

It looked to me as if the Beeman SS would do the job, so I took one and a beat-up 94 carbine to gunsmith Al Wardrop. He quickly installed a dovetail on the bolt to accept the SS's integral clamping base,

Beeman Short Scope gave Bob Bell a solution to an old problem — how to get scope onto M-94 Winchester. Dovetail rib installed on carbine's bolt made it easy to fit scope's integral clamp. Scope now rides back and forth when lever is operated, clearing the way for ejected empty.

and I took everything to the range. It worked just as I'd hoped. Zeroing was easy (something I'd never experienced before with a 94), and accuracy was good. Three-shot groups went as small as $^{11}\!/_{16}$-inch at 100 yards, with the norm being about 2½ inches. If any whitetail hunter needs more accuracy than that, I've never met him. With luck, Beeman will produce a base for the 94's bolt and anyone can try it. It's a fun outfit.

Several other SS scopes are available, the SS-2 in either 3X or 4X, and the new SS-3, a 1.5-4X variable. Beeman also has a full line of more conventional scopes, the Blue Ribbons. These have finger-adjustable silhouette-type speed dials which can be set at zero after sighting in. This makes it easy to return to the basic zero after any change made while hunting.

BAUSCH & LOMB

Bausch & Lomb has added a pair of variables to the 4X and a 3-9X introduced a couple of years back. The small one, a 1.5-6X, obviously is intended to handle any big-game situation, while the new 6-24X is ideal for varmints at any range. In case you didn't notice it, the power spread here is 4:1. Most variables work on a 3:1 spread. Lenses are multi-coated for the ultimate in light transmission and true color.

BUSHNELL

Bushnell is making several scopes in the Banner line with Lite-Site reticles for precise aiming under even the gloomiest conditions. Bushnell's forerunner of the Lite-Site appeared about a decade ago, but was not pushed commercially. Current models are definite improvements, with obvious practical applications. In use, a battery-powered red dot is superimposed on the regular reticle intersection. It is switch-operated, so it does not burn constantly.

Bushnell also supplies their popular Scopechief line and the newer Sportviews. All popular magnifications are available.

BURRIS

Don Burris has refined his extensive line by adding a 4-12X Automatic Range Compensating scope for the ultra-long-range hunters and adding an adjustable objective unit to his 4X Mini to eliminate parallax. The ARC is a trajectory-compensating reticle which allows quick adjustment of the 4-12X, so the need for holding high is eliminated at any range to 500 yards. It functions via range rings which are calibrated for most high-velocity loads.

LEUPOLD

A few years back, Leupold introduced several Compact scopes for big game. The line has grown, and two more were added in the past year, a 2-7X Vari-X as an all-round scope for a lightweight

After long absence, Bausch & Lomb got back into hunting-scope business a few years ago. This is one of current line, 4X with 40mm objective.

Several Bushnell Banner scopes have Lite-Site reticles — conspicuous red dots projected onto crosswire intersection by switch-operated battery. They make precise aim possible under even the darkest conditions.

mountain gun, say, and the 4XRF Special. This one is designed for the great hunting rimfires now available from Ruger, Kimber, and others. Its Duplex reticle is thinner than normal, to make it easy to quarter a squirrel's head at 60 yards, and it is parallax-free at 75 yards for more precision in the woods.

REDFIELD

Redfield has no new scopes this year, perhaps because it would be almost impossible to insert anything into their extensive Widefield, Tracker, and Traditional lines. Top of the Redfield line for several years now has been the 3-9X Illuminator, which features an unusual airspaced triplet objective lens unit; and a five-element erector system.

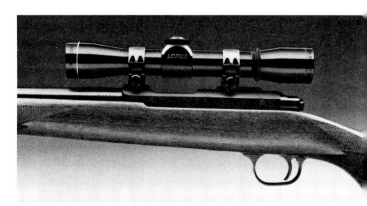

Leupold 4XRF Special is the newest Compact; it looked right at home on Ruger 77/22 — a perfect squirrel outfit.

Leupold 1.7-5X is Bob Bell's favorite variable for big game. It sits low on rifle, has excellent optics, and seems to belong on a rough-country rig. Here he's using it on fiberglass-stocked M-70 .338, a Pachmayr Lo-Swing mount tying everything together.

Everyone I know who uses the Illuminator comments on its brilliance under poor light conditions and the way it maintains point of impact during power switching. The latter is due to a nylon cam follower and thrust washers that keep everything snugged up properly.

SHEPHERD

Dan Shepherd's DRS (Dual Reticle System) scope is a highly sophisticated design that uses a series of diminishing-size circles installed on a vertical line to permit dead-on holding at extreme ranges. An important part of the original design was a rotatable .5000-inch glass cube on which four reticles were placed, one or the other matching most any high-velocity load's trajectory. It was difficult to manufacture these cubes to the accuracy required. Now, four thin glass squares are cemented into a hollow cube, significantly reducing production costs. In addition, a locking screw has been installed to prevent the cube from rotating slightly under recoil.

Soon to be available are two 6X40mm models for centerfire use — one with conventional eyepiece, one widefield — two 4X's for rimfires, and a 6-18X.

SIMMONS

Another relatively new scope line is that of Simmons Outdoor Corp. — the same Simmons family known for the excellent ventilated ribs they installed on shotguns for decades. A different American scopemaker had designed the line, to be built in Japan, then withdrew. Ernie Simmons III, who had seven years' experience as marketing manager with Tasco and wanted a line for the family company, pushed to take it over, and the result is a going operation.

Numerous models are available for big-game rifles, rimfires, silhouette and target shooting, in all normal magnifications. You can get wide-angle eyepieces, compacts, even one roof-prism 4X with illuminated reticle, as well as rubber-armored versions. Tubes are one-piece aluminum, and top-of-the-line scopes have multicoated lenses. Some have binocular-type adjustments on the ocular units, for quick and easy adaptation to individual vision.

Shepherd's DRS scope is an extremely sophisticated unit, with reticles designed to provide dead-on holding at all ranges with both centerfire and rimfire rifles. Here it is shown on M-541S Remington.

SWIFT

Eight scopes for centerfires and one for rimfires are now marketed by Swift Instruments. These include two straight 4X's, one with a 32mm objective, the other a wide-angle with 40mm lens; two 3-9X's with the same choices; a 6X40mm, and two small variables. All are good, bright scopes.

SWAROVSKI

Among the foreign scopes being seen here nowadays is the Swarovski Optik line. Several models are popular on military-type rifles, but most are slanted toward hunters. The 4X32, 6X36, and 3-9X36 have been around for some time; newer, at least here, are a 2-6X32 as a do-everything big-game scope and a 10X40 with adjustable objective for varmint shooters. All have aluminum-alloy tubes, Multiplex reticles, quarter-minute adjustments, and a spring loaded recoil system in the ocular unit to protect the forehead if you crowd too close when shooting a magnum. I've used only the 6X. It's of excellent quality, and I assume the others are too.

TASCO

Tasco calls their top scopes the World Class models, and they come in all conventional magnifications. They have so many scopes all told that I lost count of cataloged models. There's no doubt you can get a Tasco to complement any rifle or handgun cartridge, some with rubber armoring, some with illuminated or trajectory-range reticles, in an assortment of finishes. I doubt if anyone else supplies as many different scopes as Tasco.

Thompson/Center now supplies several rifle scopes as well as their older handgun models. This one is 3-9X with lighted reticle.

THOMPSON/CENTER

Thompson/Center years ago started supplying scopes to go with their popular Contender handgun (the Recoil Proof and Lobo lines), and now has several to go with the TCR 83 rifle. A battery-powered Electra Dot reticle is available in most models for use in bad light.

WEATHERBY

Roy Weatherby's third big-game scope line is called the Supremes. It consists of a 1.7-5X, two 4X's with different size objectives, and a pair of variables — 2-7X34 and a 3-9X44. They've been around a year or so, having replaced the Premiers which were introduced in 1971, which themselves had replaced the Imperial line dating from '53. I've used the smaller variables rather extensively with excellent results.

Bell's .338 Mauser wears 3-9X Shepherd, while his .338 M-70 carries small Leupold variable. The big scope has an advantage at long range, but in black timber the l.7-5X is more convenient.

Weatherby 1.7-5X Supreme is small enough to fit well on M-7 Remington, and supplies all the optical efficiency needed for its 7mm/08 chambering.

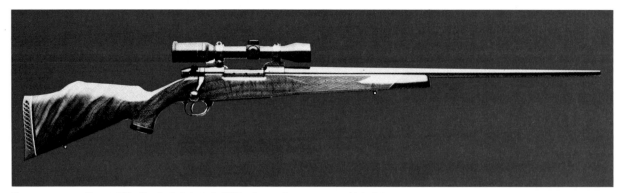

Supreme scope line is Weatherby's latest; 3-9X is shown here on one of his Magnums.

WILLIAMS

Two handgun scopes, 1½X and 2X, have been added to the Williams Twilight line, which includes rifle scopes of 2½X, 4X, 2-6X and 3-9X. The maker likes to say these Twilight models are the best in the medium-price field — such a refreshingly modest claim that we can't help quoting it. Who knows — it could well be true.

ZEISS

The Diatal C scopes — 4X32, 6X32, 10X36 and 3-9X36 — were designed for the American market by Zeiss and introduced a couple of years ago. We mention them now because this old German company isn't the kind to change a half-dozen things each year just for the sake of change. They were excellent when announced and they're excellent now. They have the constantly centered, non-magnifying reticles we like, outstanding optics, accurate adjustments. What more is needed?

For generations, Zeiss scopes have been accorded a top position on worldwide basis. Here, Andy Hufnagle uses the 10X Diatal C on South Dakota prairie-dog shoot. It's a great choice for varmint rifle.

Index

Accuracy, 18
    Computer comparison of, 130-133
    full-length vs neck-sized cases,
        143-146
Air gun accessories, 112-113
Air guns compared, 107-113
Air gun competition, 106-113
Air guns, history of, 101-105
Air gun manufacturers:
    Air Match, 110
    Beeman, 109
    Benjamin, 110
    BSA, 109
    Crosman (West Germany), 109
    Daisy, 101, (BB) 109
    Feinwerkbau, 110
    Fiocchi, 110
    Gamo (Spain), 107
    Haenel (East Germany), 107
    Marathon (Spain), 109
    RWS (West Germany), 107
    Sheridan, 110
Air gun specifications, 114-115
Air Match guns, 110
Allen, Don, 162
American Import Co. scopes. See
        Scopes
Ammunition. See Cartridge
Armson scopes. See Scopes
Armsport scopes. See Scopes

Bady, Donald B., 41
Ballistics, 6, 7, 11, 26, 117-126, 127-129,
        134-142
    categories of, 135
    performance chart, 141
Bausch & Lomb scopes. See Scopes
BB guns. See Air guns
Beeman Precision Firearms (CA), 31,
        32, 109
Beeman scopes importer,
    See Scopes
Benjamin, 110
Beretta, Ugo Gussalli, 44

Beretta USA, Corp. (MD), 45
Bianchi International (CA), 45
Bianchi, John, 44
Big game hunting, 6-13
Blackpowder guns:
    ballistics of, 86
    Mule Ear, 84
    Ozark Mountain Arms Muskrat
        rifle, 82
    Plainsman, 82, 86
    Tennessee Squirrel Rifle, 83, 84
    Thompson/Center Cherokee, 84
Bonaventure, Robert, 44
Brownell, Bob, *Gunsmith Kinks*, 161
Browning, John, 33
BSA, 109
Bullets. *See* Ballistics
Bullshooter's Supply (AZ), 52
Burris scopes. *See* Scopes
Bushnell scopes. *See* Scopes

Cartridges:
    .45 Auto, 140
    big-bore compared, 134-142
    centerfire, 46
    .38 Colt ACP, 35
    handgun cartridges, 117-126
    .375 Holland & Holland Mag.,
        6, 13, 136
    .444 Marlin, 139
    7X57mm Mauser, 139
    .358 Norma Mag., 7, 137
    9mm Parabellum, 43
    7mm Remington Mag., 16, 137
    8mm Remington Mag., 138
    .44 Remington Mag., 140
    .350 Remington Mag., 139
    .41 Remington Mag., 140
    .350 Rigby Mag., 7
    rimfire, 46, 118
    S&W Mag., 140
    .44 S&W Special, 140
    .38 Special, 46, 47

.45/70 US, 138
.30/06 US, 15, 139
    varmint cartridges, 26
.460 Weatherby Mag., 136
.300 Weatherby Mag., 138
.300 Winchester Mag.,138
.358 Winchester, 139
.308 Winchester, 139
.458 Winchester Mag., 136
.338 Winchester Mag., 7, 137
Case sizing. *See* Accuracy, full-length
        vs neck-sized cases
Charter Arms, 123
Civil-war era guns, 87-100,
    Enfield, 89
    LeMat grapeshot revolver, 94-100
    modern reproductions of, 89
    Springfields, 87
Civil-war era gun manufacturers:
    Dixie Gun Works, 92
    H & H Barrel Works, 91
    Navy Arms (NJ), 89, 98
    Springfield Firearms Corp. (MA),
        90
Colt pistols, 33
Colt Automatic Pistols, by Donald B.
        Bady, 41
Computer program for analyzing
        accuracy, 132-133
Crosman (West Germany), 109
Custom rifles and shotguns. *See*
        Rifles, Shotguns

Daisy (BB gun), 101. *See also* Air Gun
Dixie Gun Works (TN), 83, 84, 92-93

Electronic rifle. *See* Rifles, Kricotronic
English, W.H (WA), 48

Fajen, Reinhart, Inc., 64
Feinwerkbau, 110
Fiocchi, 110

Finish suppliers:
    Bivins, John, 162
    Carver Tripp, 162
    DuPont, 162
    Lowell Manley Shooting Supplies
        (MI), 162
    Pilkington Gun Co. (OK), 163
Forest Service (US), 134-142. *See also*
        Big-bore cartridges
Forgette, Val, 98

Gamo (Spain), 107
Grips, custom wood handgun, 51-52.
        See also Handgun stocks
Gun lubricants. *See* Lubricants
Gunmakers/Gunsmiths:
    Biesen, Al, 22
    Pilkington, Phil, 161
    Remington, John, 23
    Smyrl, John, 161
    Tarbox, Ross, 22
    Timmey, Allen, 65
Gunsmithing, 150-155. *See also*
        Stocks
Gunsmith Kinks by Bob Brownell,
        161

Haenel (East Germany), 107
Handguns: *See also* Silhouette guns
    automatic, 33-41
    Beretta (9mm pistol), 42-45
    Colt, 33-41
    double-action revolvers, 36
    .357 Magnum, 46-49
    .22 revolver, 46
    single-action, 36
    stocks, 51-52
    T/C Contender, 16-17
Handloading, 18-19, 25-26. *See also*
        Reloading
Harpers Ferry Armory, 101
Hawken. *See* Rifles
High Standard, 121, 123
Holland & Holland. *See* Rifles
Holsters:
    Bianchi, 44
    Huntington (CA), 48

International Handgun Metallic
        Silhouette Association
        (IHMSA), 119
Italian gunmakers:
    Beretta, 42
    Fiocchi, 110
    Perazzi, 56
Ithaca. *See* Shotguns

Kahles scopes. *See* Scopes
Krico Sporting Arms Co, The
        (Stuttgart, West Germany),
        28
Kricotronic. *See* Rifles
Kriegeskorte, Arndt, 31

Lee Precision (WI), 48
Leupold scopes. *See* Scopes
Lewis and Clark, 101-105
Lubricants, 156-160
Lydall, Inc., 149
Lyman Products (CN), 48
Lyman Reloading Handbook, 49

Mannlicher. *See* Rifles
Marathon (Spain), 109
Marlin. *See* Rifles and Shotguns
Mauser. *See* Rifles
Mayville Engineering Co., 149
McCormak, Tim, 21
Meadow Industries, 63, 65
Mequon Reloading Corp. (MRC)
        (WI), 48
Mossberg, O.F. & Sons, 63
Muzzleloaders. *See* Blackpowder guns
M-1 and M-1 Garand. *See* Rifles

National Skeet Shooting Association
        (NSSA), 53
NATO, 43
Navy Arms, 84, 89
Nikon scopes. *See* Scopes
Non-Toxic Components, 149
North/South Skirmish Association,
        93

Omark Industries (ID), 49
Open iron sights, advantages of, 10
Outers, 119
Ozark Mountain Arms, 82

Pistols. *See* Handguns

Plinking, 119-126
Pump gun. *See* Shotguns
Purbaugh, Claude, 56

Recoil reducers:
    Edwards Recoil Reducer, 62
    Griggs Recoil Redirector, 62-63
    Morgan Adjustable Recoil Pad,
        64, 65
    Recoil-Slip Pad, 63
Redfield scopes. *See* Scopes
Reloading Manual Number Nine
        (Speers), 144

Reloading supplies:
    Compact Press, 48
    Lee Improved Powder Measure
        Kit, 48
    Lee Loader, 48
    Lyman 310 Tool, 48
    Lyman Reloading Handbook, 49
    Pak-Tool, 48
    Unitized Loader, 48
Remington Custom Shop (NY), 23
Remington. *See* Rifles
Revolvers. *See* Handguns
Richland Arms, 86
Rifles:
    big bore, 6
    bolt-action, 3, 4, 24, 29,
    custom, 21-23
    doubles, 5
    glass bedding of, 150-155
    Hawken, 2, 3
    Holland & Holland, 5, 6-13
    Kricotronic, 28-32
    lever-action, 3
    Mannlicher, 4
    Marlin, 5
    Mauser, 4, 6, 8-9
    M-1, accurizing of, 166-169
    M-1 Garand, 3
    Remington, 3
    Ruger, 5, 120-121
    Sharps, 2
    single-shot, 15, 17
    Thompson/Center, 15-20
    varmint rigs, 24-27
    Weatherby, 3-4
    Winchester, 3-4
Rock Pistol Manufacturing, 120
Ruger. *See* Rifles
RWS (West Germany), 107

Schuylkill Arsenal, 104
Scopes:
    American Import Co., 176
    Armson, 176
    Armsport, 176
    Bausch & Lomb 3-9X, 20, 177
    Beeman, 176-177
    Burris, 17, 177
    Bushnell, 177
    Kahles 3-9X variable, 9
    Leupold 8X, 29, 177
    Nikon, 175-176
    Redfield, 177-178
    Shepherd, 178
    Simmons, 178
    Swarovski, 179
    Swift, 179
    Tasco, 179
    Thompson/Center, 179

Weatherby, 179
Williams, 180
Zeiss, 180
Sharps. *See* Rifles
Shepherd scopes. *See* Scopes
Sheridan, 110
Shotguns, 53-81
  BGJ Magnum, 76
  Beretta Model 680, 59
  custom, 21
  H&R Model 176, 76
  Ithaca Mag 10, 74, 75
  K-80 Unsingle, 63-64
  Kassnar/Churchill, 76
  Krieghoff Model 32, 59
  Ljutic Space Gun, 60
  Marlin, 76, 78
  Marlin 10-ga. Mag., 76
  Mercury Magnum, 76
  Mossberg Model 500, 63
  Remington, 53, 55, 59, 61
  Rottweil, 59
  Ruger, 59
  Valmet 412S, 59
  Winchester, 77
Shotguns, ballistics of, 68-70
Shotgun collecting, 81
Shotguns, comparison of 20- and
    12-ga., 71-72
Shotgun manufacturers:
  Beretta, 56
  Browning, 56
  Ithaca, 68
  Kriegoff, 55
  Mandall (AZ) supplier, 76
  Marlin, 76, 78
  Mossberg, O.F. & Sons, 63, 67
  Perazzi (Italy), 56
  Ruger, 72
  Shotguns of Ulm, 63
  Simmons Gun Specialties (KA), 55

Tradewinds (WA) importer, 76
Winchester, 56 (USRAC), 71
Shotshells, Federal ammunition, 76
Silhouette guns, 119-126
  Charter Arms Pathfinder kit gun,
    123
  High Standard Sentinel, 123
  High Standard Victor, 121-122
  Krico Model 340 Silhouette, 29
  Merrill Sportsman, 120
  Ruger Mark II Target Model, 121
  Ruger New Model Single Six,
    120-121
  S&W .22/32 Kit Gun, 123
  S&W Model 41, 121
  S&W Model 17 K-22 Masterpiece,
    121
  Thompson/Center Contender,
    119-120
Simmons scopes. *See* Scopes
Skeet guns. *See* Shotguns
Skeet gun & barrel manufacturers.
    See Shotgun manufacturers
Skeet shooting, 53-59
Skeet tube manufacturers:
  Briley, Jesse, 57
  Kolar, 57
  Purbaugh, Claude, 56
Smith and Wesson, 121
Speers, 144
Springfield Firearms Corp., 90
Spurgin, Pat, 106
Steel shot, 147-149, manufacturers of:
  Lydall, Inc., 149
  Non-Toxic Components, 149
Steel shot reloading, 149. *See also*
    Mayville Engineering Co.
Stewart, Henery M. Jr., 103
Stocks. *See* Handguns and Grips
Stocks, finish techniques, 161-165. *See*
    also Finish suppliers

Swarovski scopes. *See* Scopes
Swift scopes. *See* Scopes

Target manufacturers, 119-126: *See*
    also Silhouette guns
  Outers, 119
  Target Masters, 119
Target Masters, 119
Tasco scopes. *See* Scopes
Thompson/Center, 15, 84, 119
Thompson/Center scopes. *See*
    Scopes
Tollinger, Jim, 75
Trapguns: *See also* Shotguns
  K-80 Unsingle, 63
  Ljutic Space Gun, 60-61
  Mossberg Model 500 Hi-Rib Trap
    pump, 63
  Remington 870 Competition Trap,
    61
Trapgun stocks:
  Fajen Adjustable Trap Stock, 64
  Variable Convert-A-Stock Pad, 65
Tube sets, 56: *See also* Skeet tube
    manufacturers
  advantages of, 57

Uknalis, Bob, 58
US Forest Service. *See* Forest Service
  (US)

Varmint guns. *See* Rifles
Varmint hunting, 24-27

Weatherby. *See* Rifles
Weatherby, Roy, 52
Weatherby scopes. *See* Scopes
Williams scopes. *See* Scopes
Winchester. *See* Rifles and Shotguns
Wood. *See* Handgun stocks

Zeiss scopes. *See* Scopes